# The Revolutionary Guide to
# Turbo C++

### Valery Sklyarov

WROX PRESS LTD

# The Revolutionary Guide to Turbo C++

*Published by WROX Press Ltd. 1334 Warwick Road, Acocks Green,
Birmingham, United Kingdom.*

*Printed In the UK by Eyre and Spottiswoode Ltd.*

*ISBN 1 - 874 - 41610 - 9*

## About the Author

*Professor Valery Sklyarov is a Doctor of Science and
Head of the Computer Department at the Minsk Radio Engineering Institute.
The Institute is one of the largest graduate and postgraduate establishments
for teaching electronics in the Commonwealth of Independant States
(formerly the USSR), with a total student population of around ten thousand.
Professor Sklyarov has extensive experience of teaching Object Oriented
Programming, C and C++ and Assembler, with particular application to the
design and synthesis of electronic circuits.*

*In his native Russian, Professor Sklyarov is a prolific and renowned author,
with books published on personal computer hardware, programming,
Computer Aided Design and the Theory of Finite Automata.*

*Together with his wife and daughter, he is an inveterate explorer of the more
remote and uninhabited regions of Russia, especially the Urals. His exploits
in these areas include climbing, fishing, and white water rafting!*

*Tecnical Editor* **Ivor Horton**

*Translation* **Sergei Ponomariov**

*Book Design* **Nina Barnsley and Paul Hougham**

*Cover Design* **Paul Hougham**

*Воля и труд человека дивные дива творят.*

*Н. А. Некрасов*

**Acknowledgements**

**Thanks to my wife Tatyana for her patience and support, and for endless supplies of cups of tea throughout the production of this book. Thanks also to Eve Horton for being so understanding about Ivor's long hours and frequent absences.**

# Contents

## CHAPTER NINE

## CHAPTER TEN

### SECTION THREE

## CHAPTER ELEVEN

# INTRODUCTION

# *INTRODUCTION*

**The Revolutionary Guide To Turbo C++** teaches the concepts of Object Oriented Programming (**OOP**) and **C++**, one of the latest and most exciting languages to incorporate these capabilities. The book is aimed at teaching you effective programming in **C++** using object oriented methods in the fastest possible way.

To make things easy, a disk is included containing all the sample programs given in the book. Also included on the disk is a specially developed interactive tutorial. This shows, with animated illustrations linked to code examples, all the principle concepts necessary to understand **C++**.

Many of these ideas can be difficult to grasp in the abstract, but the programs on this disk will provide you with an instant, understandable and direct illustration of the concepts to complement the material in the book. We strongly recommend you have this on hand when you get to the **C++** specific sections of the book. It will really help you get to grips with all of the notions involved in Object Oriented Programming.

**C** is one of the most widely used programming languages. Since its appearance in the 1970's it has passed through several phases of development resulting in the 1989 **ANSI** standard for **C**. Beginning in 1980 a range of extensions to **C** were developed, incorporating Object Oriented Programming capabilities. The resulting language was called **C++**. It provides the following advantages:

- programs are easier to understand and modify
- debugging is considerably simplified
- the design and development of complex programs is easier
- the potential for re-useable code is extended
- software reliability is enhanced

The advantages realised from having Object Oriented Programming facilities in **C++** have resulted in a trend towards extending other programming languages to provide similar facilities.

# The Characteristic Features of the Book

With the main objectives being to teach you **C++** and Object Oriented Programming as quickly and easily as possible, there is an emphasis on teaching by example. There is also extensive use of illustrations to augment the sample programs. The major features of the book are:

1. It has specially designed sample programs showing the advantages of **OOP** technology.

2. It has many simple examples explaining all the basic constructions of **C** and **C++**. All programs have been executed in the **Turbo C++** environment (manufactured by *Borland International Inc.*). You can also use the **Borland C++** environment from the same company.

3. The book is extensively illustrated. Many language constructions are explained using simple diagrams. This makes the material easier to understand and considerably shortens the time required to learn the language. Most programming examples are accompanied by diagrams.

4. The inclusion of a disk with demonstration and teaching programs is intended to make learning **C++** as easy as possible. The disks include:

   - Source code of all the programs from the book.

   - A comprehensive, interactive, graphical tutorial program on **C++** and object oriented concepts.

Where library functions are used in examples their principle features are described in sufficient detail to enable the operation of the example to be understood. For a comprehensive description of the library functions you can consult your Turbo C++ library reference manual.

## Who is this Book Aimed at?

This book is intended to teach the new **C++** programming language to a broad spectrum of prospective users, but with a special emphasis on beginners. In particular, it deals with the **Borland Turbo C++** Compiler and development environment. It is designed to be effective for you, whether you are an experienced programmer or a beginner to **C++** . If you want to learn **C++** this book is for you.

# Conventions Used in the Book

We have used a variety of type styles and other devices to identify and distinguish particular entities. Throughout the book, to make the dialogue between you and your computer clearer, any output from your computer on the screen is represented thus:

**Typical computer output**

Where the information should be entered by you on the keyboard, it will appear thus:

*Your input*

The symbol, *<Enter>*, means that you should press the *Enter* key. An example of a **DOS** command input that you are certainly familiar with, could appear using this notation as:

C>*dir<Enter>*

Throughout the book, we have programming examples which will appear in the form:

```
This is how
an example of
a sample program
looks in the book
```

It is frequently necessary to refer to program code in the text of the book. Where specific fragments of code appear, to separate them clearly from the text, they will look like a fragment of code. It should be emphasized that the programs in the book are designed to demonstrate the capabilities inherent in **C++**. Many of the programs could be written in a much more concise manner but then they may not illustrate the programming features under discussion.

References to your keyboard function and control keys in the text are highlighted: for example, *F4* . The cursor control keys are referred to as arrow keys. The Escape key, which is usually situated at the top left hand side of your keyboard, is denoted in the text as *Esc* .

# *The Contents of this Book*

The book is organised into four major sections. These are self contained units designed to be read in sequence or independently of one another, so you can dip in as your particular needs, interests and programming experience dictates.

The first section provides an introduction to programming in **C** and **C++**. It provides simple program examples designed to illustrate basic concepts. Writing and executing programs is the way to learn any programming language, so you should run these on your own computer.  This section also deals with the Interactive Development Environment provided with the **Turbo C++** compiler. It will teach you how to enter and edit your **C** and **C++** programs and how to compile and execute them. You will also learn how to use the extensive tracing and debugging facilities of the Interactive Development Environment (**IDE**).

The second section covers the common **C** and **C++** language constructs and reflects the basic ideas of modern programming style. It also provides an initial taste of Object Oriented Programming. If you are already a reasonably experienced programmer and already have an understanding of how the Interactive Development Environment works, then you could start with this section if you wish.

The third section is dedicated to the new capabilities offered by **C++** that are not found in **C**. The various aspects of Object Oriented Programming are covered, illustrated with programming examples.

The fourth section includes a range of practical examples of programming in   **C++**. You should find that these not only provide an effective illustration of **C++** programming in a variety of contexts, but also furnish you with a range of useful programs in their own right. The examples given will enable you to:

- Create Screen Menu Systems
- Display a Watch and Notepad
- Create a Graphic Simulation of a Calculator

At the back of the book you will find a comprehensive index, plus the disk we have already mentioned containing all the examples used in the book. The disk will save you time and make the reading more interesting and absorbing. You will be able to develop your **C++** skills that much quicker. We wish you every success.

## *How to Use the Disk*

You will need about 1.5 megabytes free on your hard disk, of which about 200 kilobytes are required for the source files of the examples in the book. First you need to run the installation program (**INSTALL.EXE**) provided on the disk. You will have a choice of installing the Tutor program or the examples, or both. The **INSTALL** program will create a directory **\CPPTUTOR** for the Tutor program and a directory **\EXAMPLES** for the source files of the examples. The directory **\CPPTUTOR** will also have two subdirectories. The installation program will unpack and move all the required files into the appropriate directories. You can use any IBM compatible computer with 640Kb RAM and a hard disk. We assume that all operations will be carried out in the **MS-DOS** environment, booted from the hard disk with logical name **C:**. In this case, you can proceed as follows:

1. Turn on your computer and load **MS-DOS**
2. Insert the disk into drive A:
3. Make drive A: current by typing:

   C>*A:<Enter>*
   **A>**

4. Now key in:

   A>*INSTALL<Enter>*

During the installation, the **INSTALL** program will give you the option of choosing an alternative hard disk for installation instead of the default drive C: . The program default is to install both the set of source code examples and the tutor program. You can toggle Yes/No for either of these choices by positioning the cursor on the appropriate line using the up and down arrow keys and pressing *<Enter>*. To start the unpacking and file transfer process, move the cursor to the line "Start Installation" and press *<Enter>*. On completion, all the necessary subdirectories will have been created and all the source files will have been transferred. To view the directory **EXAMPLES** you should enter :

A>*C:<Enter>*
C>*CD EXAMPLES<Enter>*
C:\EXAMPLES>

If instead of the last prompt you get:

C>

You should be able to fix it by entering:

C>*PROMPT $p$g<Enter>*
C:\EXAMPLES>

Now if you enter:

C:\EXAMPLES>*DIR<Enter>*

you will see the contents of subdirectory **EXAMPLES**. The examples have the same file names on the disk as in the book. So for section 1, the names are **EX1_1**, **EX1_2**, etc. The names of the examples appear in the program listings in the text as program comments:

```
/* example EX1_1 */
```

Suppose you want to execute the program **EX1_1.C**. You simply enter:

C:\EXAMPLES>*TC EX1_1.C<Enter>*

This will result in automatic loading of the **Turbo C++** programming system (the **TC.EXE file**), and you will see in the editor window the

**EX1_1.C** program source code. Now press *Ctrl-F9* for automatic compiling, linking, loading and execution of the program. Press *Alt-F5* to see the results and then press any key to return to the **Turbo C++** Main menu. To exit to **MS-DOS** press *Alt-X* .

To run the Tutor program enter **CPPTUTOR** from the directory **\CPPTUTOR** :

### C:\CPPTUTOR>*CPPTUTOR<Enter>*

A few seconds after the initial panel is displayed, the program will automatically switch to an index of topics in a window. If you are using a mouse you can select a topic by clicking on the selector button at the right hand end of the topic line you want. To space the menu up or down click on the appropriate arrow on the scroll bar on the right hand side of the window. To exit the Tutor program click on the door marked exit at the bottom left of the screen. Within a topic you can move forward through the material by clicking on the More button. To go back to the beginning of a topic click on the Home button. To return to the topic index click on **C++** at the bottom left corner of the screen.

If you do not have a mouse you can use the keyboard. The *Tab* key will move the selector down through the topic buttons. The currently selected topic is indicated by a circle on the selector button. To scroll the topic index in the window you use the up or down arrow keys. To choose the selected topic press *<Enter>*. If you wish to terminate the Tutor program press *Esc* from the panel with the topic index. Within a topic, pressing the *Spacebar* will move forward through the topic, and pressing the *Home* key will return you to the beginning of the current topic. To return to the topic index press *F10*.

That is practically all you need to know for the beginning. You will find more detailed explanations of how to work with the examples later on. While working with the program examples, try changing them in various ways to use alternative methods or to extend their function. You should find it instructive and entertaining and you will have a chance to see what you have learned. Don't be afraid if you don't get it right the first time, after all, practice makes perfect!

# SECTION ONE

*Writing, Compiling,*

*Linking, Debugging*

*and Executing C++*

# SECTION ONE

# YOUR FIRST PROGRAMS IN C AND C++

## Program Structure in C and C++

### Functions

In **C**, any program consists of one or more **functions**. A function is a self-contained block of code which is referenced by name. In general, different functions may be assigned any names you like, but there must be one function called **main** in every program. Execution of any program starts with the function **main**. A simple C program structure, consisting of only the function **main**, may be presented as:

```
main()
    { Body of function
    comprising one or more statements
    }
```

Arguments are one of the interaction mechanisms between the functions of a program. A list of the arguments in round brackets follows the function name. Our function **main()** has no arguments, that's why the list looks like **()**. The curly brackets, **{}**, enclose the start and the end of the function body. Later we will see that they are also used for other purposes.

A function body comprises a sequence of **statements** defining what actions must take place when the program is executed. These actions may include: assigning a variable value, checking dependencies and so on. A statement consists of **operands** and **operators**. An operand might be a number or a variable. An operator causes some computation or other to occur, such as

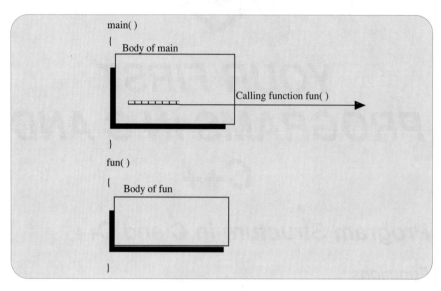

*Figure 1.1*
**A C Program
Calling a
Subprogram**

addition or subtraction. Keywords are used to define operands that can
vary in value. For example, there is a keyword to define a variable as
being of **integer type**. All keywords are reserved words which must not
be used as variable or function names. All statements defining actions
end with a semicolon. The first line of a **C** function, which defines its
name among other things, does not require a semicolon terminator. Neither
do lines called **preprocessor directives** which are instructions to the
compilation process, but we shall come to those later.

Figure 1.1 shows a simple program structure, where the function **main**
calls the function **fun**, which is a subprogram with no arguments. In its
turn, the function **fun** could call another function. As we shall see, a
function is called simply by using the function name followed by its
arguments enclosed within parentheses.

Figure 1.2 shows the interaction mechanisms and the sequence of execution
of statements occurring in programs typically structured in a modular
fashion as a set of functions. If there is a call statement in the program, it
invokes the execution of the corresponding function or subprogram. After
termination of the function, the statement following the call is executed.
The same function may be called repeatedly from another function.
Structuring programs into subprogram modules in this way enables
complex systems to be developed efficiently. It also makes testing and
debugging very much easier.

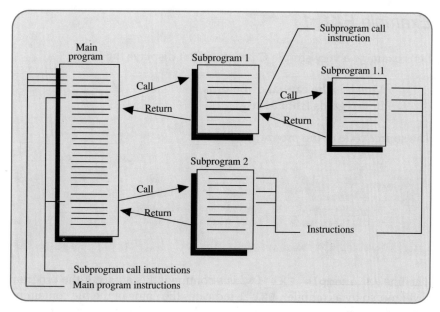

*Figure 1.2*
**A Demonstration Program Designed on a Module Basis**

Functions in **C** can acquire arguments and return values. There is a special key word, **void**, that is used to indicate the absence of arguments or return values. Consider an example:

```
void main(void)
   {  Body of function
   }
```

Here the function **main** neither receives nor returns any values.

There is an important notion in **C++**. It is called a **function prototype** and defines the form and name of the function. Within the function prototype, the presence of the return values types and the types of all arguments is mandatory. Consider an example:

```
int fun(int, char);
```

In this case, the first argument and the return value are integers (**int**), and the second argument is a character (**char**). The type of the return value is defined by the specifier preceding the function name.

## Example EX1_1

Let's examine a very simple **C** program that displays the lines:

> **Minsk is the capital of Belorus**
> **Best regards from Minsk**

The source code of the program will be:

```
/* example EX1_1*/
#include <stdio.h>
  {  printf("Minsk is the capital of Belorus\n");
     printf("Best regards from Minsk");
  }
```

The line **/\* example EX1_1\*/** is a comment. It's a part of the program text ignored by a compiler. **EX1_1** indicates the name of the file containing the sample program on the enclosed disk. A preprocessor instruction **#include** on the second line brings into our program the **Turbo C++** file **stdio.h** that describes the library function **printf**. We actually need only one line from the file **stdio.h**:

> **int_Cdecl printf(char \*_ _format,...);**

If we include this line in our program, we could omit the include statement that brings in the file **stdio.h**. However, besides the function **printf**, this file describes other library input/output functions. That's why it's usually easier to include this one file, instead of trying to remember all the lines for the various facilities that we might need in a complicated program. The input/output functions described in the file **stdio.h** are C functions that can also be used in **C++**.

The first call to the function **printf** enables us to display the text: **Minsk is the capital of Belorus** and move the cursor to the beginning of the next line. The cursor movement is controlled by a special symbol, **\n**. The second use of the function **printf** displays the text **Best regards from Minsk**.

It's very simple to execute this program. First make the directory holding the source code of the examples current. Then load it into the **Turbo C++** Window editor using the instruction:

> C:\EXAMPLES>*TC EX1_1.C<Enter>*

Now press *Ctrl-F9* . Press *Alt-F5* to view the results. Should any problems arise, consult the section titled "How to Use the Disk", and see if you made a mistake in installing the sample programs.

The source file **EX1_1.C** is a **C** program and not **C++**. This is identified by the extension **C** after the decimal point in the file name. We may create a new file with the same file contents but with the name **EX1_1.CPP**. Disregarding the absence of any changes in the program itself, it's now a **C++** file! You can load it into the **Turbo C++** Window editor using the command:

> C:\EXAMPLES\EX1>*TC EX1_1.CPP<Enter>*

The executing statements are identical to the **C** language version so of course, none of the **OOP** characteristics are revealed in the example. We just wanted to show you how to run **C** and **C++** programs in the **Turbo C++** programming system. Now we can draw some conclusions:

▲ If the program source code file has the extension C, it allows the user to employ only **C** language constructions and none of the new **C++** constructions may be used.

▲ If the program source code file has the extension CPP, it is a **C++** program and therefore permits the use of new **C++** constructions, as well as most **C** language constructions.

▲ You will find that most **C** programs will execute in the **C++** environment although in some cases minor changes will be necessary. Some old **C** language constructions, for example those lacking function prototypes, will not compile as **C++** programs without modification.

## Example EX1_2

Let's take a look at an elementary sample program incorporating some typical **C++** constructions:

```
/* example EX1_2 */
#include <iostream.h>
void main(void)
{   cout << "Minsk is the capital of Belorus\n";
    cout << "Best regards from Minsk";
}
```

This program does the same as the program **EX1_1**, but employs a different mechanism for displaying the data. It introduces the idea of an output data stream which is called **cout**. The symbols, **<<**, direct the data to the output stream, which is connected by default to the monitor screen. We shall see a lot more of stream input/output later on. The **#include** preprocessor statement brings the **C++** file **iostream.h** into our example. This provides the declarations for the stream input/output facility. This is specific to **C++**. You will find the **C++** stream input/output easier to use than the **C** functions in **stdio.h**. They have some other advantages as we shall see. To run this program you can make use of the enclosed disk.

# CHAPTER 2

# AN INTRODUCTION TO THE TURBO C++ INTEGRATED DEVELOPMENT ENVIRONMENT

## Using the Turbo C++ Main Menu

When **Turbo C++** begins execution you will see the **Main menu** screen shown in Figure 1.3. It consists of three parts: **the menu bar** at the top, **the window area** in the middle, and **the status line** at the bottom. **The menu bar** lets you access all the menu commands in the **Turbo C++** Integrated Development Environment (**IDE**).

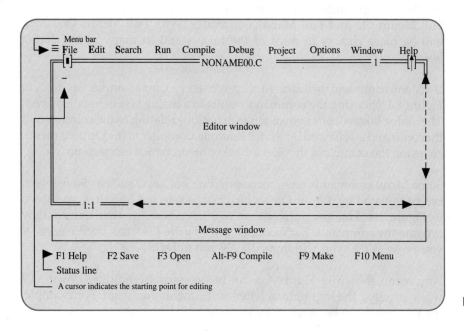

Figure 1.3
**The Main
Menu Screen**

Press the *F10* key to make the menu bar active. You'll see that one of the menu titles (for example, File) will be highlighted. Using the arrow keys you may move the highlight to select the other menu titles.

For example, select the File menu. Press *<Enter>* to activate the File pull-down menu. It contains either a full set or a simpler subset of the file manipulation functions. You can alternate between the two sets by choosing either Full Menus On or Full Menus Off in the **O**ptions menu. When you want to exit the File menu press the *Esc* key. You may cancel any action by using the *Esc* key.

Now choose the **O**ptions menu. Move the highlight to the **O**ptions title using the arrow key and press *<Enter>*. The first **O**ptions menu line may be set as follows:

Full Menus On

Move the cursor to it using the arrow keys and press *<Enter>*. The **O**ptions menu will disappear. However, if you choose it again the menu line will be:

Full Menus Off

To illustrate the difference, Figure 1.4 shows you the File menu in both Full Menus On and Full Menus Off modes. With Full Menus On, there will be more choices in most of the menus and in many of the dialog boxes.

If a Menu command includes an ellipsis mark (...), for example, Save as... in Figure 1.4, choosing the command results in a dialog box being displayed. The dialog box will offer you a range of options relating to the command. If the command is followed by ↓ , for example Compiler in the **O**ptions menu, choosing the command invokes a further menu which is a pop-up.

Some Menu commands have corresponding hot keys, such as **S**ave which can be initiated by *F2* , or **Q**uit which can be selected by *Alt-X* as shown in Figure 1.4. Hot keys are one or two key shortcuts that immediately activate the command. For example, after **Turbo C++** has been loaded, if you press *Alt-X* you will immediately exit to **DOS**.

Any menu shown in Figure 1.3 can be accessed by holding down *Alt* while pressing the highlighted letter of the menu you want. For example, the File menu can be invoked by pressing *Alt-F* .

The **Turbo C++** Integrated Development Environment also allows for using a "mouse" manipulator. In order to use your mouse you obviously must have installed an appropriate mouse driver. By default **Turbo C++** uses only the left button for carrying out various operations, although you can choose to have the right button as the active one.

We will assume that the left button is active. To choose a desired menu item, position the mouse marker on it and press the left button. This is referred to as "clicking" the menu item. Any menu command may be selected in the same manner.

For some functions you can also hold down the left button while moving the mouse. This is called "dragging". Generally, it is used for moving or changing the size of things, such as windows, on screen.

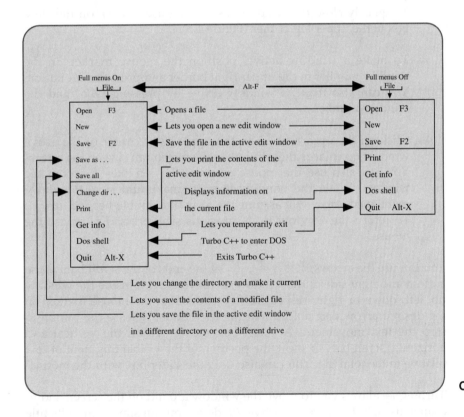

*Figure 1.4*
**Full Menu
On/Off Modes**

# *Using the Development Environment Windows*

Windows play an important role in the **Turbo C++** Integrated Development Environment. You can create (open) or destroy (close) them. You can have any number of windows open at any time, but only one of them can be active. On the screen, the active window is always placed on top of all the others and has a double-lined border around it.

Any text you type, or any command you choose, generally applies to the active window. Figure 1.5 shows the features that a window can have, although not all windows will have all the features illustrated. Here are some examples of how to use the mouse while working with windows:

▲ To quickly close the window, use the mouse to click on the close box in the upper left corner (Figure 1.5).

▲ To make a window active, position the mouse marker on the window number in the upper right border and press the left button. You can also make a window active by pressing *Alt* and the window number.

▲ Click on the up arrow ↑ , in the upper right corner of the active window, to enlarge the window to the maximum size on the screen. You can also use the mouse or press the *F5* key to zoom the window. When the window is at its maximum size, the above mentioned arrow will assume the form of a double-headed arrow . To return the window to its previous size, press *F5* or use the mouse.

You can use the arrows, ↑, ←, ↓ , → at the ends of the scroll bars at the bottom and right side of the window, to move the text inside the window up, left, down or right, respectively. Just position the mouse marker on the desired arrow and hold down the left button. Release the button to stop the text movement. A slider box moves within the vertical and horizontal scroll bars to show the position of the visible fragment of text relative to the total file. You can also drag the slider box with the mouse.

**Turbo C++** allows you to move the window around on the screen and to change its size. To move the active window, you can simply drag its title bar or alternatively, choose the **W**indow menu (Figure 1.6). Its commands are very simple. We shall come to them later.

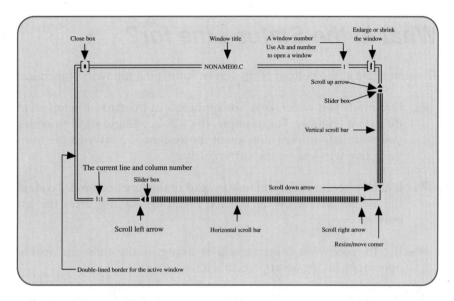

*Figure1.5*
**Window Format**

To resize a window, position the mouse marker onto the single-line border in the lower right corner of the window. Hold down the active button and move the mouse. Moving the mouse with the button held down makes the window larger or smaller. Release the button when it's at the size you want.

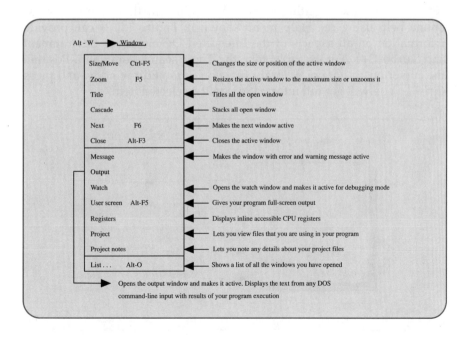

*Figure 1.6*
**The Window Menu**

# *What is the Status Line for?*

The status line at the bottom of the screen fulfills the following functions:

▲ It reminds you which keys are applicable at the current moment in the active window. For example, the *F1* key (Figure 1.3) provides you with help information about the system, *F2* saves a file from the active window on the current drive.

▲ It allows you to use the mouse instead of the function keys. Position the mouse marker on the desired menu option and press the left button.

▲ It tells you what the program is doing at the moment during operations taking an appreciable time.

▲ It suggests hints on the currently selected menu commands and dialog box choices.

▲ You will see that the status line changes as you switch windows and commands.

Now, a brief look at getting hints and help information. You can access online help using the **Help** menu shown in Figure 1.7. It can provide information on all aspects of the Integrated Development Environment and **Turbo C++**. For example, take the **Topic** search command. Position the cursor on an item or a library function in the **Edit** window and press *Ctrl-F1* . You will get full information on the selected item.

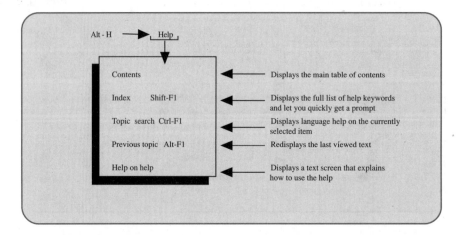

*Figure 1.7*
**The Help Menu**

# *Setting the Environment Options*

## *The Include Directory*

**Turbo C++** uses a variety of standard files it expects to find in libraries defined within the programming system. We've already met two of them: **stdio.h** and **iostream.h**.

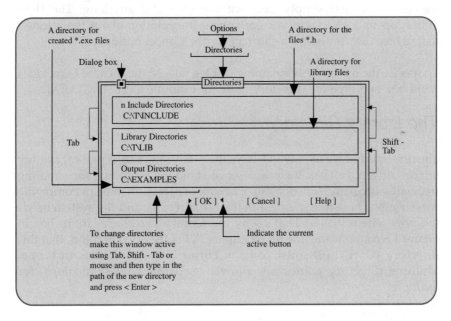

*Figure 1.8*
**The Options/
Directories
Selection**

All files with the extension **.h** are held in the INCLUDE Directory. They contain descriptions of the library functions, global variables and so on. The statement:

```
#include <file_extension_h>
```

will include the file named between the angle brackets into the program from a standard directory. The directory name, which in our case is INCLUDE, together with its path, must be known to the system. Consider Figure 1.8, where the **O**ptions menu and its **D**irectories command are selected consecutively. This command will open a dialog box which allows you to specify the directories that **Turbo C++** should search for the files it needs. Having entered the directory path names you select one of three standard choices: (OK), (Cancel) or (Help). Using *Tab* or *Shift-Tab* you can move the highlight to select the one you want. If you are using a mouse, just click on your choice. You can also press *Alt* and the highlighted letter of an item to select it. For example, to activate the **OK** button, press *Alt-K* .

If you choose **OK**, **Turbo C++** will activate the choices in the current dialog box. **Cancel** simply exits without changing anything. The **Help** button opens a **Help** window containing information about the selected dialog box. *Esc* is always a shortcut for the **Cancel** button.

To specify the directories containing `.h` files, choose the Include Directories input box and type the directory path, for example C:\T\INCLUDE.

## The Library Directory

The run-time library files, which have the extension `.LIB`, represent another important group. They include a set of standard programs for handling frequently occurring functions such as square root extraction, or comparing two strings. These files are held in the LIB directory and the system needs to know where that is. That's why the Library Directories input box in Figure 1.8 contains the line for example C:\T\LIB. Keep in mind, that this directory (C:\T\LIB) must contain **Turbo C++** object files `C0?.OBJ`. Multiple directory names are allowed, separated by semicolons, for example:

C:\T\LIB; C:\T\MYLIB

## The Output Directory

The **Output** Directory input box specifies the directory in which **Turbo C++** should store object files with the extension `.OBJ`, and executable files with the extension `.EXE`. If you want to store the files on a floppy disk, you must specify its logical name, for example, A:. All the environment options shown in Figure 1.8 will be set during installation. So this Chapter is aimed at showing you how to change options, if it becomes necessary.

Some dialog boxes may contain so-called **check boxes** and **radio buttons**. **Check boxes** simply offer you a range of choices. The chosen check boxes are marked with the symbol **x** to show that they are in "on" mode, for example:

[X] **W**hole words only

An empty check box, for example:

[ ] **W**hole words only

indicates this option has not been selected. You can toggle between on and off either by clicking a check box or its text, or pressing *Tab* ( *Shift-Tab* ) until the box is highlighted and then pressing the Spacebar. You can also use *Alt* and the highlighted letter. Radio buttons differ from check boxes in that they give mutually exclusive options. The chosen radio button is indicated by an asterisk (∗). For example, in a group:

(∗) **F**rom cursor
( ) **E**ntire scope

you can choose either the first or the second line, but not both. Setting radio buttons on or off is achieved by selecting a required group and using the arrow keys or clicking your selection.

Figure 1.9 gives you an overview of all the **O**ptions menu commands. Some commands have already been described. The **O**ptions menu allows you to view and modify various settings in the **Turbo C++ IDE**. If you

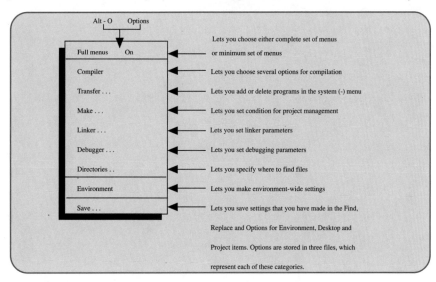

*Figure 1.9*
**The Options Menu**

have just started using **Turbo C++,** it would be better to leave the settings as they are.

There is one more menu, the **S**ystem menu, that appears at the far left of the menu bar. You can invoke it by pressing *Alt-Spacebar.* The menu includes commands that will give you information about **Turbo C++** (**A**bout), and close all windows (**C**lear Desktop). Some of the other commands in the menu will be relevant when you have a deeper knowledge of **Turbo C++** programming.

# CHAPTER 3

# *RUNNING C++ PROGRAMS*

## *Writing Program Source Code*

You write and alter your program source code using an **Edit** window. You can start working with a new file using the **File** menu commands. Figure 1.4 shows the complete set of commands in the **File** menu. Choose the **New** command shown in Figure 1.10. It will let you open a new **Edit** window with the name NONAME*xx*.C. Any number from 00 to 99 may be substituted instead of *xx*.

Now you can enter source code for your program. As an exercise you could key in EX1_1.C from the previous chapter. By pressing the *F2* key to save the file in the current directory, you will invoke a dialog box. It

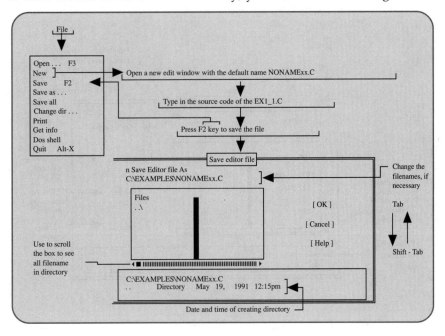

*Figure1.10*
**The File/
New
Command**

will prompt you to rename the file instead of NONAMExx.C and permit you to save it in a different directory if you wish. Here you can also see what is held in a selected directory. For example, Figure 1.10 shows that directory C:\EXAMPLES is empty.

## Creating a New File

You can create a new file using the **O**pen command in the File menu. It also allows source code of a previously written program to be loaded into the **E**dit window. Suppose we have executed the operations shown in Figure 1.11 (i.e. we've selected the **O**pen command in the File menu). The dialog box shows the current directory name (C:\EXAMPLES) and all the files held in it  (EX1_1.CPP and EX1_2.CPP).

You can choose any file from the displayed list by moving the highlight to the desired name using the arrow keys. Then press *Tab* or *Shift-Tab* to highlight the desired button. Alternatively, you may use a mouse to click on the selection you want. The **O**pen button opens up a new **E**dit window with the selected file. The **R**eplace button replaces the file in the active **E**dit window with the file selected in the dialog box (Figure 1.11).

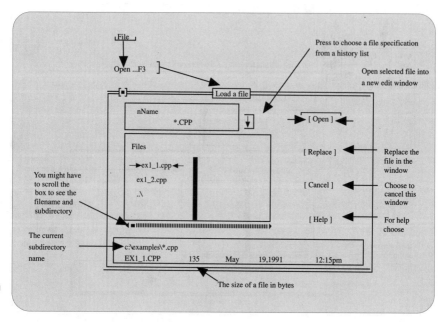

*Figure 1.11*
**The File/Open Command**

If you enter a file name in the **Name** input box in the **O**pen command that is not in the file list, a new file will be created as a result. The sequence of operations is similar to that in the **New** command shown in Figure 1.10.

Apart from the actions mentioned above you may also:

▲ Enter a file name with standard DOS wildcards * and ? (for example, MY*.CPP). It will filter the names in the **File** window according to the specified pattern.

▲ Press ↓ key (when the cursor is blinking in the **Name** input box) or click a desired dialog box button. You will see a history list of the last eight file names you've entered.

▲ View the contents of a subdirectory of the current directory by selecting the name of the current directory in the file list displayed.

## Editing Source Code

Now we can look at editing source code. The **Turbo C++** Editor commands are given in Table 1.1. Many text handling procedures involve moving or copying chunks of text around. This is achieved using the concept of **a block**. A block is any contiguous text fragment ranging from a single character to hundreds of lines. There can be only one block at a time. You mark its beginning and end. Once marked, the block may be written to a disk, printed, copied to a temporary buffer called the clipboard and moved or copied to another point in the file.

| Command | Action |
|---------|--------|
| **Cursor Movement Commands** | |
| ← or *Ctrl-S* | Left one character |
| → or *Ctrl-D* | Right one character |
| *Ctrl -* ← or *Ctrl-A* | Left one word |
| *Ctrl -* → or *Ctrl-F* | Right one word |
| ↑ or *Ctrl-E* | Up one line |

*TABLE 1.1*

| *Command* | *Action* |
|-----------|----------|

| **Cursor movement commands** | |
|------------------------------|---|

| ↓ or *Ctrl-X* | Down one line |
| *Ctrl-W* | Scroll up one line |
| *Ctrl-Z* | Scroll down one line |
| *PgUp* or *Ctrl-R* | Up one page |
| *PgDn* or *Ctrl-C* | Down one page |
| *Home* or *Ctrl-Q-S* | Beginning of line |
| *End* or *Ctrl-Q-D* | End of line |
| *Ctrl-Home* or *Ctrl-Q-E* | Top of screen |
| *Ctrl-End* or *Ctrl-Q-X* | Bottom of screen |
| *Ctrl-PgUp* or *Ctrl-Q-R* | Beginning of file |
| *Ctrl-PgDn* or *Ctrl-Q-C* | End of file |
| *Ctrl-Q-B* | Beginning of block |
| *Ctrl-Q-K* | End of block |
| *Ctrl-Q-P* | Last cursor position |

| **Insert and delete commands** | |
|--------------------------------|---|

| *Ins* or *Ctrl-V* | Insert mode on/off |
| *Ctrl-N* | Insert blank line |
| *Ctrl-Y* | Delete entire line |
| *Ctrl-Q-Y* | Delete to end of line |
| *Backspace* or *Ctrl-H* | Delete character left of cursor |
| *Del* or *Ctrl-G* | Delete character at cursor |
| *Ctrl-T* | Delete word right |

**TABLE 1.1 CONT'D**

## Block commands

| | |
|---|---|
| *Shift* ↑ ↓ →← or *Ctrl-K-B* | Mark the beginning |
| *Shift* ↑ ↓ →← or *Ctrl-K-K* | Mark the end |
| *Ctrl-K-T* | Mark word |
| *Ctrl-Ins , Shift-Ins* or *Ctrl-K-C* | Copy block |
| *Shift-Del , Shift-Ins* or *Ctrl-K-V* | Move block |
| *Ctrl-Del* or *Ctrl-K-Y* | Delete block |
| *Ctrl-K-H* | Hide or display block |
| *Ctrl-K-W* | Write block to disk |
| *Ctrl-K-R* | Read block from disk |
| *Ctrl-K-P* | Print block |
| *Ctrl-K-I* | Indent block |
| *Ctrl-K-U* | Unindent block |

## Miscellaneous commands

| | |
|---|---|
| *Ctrl-U* | Abort |
| *Ctrl-O-I* | Auto indent on/off |
| *Ctrl-P* | Control character prefix |
| *Ctrl-Q-F* | Find |
| *Ctrl-Q-A* | Find and replace |
| *Ctrl-Q-n* | Find place-marker(n-number 0-9) |
| *Ctrl-K-D* or *Ctrl-K-Q* | Exit without saving |
| *Ctrl-L* | Repeat last search |
| *Ctrl-Q-L* | Restore line |
| *F2* or *Ctrl-K-S* | Save text |
| *Ctrl-K-n* | Set place-marker(n-number 0-9) |
| *Tab* or *Ctrl-I* | Tab |
| *Ctrl-O-T* | Toggle tab mode |
| *Ctrl-Q-[* | Find previous match |
| *Ctrl-Q-]* | Find subsequent match |

*TABLE 1.1*
*CONT'D*

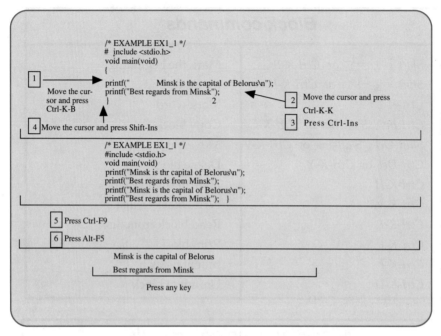

*Figure 1.12*
**An Example of Editing**

Take a look at Figure 1.12. It illustrates the following operations numbered 1 through 6:

1. Marking the beginning of a block. Position the cursor at the desired place and press  *Ctrl-K-B* , or use the arrow keys while holding down  *Shift* .

2. Marking the end of a block. Position the cursor at the end of the block and press  *Ctrl-K-K* , or use the arrow keys while holding down  *Shift* . Marked text will be displayed in a different intensity.

3. Copying the marked text to the Clipboard. Press  *Ctrl-Ins* .

4. Copying the block from the clipboard to the cursor position at a new place in the screen. Position the cursor on the closing figure bracket and press  *Shift-Ins* . The previously copied block will be pasted from the Clipboard to the screen. You could copy the block while copying it to the Clipboard by pressing  *Ctrl-K-C* . However, using the Clipboard allows you to move the marked block from one window to another.

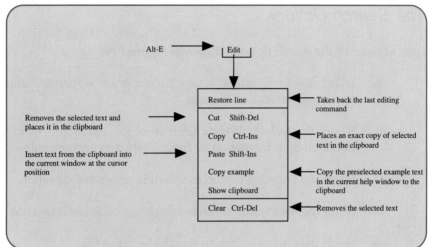

*Figure 1.13*
**The Edit Menu
Commands**

5. Pressing *Ctrl-F9* will initiate compiling, linking and executing your program.

6. Pressing *Alt-F5* will view the changed program on a full screen.

You can also mark a block using a mouse. Move the mouse marker to the beginning of a block, hold down the left button and move the marker to the end of the block. Then release the button.

To edit text you may use the Edit menu commands shown in Figure 1.13. To better understand how they work, try to manipulate some text. For example, mark copy to the Clipboard, delete and paste fragments of the program EX1_1.C. Try using some of the various editor commands given in Table 1.1.

## Searching Through Text

While editing text you may often need to search for specific occurrences of words, sentences, or any other string and, probably, replace them. For that you may use the editor commands, or you can use commands from the Search menu shown in Figure 1.14. The Find command displays the dialog box shown in Figure 1.14 that lets you enter the text pattern you are looking for, and set options that affect the search. The same dialog box will appear when pressing *Ctrl-Q-F* .

## The Search Options

Look at some of the search options shown in Figure 1.14:

- Select the **C**ase sensitive box to recognise uppercase and lowercase letters as different.

- Select the **W**hole Words Only box to search for words bounded by punctuation or space characters on both sides.

- Select the Forward button to search in a forward direction.

- Select the **B**ackward button to search in a backward direction.

- Select the **G**lobal button to search the entire file.

- Activate the **S**elected text button to search only the text you have previously blocked.

- Select the **F**rom the cursor button to activate Forward and **B**ackward search from the current cursor position.

- Check the **E**ntire scope button to search the entire file, regardless of the current cursor position.

If you choose the **F**ind command from the **S**earch menu, you can search for the word that the cursor is currently placed on. Pressing the right arrow key will pick up the succeeding characters and add them to the Find box.

The **R**eplace command displays a similar dialog box. As well as the text you want to search for, it enables you to enter the text you want to substitute. Select the Change All button to make the substitution throughout the entire text. An additional checkbox, **P**rompt on replace, controls whether you are prompted for each change.

Other **S**earch menu commands are briefly illustrated in Figure 1.14.

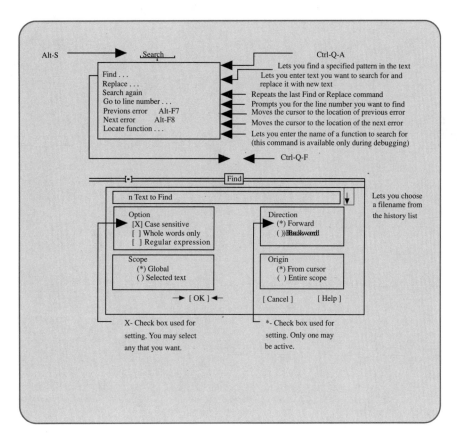

Alt-S

Search

Ctrl-Q-A

Find . . .
Replace . . .
Search again
Go to line number . . .
Previous error    Alt-F7
Next error        Alt-F8
Locate function . . .

Lets you find a specified pattern in the text
Lets you enter text you want to search for and
replace it with new text
Repeats the last Find or Replace command
Prompts you for the line number you want to find
Moves the cursor to the location of previous error
Moves the cursor to the location of the next error
Lets you enter the name of a function to search for
(this command is available only during debugging)

Ctrl-Q-F

Find

n Text to Find

Lets you choose
a filename from
the history list

Option
[X] Case sensitive
[ ] Whole words only
[ ] Regular expression

Direction
(*) Forward
( ) Backword

Scope
(*) Global
( ) Selected text

Origin
(*) From cursor
( ) Entire scope

[ OK ]

[ Cancel ]        [ Help ]

X- Check box used for
setting. You may select
any that you want.

*- Check box used for
setting. Only one may
be active.

*Figure 1.14*
**The Search/
Find Menu**

# CHAPTER 4

# COMPILING, LINKING, DEBUGGING AND EXECUTING A PROGRAM

## Developing a Program

Suppose we are to develop a program with the name MYPROG. The process we must go through in **Turbo C++** may be presented in the form of a simple schematic:

`MYPROG.CPP` → `MYPROG.OBJ` → `MYPROG.EXE`

First we must create a file **MYPROG.CPP**. Then, using the editor, we need to key in the source code for the program and save it in that file. From the source code, the compiler will create an object file, **MYPROG.OBJ**, and the linker will create an executable file, **MYPROG.EXE**. This latter file you can load and execute.

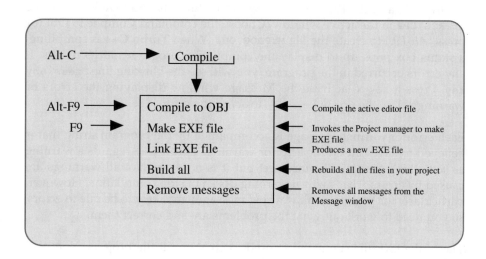

Figure 1.15
**The Compile Menu**

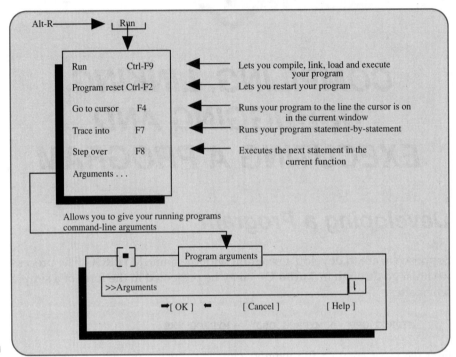

*Figure1.16*
**The Run Menu**

## The Compile Menu

For compiling, linking and executing you use the **C**ompile menu shown in Figure 1.15, and the **R**un menu shown in Figure 1.16. Say we have the file **MYPROG.CPP** in the active window. Choose the command **C**ompile to OBJ (or press *Alt-F9* ) to create the file **MYPROG.OBJ**. When **Turbo C++** is compiling, a status box pops up to display the compilation progress and its results. If any errors occurred in the program, you will see the blinking line **Press any key**. Press a key to activate the **M**essage window displaying the errors or warnings. Use the arrow keys ↑↓ to scroll the errors.

Each error or warning message is accompanied by the program string that is believed to have caused the error or warning. **Turbo C++** regards a warning as something that may be incorrect but it is not sure. Not all warnings are caused by errors. That's why a warning does not stop compilation. However, particularly for beginners, all warning messages are likely to be due to errors, so you need to work out what the problems are and correct them.

The **M**ake EXE file command is used to create multifile projects. Note that this command rebuilds only those files with revised source code.

The Link EXE file command uses the current object (`.OBJ`) and library (`.LIB`) files and builds an executable (`.EXE`) file. The **B**uild all command rebuilds all the files in your project regardless of whether they are out of date or not.

## The Run Menu

The **R**un menu (Figure 1.16) runs your program and also starts and ends debugging sessions. We have already met the command *Ctrl-F9* . It runs your current program and passes arguments to it that you've selected in the dialog box (see Figure 1.16). If the source code has been modified since the last compilation, it recompiles and links your program. We will see more of the commands shown in Figure 1.16 in Chapter 5, in the section 'Working in the **Turbo C++ IDE**'.

## The Project Menu

Consider the **P**roject menu that allows you to create multifile projects. It is illustrated in Figure 1.17. It allows you to combine several files into a single **project** and then control this project as a single entity. This can be very useful for managing complex programs comprising many functions. The **O**pen project command displays the Load Project File dialog, which enables you to select and load a project, or create a new project by typing in a name (`.PRJ`). You select a file in a similar fashion to the mechanism used in the **O**pen command in the File menu.

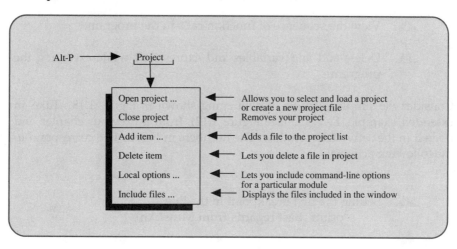

Figure 1.17
**The Project
Menu**

The **A**dd Item or **D**elete Item commands are used when you want either to add a file to the project list, or delete a file in the **P**roject window. These commands display a dialog box where you key in a file name to add or delete.

A brief summary of other commands in the **P**roject menu is given in Figure 1.17. Remember, if you have defined a project, **Turbo C++** will use its name when creating an executable file .**EXE**.

## *Debugging Programs*

During a debugging session you can:

1. Perform single-step execution of the program. Execution of each line will be followed by a breakpoint that will let you analyze the results obtained so far, the contents of program-accessible registers and so on. You can set breakpoints at every line of the program, at previously specified lines, or at lines where the cursor is placed during debugging.

2. Check the value and address of a variable while executing the program.

3. Analyze the values of variables and expressions and change them while executing the program.

4. View the sequence of function calls in the program.

5. Delete and add variables and expressions while executing the program.

Consider the simple example of debugging shown in Figure 1.18. Take an extended example, EX1_1.C (see Figure 1.12), from a previous chapter and open it in the active **E**dit window. The numbers in Figure 1.18 correspond to the following actions:

1. Setting the first breakpoint in the line:
              printf (**Best regards from Minsk\n**).

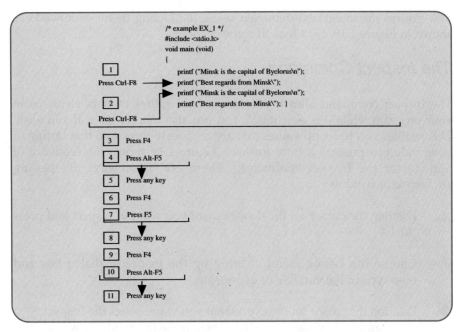

*Figure1.18*
**An Example of Debugging**

2. Setting the second breakpoint in the line:
   printf (**Minsk is the capital of Belorus\n**).

3. Executing the program up to the first breakpoint.

4. Viewing the results of the program up to the first breakpoint.

5. Switching over to the active Edit window.

6. Executing the program up to the second breakpoint.

7. Viewing the results of the program up to the second breakpoint.

8. Switching over to the active Edit window.

9. Executing the program from the second breakpoint to the end.

10. Viewing the results of program execution.

11. Switching over to the active Edit window.

You control the integrated debugger using the **Debug** menu commands as shown in Figure 1.19. Let's look at some of them.

## The Inspect Command

The Inspect command allows you to examine values of data elements in your program while it is executing. You can also modify them if you wish. This enables you to fix up values that are obviously wrong so that testing of your code can proceed a little further. Figure 1.19 shows the sequence of options for the Inspect command. There are three ways of opening an Inspector window:

▲ Position the cursor on the data element you want to inspect and press *Alt-F4.*

▲ Choose the **Debug** menu to bring up the Inspector dialog box and then type in the variable or expression.

▲ Position the cursor on the expression you want, select the Inspect command and, while in the dialog box, press the right arrow key to bring in more of the expression. To select the expression for inspection, press *<Enter>*.

Alternatively, position the cursor on the expression you want, select the Inspect command and, while in the dialog box, press the right arrow key to bring in more of the expression. To select the expression for inspection, press *<Enter>*.

When the Inspector window item can be modified, the status line displays " *Alt-M* Modify Field". If you now press *Alt-M* , a dialog box will prompt you to enter a new value for the item being inspected.

The Inspector window displays the variable value in decimal, with the hexadecimal value in parentheses with the standard **C** and **C++** prefix for hexadecimal numbers, 0x. If the displayed variable is of type **char**, the character equivalent is also displayed.

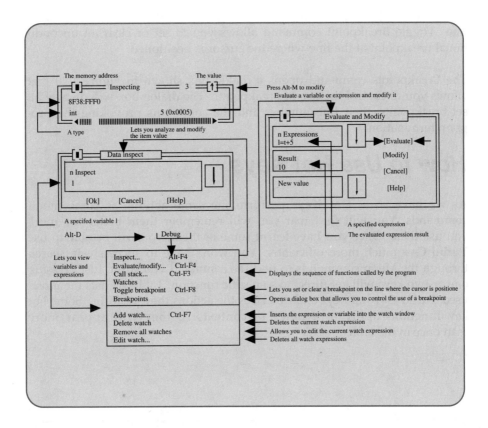

*Figure 1.19*
**The Debug
Menu**

## The Evaluate/modify Command

The Evaluate/modify command evaluates and displays a variable or expression and lets you change it. The Expression field (see Figure 1.19) shows the word at the cursor in the Edit window. You can evaluate it by pressing *<Enter>*, or you can edit it. You can also press the right arrow key to bring in additional characters from the Edit window. When you press *<Enter>* the Evaluate button is activated, and the value will be displayed in the Result field. In the New Value field you can enter a new value for the expression. You must select Modify to make it effective.

## The Watches and Breakpoints Commands

The Watches command opens the pop-up menu shown in Figure 1.19. It lets you insert, delete or edit variables and expressions in the Watch window.

The  Toggle **B**reakpoint command allows you to set or clear an uncondi-tional breakpoint at the line where the cursor is positioned.

The **B**reakpoints command opens a dialog box shown in Figure 1.20 that allows you to control the use of breakpoints. The dialog box will display all set breakpoints, their line number and the conditions provoking the pro-gram termination.

## How to Use Hot Keys

As we have seen, **Hot Keys** perform the same actions as some menu commands. You will find that you will remember them better the more you use them. Once you have learnt some of them, you will be able to use **Turbo C++** much more efficiently. You won't have to successively search through the Menu commands to find the command you want. Just pressing one or two keys will get direct to a specific function. Table 1.2 lists the most-used **Turbo C++** hot keys and describes the actions they perform.  Some hot key functions apply to a range of contexts so they will appear more than once in the table.

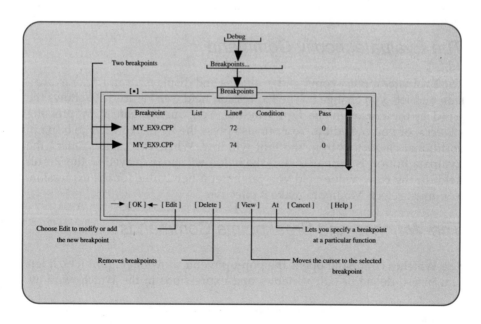

*Figure 1.20*
**The**
**Breakpoints**
**Command**

| Key(s) | Function |
|--------|----------|
| | ***General Hot Keys*** |
| F1 | Displays a help screen |
| F2 | Saves the file currently in the Edit window |
| F3 | Loads a file |
| F4 | Runs your program to the line where the cursor is placed |
| F5 | Zooms the active window |
| F6 | Cycles through all open windows |
| F7 | Runs your program in debug mode (tracing into functions) |
| F8 | Runs your program in debug mode (stepping over function calls) |
| F9 | Makes the current window or project |
| F10 | Turbo C++ Menu bar |

| | ***Menu Hot Keys*** |
|--------|----------|
| Alt-Spacebar | Takes you to the -(System) menu |
| Alt-C | Takes you to the Compile menu |
| Alt-D | Takes you to the Debug menu |
| Alt-E | Takes you to the Edit menu |
| Alt-F | Takes you to the File menu |
| Alt-H | Takes you to the Help menu |
| Alt-O | Takes you to the Options menu |
| Alt-P | Takes you to the Project menu |
| Alt-R | Takes you to the Run menu |
| Alt-S | Takes you to the Search menu |
| Alt-W | Takes you to the Window menu |
| Alt-X | Exits Turbo C++ to DOS |

*TABLE 1.2*

### Window Management Hot Keys

| | |
|---|---|
| *Alt-#* | Displays the window with given number |
| *Alt-O* | Displays the open windows list |
| *Alt-F3* | Closes the active window |
| *Alt-F4* | Opens an Inspector window |
| *Alt-F5* | Displays User Screen |
| *F5* | Zooms/unzooms the active window |
| *F6* | Switches the active window |
| *Ctrl-F5* | Changes the size of the active window or its position |

### Online Help Hot Keys

| | |
|---|---|
| *F1* | Displays a help screen |
| *F1 F1* | Brings up Help on Help (Press F1 when you're already in Help) |
| *Shift-F1* | Brings up Help index |
| *Alt-F1* | Displays previous Help screen |
| *Ctrl-F1* | Gives language-specific help |

**TABLE 1.2
CONT'D**

## Debugging/Running Hot Keys

| | |
|---|---|
| *Alt-F4* | Opens an Inspector window |
| *Alt-F7* | Takes you to previous error |
| *Alt-F8* | Takes you to next error |
| *Alt-F9* | Compiles a program and builds a file .OBJ |
| *Ctrl-F2* | Resets running program |
| *Ctrl-F3* | Brings up call stack |
| *Ctrl-F4* | Evaluates an expression |
| *Ctrl-F7* | Adds a watch expression |
| *Ctrl-F8* | Sets or clears conditional breakpoint |
| *Ctrl-F9* | Compiles, links and runs a program |
| *F4* | Runs program to cursor position |
| *F7* | Executes tracing into functions |
| *F8* | Executes skipping function calls |
| *F9* | Compiles file (or project) in the active window |

*TABLE 1.2*
*CONT'D*

# CHAPTER

## 5

# *EXAMPLES*

Consider some simple **Turbo C++** programs we can use to exercise the Interactive Development Environment.

## *Example EX1_3*

The source code of this first example is:

```
/* example EX1_3 */
#include <iostream.h>
void main (void)
{   int a=20, b=30;
    char c;
    c = a + b;
    cout << "c = " << c << "\n";
    cout << "a + b = " << a + b << "\n";
    c = c + 4;
    cout << "c = " << c << "\n";
}
```

The statement:

```
int a=20, b=30;
```

declares two integers a and b and assigns the values 20 and 30 to them. The statement:

```
char c;
```

declares the variable c to be of type **char**. The next statement:

```
c = a + b;
```

will assign the variable c with the value 50 which will be interpreted as representing a character. The **ASCII** character code with the decimal value of 50 corresponds to the digit 2. The statement:

```
cout << "c = " << c << "\n";
```

will display the string  c = , followed by the value of the character variable
**c**, which is the digit 2. Then, because of the inclusion of the control
character **\n**, it will move the cursor to the beginning of the next line. The
next statement:

```
cout << "a + b = " << a + b << "\n";
```

will display the string a + b = , the value of  a + b  and move the cursor to
the beginning of the next line. The statement:

```
c = c + 4;
```

will increase the value of c by 4. Now c has the value 54 , which
corresponds to the digit 6. The construction

```
c + = 4;
```

is also allowed in **C** and **C++** and does the same as the previous statement. We will discuss this construction in the next chapter.

## Working in the Turbo C++ IDE

Try working in the **Turbo C++ IDE** using the previous example. Run the
program EX1_3.CPP after keying in the corresponding text in the active
**Editor** window and pressing  *Ctrl-F9* . Alternatively, you could load it
into the **Edit** window from your hard disk if you have installed the sample
programs.

To view the results, switch the screen using  *Alt-F5* . You can also adjust
the screen to see the source code and the results at the same time. To do
this proceed as follows:

1. Choose the **Output** command from the **Window** menu.

2. Using the **Size/Move** commands from the **Window** menu
   (or press  *Ctrl-F5* ) position the windows as shown in
   Figure 1.21.

3. Make the window with the source code active and press *Ctrl-
   F9* . After the program finishes executing, the **Output** window
   will display the results (Figure 1.21).

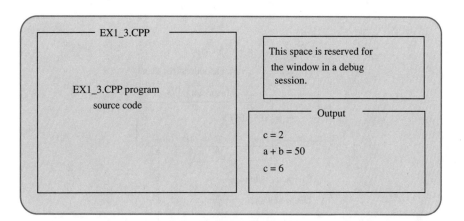

Figure 1.21
**The Output
Window**

To make Figure 1.21 simpler we have omitted some window management commands. We'll do the same with all the figures. Don't forget that to move windows you can use the arrow keys, ↑, ↓, →, ←.

To resize windows, use the same arrow keys while holding down *Shift* . Before manipulating a particular window, you need to make it active by pressing the key corresponding to the window number while holding down *Alt* .

Let's discuss some operations used during debugging sessions. For example, to choose the **Step over** command from the **R**un menu, press *F8*. This command executes the next statement in the current function. Pressing *F8* , you'll see how each string is handled.

As we shall see later, you can also analyze the value of selected variables and examine the contents of program-accessible registers (as long as the **R**egister command from the **W**indow menu has been previously chosen). By pressing *F8* you highlight the string you are currently watching. For example, highlight the first string

```
cout << "c = " << c << "\n";
```

Using the arrow keys position the cursor on the character c in **char c;**. Select the **Inspect** command in the **D**ebug menu (or press *Alt-F4* ). It will open the Inspector window shown in Figure 1.22. You can position it conveniently on the screen. Press *F8* again and watch the value of c changing.

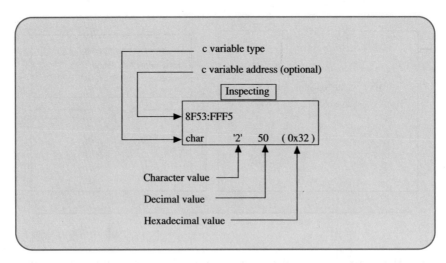

Figure 1.22
**The Inspector
Window**

Close the Inspector window. To do this you just make the window active
and press *Esc* . Choose the **Watch** command from the **Window** menu and
position the windows in the manner shown in Figure 1.23. Using the
sequence of commands:

> Debug menu - **Watches** command - **Add watch** command

add variables a, b and c to the **Watch** window. You will see the following
lines on the screen:

> **a: Undefined symbol 'a'**
> **b: Undefined symbol 'b'**
> **c: Undefined symbol 'c'**

At this point this is correct.

Now we'll show you how to delete a variable from the **Watch** window.
First, make the window active. Then move the marker, for example, to
the second string (with the variable b) and press *Del* . You can also use
the sequence of steps:

> Debug menu -**Watches** command - **Delete watch** command.

Make the Edit window with your program active and press *F8* . In the
Watch window you will see how the variables a and c change their values during the execution of the program. After the program ends the
values of a and c will be as shown in Figure 1.23.

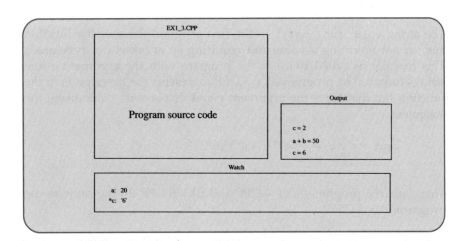

*Figure1.23*
**Closing the
Inspector
Window**

## Example EX1_4 and Example EX1_5

Turn now to creating a project. For that, we have to change our previous program somewhat:

```
/* example EX1_4 */
#include <iostream.h>
void main(void)
{   int a=20, b=30;
    char c;
    void fun(char);
    c = a + b;
    fun(c);
    cout << "a + b = " << a + b << "\n";
    c = c + 4;
    fun(c);
}
```

We need to create the function **fun**:

```
/* example EX1_5 */
#include <iostream.h>
void fun(char c)
{     cout << "c = " << c << "\n";     }
```

The string **void fun(char);** in the first program declares the function **fun**, as not returning a value and requiring an argument of type **char**. This function is called twice in the program with the argument c (the strings fun(c)). The program EX1_5.CPP represents the description of the function fun that takes the argument c and displays its value using the statement:

```
cout << "c = " << c << "\n";
```

Therefore, the programs EX1_4.CPP and EX1_5.CPP do the same as the program EX1_3.CPP.

Now we choose the **O**pen project command in the **Project** menu and create the project EX1_6.PRJ. You can simply type in EX1_6 and press Enter. Then select the **A**dd item command in the **Project** menu to add to the project the file names EX1_4.CPP and EX1_5.CPP. Press *Ctrl-F9* to compile and link the project. As a result, you'll get an executable file EX1_6.EXE.

Return to the debug mode again. Note that by pressing *F8* you'll skip the function fun, and by pressing *F7* you won't. (Pressing *F7* you'll also trace into the function of the file **iostream.h**). Suppose that, during the debugging session the marker moves to the string **c = c + 4;** and you want to start a new debugging session or terminate the program. All you need to do is press *Ctrl-F2* (see Figure 1.16). If now you press *F7* or *F8*, you will start a new debugging session from the beginning of the program. At this stage you can select the **Call** stack command from the **Debug** menu (or press *Ctrl-F3* ). You will see the call sequence of the functions **main** and **fun** in the program EX1_6.
For example, when the function **fun** is called for the first time, press *Ctrl-F3* to see the following lines in the **Call** stack window:

```
fun('2')
main()
```

The **Call** stack window will disappear when you press *Esc* . When the function **fun** is called for the second time, press *Ctrl-F3* and you'll see the following lines:

```
fun('6')
main()
```

If you choose the string **cout** in the program EX1_5, a function from the file **iostream.h** will appear in the stack.

Try to create a more complex project. Add, for example, new functions, set watches in the program so you can trace what is happening, use **G**o to cursor command in the **R**un menu. After a bit of practice, you'll be able to solve the more complicated problems that will be discussed in further chapters.

# SECTION TWO

C and C++

Common

Constructions

# *SECTION TWO*

# CHAPTER
## 6

# PROGRAMS AND DATA TYPES

## Basic Concepts of a Programming Language

### Statements and Character Sets

As has already been mentioned, **C** and **C++** program bodies consist of **statements**. Each statement defines the actions to be carried out at that particular position in the sequence of program execution. For writing statements you must use a specific set of characters that constitute the ABC of the programming language.

The character set includes Roman capital and small letters, the digits 0 to 9, and special symbols. These symbols include for example, (.) point, (,) comma, (:) colon, (;) semicolon and other special characters. The internal representation of the character set in a **PC** is implemented through a coding system known as the **American Standard Code for Information Interchange**, usually referred to as **ASCII**. The **ASCII** standard is defined by a code chart that matches each character with its unique code. The character codes are called **ASCII**-codes.

Within the **ASCII** character set there are visible characters and control characters. The former can be displayed on the screen and printed. The latter can cause your computer to carry out certain actions. These control characters are represented by decimal values **0** to **31**, and **127**. For example, decimal code 7 causes a beep sound, decimal code 8 returns the screen cursor one step back, decimal code 9 is a horizontal tab and decimal code 13 returns the cursor to the beginning of a line.

Personal computers use a byte consisting of eight binary bits to represent each character. Thus, the total number of possible different characters amounts to $2^8 = 256$, and the conversion chart defining the code for each of the characters will have 256 lines of the form:

**character_code - character**

An example would be: $33_{10}$ - !.

The first part of the **ASCII** character set containing 128 characters is standard and the second part is used to represent characters of the various national alphabets, graphic characters and so on. Further on in the book you will find a program that will enable you to display the conversion chart on the screen and print it.

## Identifiers

An **Identifier** is a very important programming language notion. It is used as an object's name, where an object might be a function, a variable, a constant, or some other language element that is referred to by name. Identifiers must be chosen keeping in mind the following restrictions:

1. The first character must be alphabetic (a, ..., z, A, ..., Z) or an underscore (_).

2. Identifiers can contain Roman letters, the underscore character (_), and the digits 0 to 9. Use of any other characters is prohibited.

3. C and C++ identifiers are case sensitive, so that Prog, ProG, PROG, pRoG are distinct identifiers.

4. Identifiers can be of any length, but only a limited number of characters are recognized and used to differentiate between objects (functions, variables, constants and so on). Different compilers will support different limits on the number of characters recognised. **Turbo C++** recognizes only the first 32 characters as significant. Suppose, in a hypothetical case, the number of characters recognised in an identifier was limited to five. In this case, the identifiers **count** and **counter** would be identical, since the first 5 characters coincide.

5. Identifiers must not coincide with language keywords or standard library function names.

## Comments

**Comments** play a significant role in **C** and **C++**. Good explanatory comments make a program more readable and easier to understand. In **C** and **C++** comments are placed between the symbols /* and */. You can write them in any part of the program. **C++** also allows an additional form of comments. Everything written after two adjacent slashes is considered a comment and is ignored by the compiler. For example:

```
// this is a comment.
```

In many of our examples, comments will be used extensively for explaining the function of particular language statements. If you are keying in the source code of sample programs, you can type them either with or without the comments since the comments in no way affect program execution. However, they will be much easier to understand later if you include the comments. Including explanatory comments in your programs as you write them is a very good habit to acquire. What may be perfectly clear coding today, may seem quite obscure a month hence.

In **C** and **C++** programs, spaces, horizontal and vertical tabs and newline characters are ignored. This allows you to write program statements in a more readable way since you can space them out as you please. By starting program lines at appropriately chosen positions, you can clearly separate different blocks of code.

# Declarations and Data Types

Programs operate with different kinds of data organised in a variety of ways. Data items can be simple or structured and can be of different types. Simple data items are integers, real numbers, characters and pointers. Pointers are the addresses of objects in memory. Integers, unlike real numbers, have no fractional parts. Structured data items are arrays, structures and files. We will be looking at these in detail later.

## Declarations

Variables and other objects are specified by means of **declarations**. The **C** and **C++** programming languages distinguish between **defining declarations** and **reference declarations** of variables. With a **reference declaration** for a variable, you simply introduce its identifier and its type, for example, integer. When defining a variable through a **defining declaration** you will do the same, but you will also allocate space in memory, usually by assigning an initial value. When defining variables there are **type specifiers**, which determine the kind of data values the variable can have and **type modifiers**. Let's first take a look at the former.

## The Five Basic Types

There are five basic types in **C** and **C++**, which you define by the following keywords: **char** - character; **int** - integer; **float** - real; **double** - double precision real; **void** - no value. Now we can summarise their basic characteristics:

1. A variable of type **char** is 1 byte in size. It has as its values different characters from the **ASCII** code chart, for example: 'w', '*', 'G' (they are included in single quotes as they would be in a program).

2. A variable of type **int** is 2 bytes in size. The value of the variable lies within the range from -32768 to 32767.

3. The keyword **float** allows you to declare variables which may have real values. That is, their values may have fractional parts following a decimal point, for example; 3.8 or 67.91. Real numbers can also be written in floating point format or, as it is sometimes called, scientific notation, with a decimal value followed by an exponent. An example would be 1.26e+2 representing -1.26 $10^2$ or -126. A variable of type **float** occupies 4 bytes which is 32 bits of memory. It can have values from 3.4e-38 to 3.4e+38 with 7 decimal digits precision.

4. The keyword **double** lets you declare a variable which is also real, but of double precision. It needs 64 bits of memory which is twice that of a variable of type **float**. It can have values from 1.7e-308 to 1.7e+308 with 15 decimal digits precision.

5. The keyword **void** is used to define an object value as empty or null. A common use is for declaring a function that returns no values.

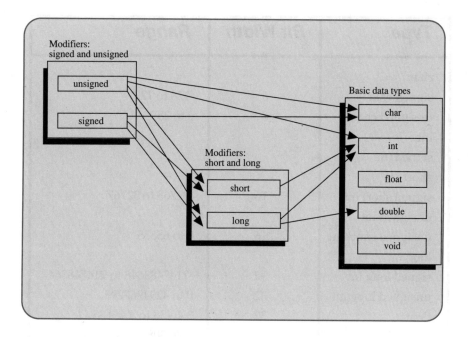

*Figure 2.1*

**Combining Modifiers with Type Identifiers**

## Modifiers

The keywords called **type modifiers**, which we have mentioned on the previous page, can be applied to several base types. This chapter deals with only four of them: **unsigned**, **signed**, **short** and **long**. In the case of the data type **int**, the modifier can be either **signed**, meaning presence of a sign, or **unsigned**, meaning absence of a sign. Fairly obviously, an integer with a sign can be of positive or negative value, whereas an integer with no sign can only be positive. Modifiers precede the type identifiers, for example: **unsigned int**.

Figure 2.1 shows all admissible combinations of these modifiers and associated type identifiers. If there is no type identifier following a modifier, the compiler assumes the type identifier to be **int**. Therefore the declarations:

```
long  a;
long int  a;
```

are identical and declare the variable **a** as long integer. Table 2.1 (overleaf) also shows the effects of the type modifiers on the size and range of values of the declared object.

| Type | Bit Width | Range |
|------|-----------|-------|
| char | | |
| signed char | 8 | -128 to 127 |
| unsigned char | 8 | 0 to 255 |
| int | | |
| signed int | | |
| short int | | |
| signed short int | 16 | -32768 to 32767 |
| unsigned int | | |
| unsigned short int | 16 | 0 to 65535 |
| long int | | |
| signed long int | 32 | -2147483648 to 2147483647 |
| unsigned long int | 32 | 0 to 4294967295 |
| float | 32 | 3.4e-38 to 3.4e+38 |
| double | 64 | 1.7e-308 to 1.7e+308 |
| long double | 80 | 3.4e-4932 to 1.1e+4932 |

**TABLE 2.1**

# Declaring Global and Local Objects

Let's examine where in a program you can declare objects. **C** and **C++** have **global** and **local** objects. **Global** objects are declared outside functions and as a result are accessible to any of them. **Local** objects are internal to a particular function. They start their existence in the beginning of a function upon entry and are destroyed when the function is exited. Figure 2.2 shows the place in a program where you can declare global variables. It also shows their scope. Figure 2.3 gives the possible location for the declaration of local objects. In **C**, all declarations must precede the statements that constitute the function body. In **C++** this restriction does not apply and you can place declarations in any part of the program. If you position them inside a function, the declared objects will be local to that function. If you place them outside all the functions, they will be global.

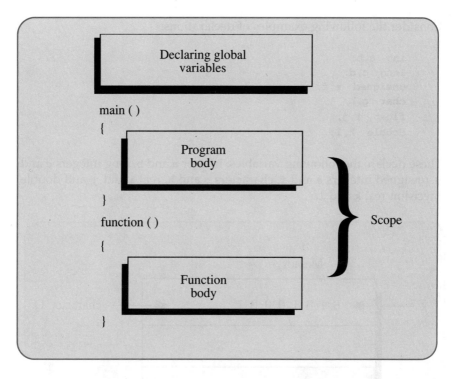

*Figure 2.2*
**Declaring
Global
Objects**

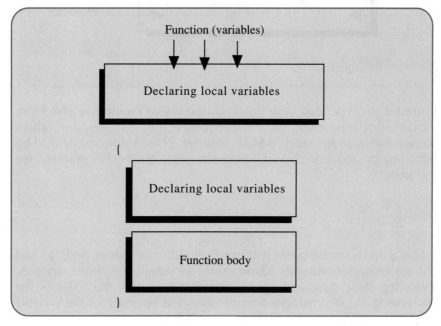

*Figure 2.3*
**Declaring
Local
Objects**

Consider the following examples of declarations:

```
int  a,b;
long  c,d;
unsigned  e,f;
char  g,h;
float  i,j;
double  k,l;
```

These declare the following variables: integer **a** and **b**, long integers **c** and **d**, unsigned integers **e** and **f**, characters **g** and **h**, real **i** and **j**, and double precision real **k** and **l**.

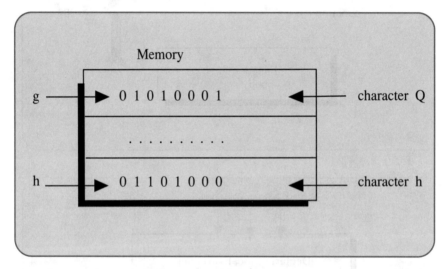

*Figure 2.4*

**ASCII Codes Stored for Characters 'Q' and 'h'**

Consider the type **char** once more. In the above example, **g** and **h** are variables of type **char**. As a consequence they can acquire values corresponding to any single **ASCII** character. These values are defined by including the required character between single quotes. For example, we can write:

```
g = 'Q';
h = 'h';
```

where **g** and **h** are variables that can have different values, and '**Q**' and '**h**' are character constants whose values are assigned to those variables. Executing these statements, your computer will store the codes of the character **Q** and the character **h** in memory cells reserved for the variable

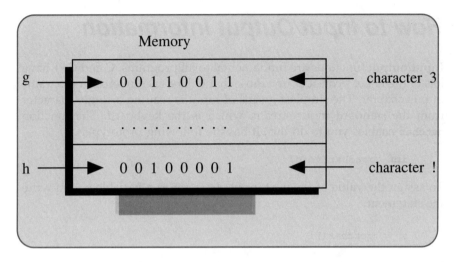

*Figure 2.5*

**ASCII Codes
Stored for
Characters
'3' and '!'**

**g** and **h** respectively, as illustrated in Figure 2.4. We can assign new values
to the variables **g** and **h**, for example:

```
g = '3';
h = '!';
```

Figure 2.5 shows which codes will be put in the corresponding memory
cells.

In **C**, you can initialize variables within the declaration statement. Some
examples of how you can do this are as follows:

```
int   a=10,b=20;
char  c='R',ch='*';
float f=1.87;
```

You simply follow the variable name with an equals sign, then the value
you wish to set initially.

# How to Input/Output Information

**Input/output** functions are fundamental to all programs. **C** and **C++** have lots of them. Let's consider first those that will be encountered in programs in this chapter. The simplest means of input is reading a single character from the standard input stream, which is the keyboard. The function **getchar** enables you to do this. It has the following prototype:

```
int  getchar(void);
```

To assign the value of the next input character to a variable **x**, you write the statement:

```
x  =  getchar();
```

The variable **x** must be of type **char** or **int**. Another function, **putchar(x)**, outputs the value of the variable **x** to the standard output stream, which is the screen. The function **putchar** has the following prototype:

```
int  putchar(int);
```

## Example EX2_1

Consider a sample program:

```
/*  example  EX2_1  */
#include  <stdio.h>
void  main(void)
{   char  x;
    printf("Enter  any  character:  ");
    x  =  getchar();
    printf("\nA  character  entered:  ");
    putchar(x);
    printf("\n");
}
```

When you start running the program, you will see a prompt on the screen:

**Enter any character:**

Press the *W* key followed by *<Enter>*. You will then see the message:

**A character entered: w**

The function **printf**, which is used in the program to output the prompt and the message, will be discussed in detail later. The necessary declarations for **getchar** and **putchar** are made in the standard include file **stdio.h**.

Note, that the function **getchar** requires that you press *<Enter>* after keying in a character. Sometimes this is not very convenient. The functions **getch** and **getche** can help you in this instance. They have the following prototypes:

```
int  getch(void);
int  getche(void);
```

Both these functions read in a character as soon as you press the corresponding key, so there is no need to press *<Enter>*. The difference between them is that **getche** displays the input character on the screen, and **getch** does not. Replace the function **getchar** in the program EX2_1 with **getch** and **getche** and you'll see how they work. Since the prototypes for these functions are held in the file **conio.h**, this file must be included in the program using the statement:

```
#include  <conio.h>
```

# Formatted Data Output

The function **printf** provides formatted output to the standard output stream which is the screen. It can be written in the following formal form:

```
printf("control  string"  ,  argument_1,  argument_2,...);
```

The control string contains items of three types: **ordinary characters** that are copied to the standard output stream and thus displayed on the screen, **format specifiers** which determine how the arguments of the succeeding list are displayed and **control character constants**.

## Format Specifiers

Each format specifier starts with a **%** symbol and terminates with a format setting character. You can put a variety of symbols between the **%** symbol and the format setting character, so let's first explain those.

Format Specifiers can be any of the following:

▲ (-) Indicating that the formatted item must be left-justified in its field.

▲ A string of digits setting the minimum field size.

▲ A point (.), dividing a field size from the next string of digits.

▲ A string of digits, setting either the maximum number of characters to be output from a string, or the number of digits to be output to the right of the decimal point in values of type **float** and **double.**

▲ The character l, indicating that the corresponding argument is of type **long.**

▲ The character # preceding the format characters **g, f** or **e**, forcing a decimal point to be output even if no digits follow it. When the # symbol precedes the character **x** a prefix **0x** will be inserted in front of the corresponding hexadecimal value displayed. The example EX2_6 demonstrates the use of the character **#.**

▲ The character * that lets you to define the minimum field length and precision of the corresponding output number. The example EX2_6 also shows the use of the character *.

## The Format Setting Characters

The format setting characters may be any of the following:

c    The argument value is a character.

d    The argument value is a decimal integer.

i    The argument value is a decimal integer.

e    The argument value is a decimal integer and is to be displayed in scientific notation.

f    The argument value is decimal floating point and is to be displayed as a decimal.

g      Uses **e** or **f**, whichever is shorter.

o      The argument value is an octal integer.

s      The argument value is a character string, and the characters of the string are to be displayed until an end-of-line character is encountered, or the number of characters specified by precision is reached.

u      The argument value is an unsigned decimal integer.

x      The argument value is a hexadecimal integer.

p      The argument value is a pointer.

n      Used in format operations. The argument corresponding to this character specifier must be an integer pointer. A value is returned to the argument corresponding to this specifier, which is the present screen character position. The first position in a line is 0, the second is 1 and so on. Example EX2_3 shows how this specifier is used. The values assigned for the position in the output line, are displayed on the screen.

If the **%** symbol is followed by a character that is not a format setting character, this character will be displayed on the screen. Thus, the string **%%** displays the **%** symbol.

The function **printf** uses the control string to define the number of arguments and their types. Variables, constants, expressions, function calls can all be arguments. The only constraint is that their values must correspond to the specifiers. If the number of arguments or their types do not correspond with the control string specifications, the results will be incorrect.

The control character constants you are likely to use most often are as follows:

| | |
|---|---|
| \a - Audible bell | \b - Backspace |
| \f - Formfeed | \n - Linefeed |
| \r - Carriage return | \t - Horizontal tab |
| \v - Vertical tab | \\ - Backslash |
| \' - Single quote | \" - Double quote |
| \? - Question mark | |

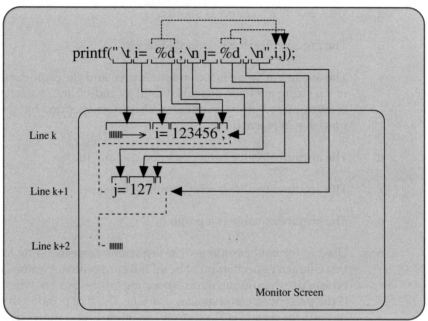

*Figure2.6*

**Using the Function Printf**

Let's take a look at a **printf** statement using some of these. When the statement:

```
printf("\tIBM\n%d\n",i);
```

is executed the following sequence of events occur:

1. The tab operator **\t** causes the cursor to move one tab position.

2. The three letters **IBM** appear on the screen.

3. The **\n** causes the cursor to move to the beginning of the next line.

4. The value of the integer **i** is formatted according to format **%d**.

and, finally,

5. The **\n** causes the cursor to move to the beginning of the next line.

Figure 2.6 shows the operation of the function **printf** assuming that i = 123456 and is of type **long** and j = 127 and is of type **int**.

## *Formatted Data Input*

The function **scanf** provides formatted input. It can be written in the following formal form:

```
scanf("control string", argument_1, argument_2,...);
```

The **scanf** arguments must be pointers to values corresponding to the control string specification. We will discuss pointers in more detail later. For the moment it is sufficient to understand that a pointer contains the address of the memory location containing the value of a given variable. The character **&** preceding a variable name, denotes the pointer corresponding to that variable. Figure 2.7 shows how the character **&** is interpreted when it precedes the name of a variable **i**.

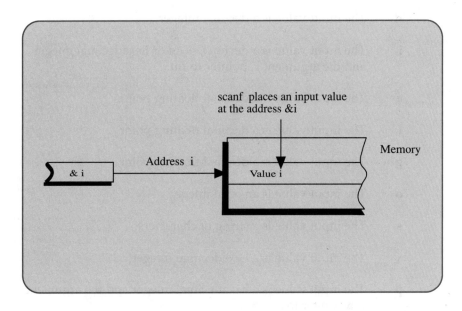

*Figure 2.7*

**A Sample Operation of Taking an Address**

As in the case of **printf**, the control string contains the **format specifiers** and is used to define the number and types of the arguments. It can include:

▲ Whitespace characters, which are blanks, tab symbols **\t**, and newline symbols **\n**. The occurrence of these in the control string causes all consecutive whitespace characters in the input string, up to the next non-whitespace character, to be ignored.

▲ Format specifiers consisting of the symbol **%**, an optional character **\***, and a format setting character. Inclusion of the **\*** causes the input field to be skipped.

▲ Non-whitespace characters, which are all other characters except **%**. They will each cause a matching non-whitespace character to be read but not stored.

Consider the format characters of the function **scanf**:

| | |
|---|---|
| **c** | The input value is a character. |
| **d** | The input value is a decimal integer. |
| **i** | The input value is a decimal, octal or hexadecimal integer and the argument is pointer to **int**. |
| **e** | The input value is a decimal floating point. |
| **f** | The input value is a decimal floating point. |
| **g** | The input value is a decimal floating point. |
| **o** | The input value is an octal integer. |
| **s** | The input value is a string of characters. |
| **x** | The input value is a hexadecimal integer. |
| **p** | The input value is a hexadecimal integer and the argument is a pointer to an object. |

**n**    The argument corresponding to this character specifier must be a pointer to **int**, and the number of characters read successfully up to the %n is stored. Example EX2_4 shows the usage of this specifier.

**u**    The argument value is an unsigned decimal integer.

**[ ]**   Scan for characters from the set contained between the square brackets.

The letter **l** can precede the characters **d, o, x,** and **f**. In the first three cases variables must be of type **long**, and in the last case of type **double**.

Figure 2.8 illustrates an example of using **scanf**, and shows the correspondence between the arguments and the specifier characters. In the example,the last argument **l**, has no **&** symbol in front of it. This is because **l** is a character array declared as **char l[20];**, where the number 20 in square brackets defines the number of array elements. In **C** and **C++**, an array name is always a pointer containing the address of the first element in the array. We will see more about arrays in Chapter 8.

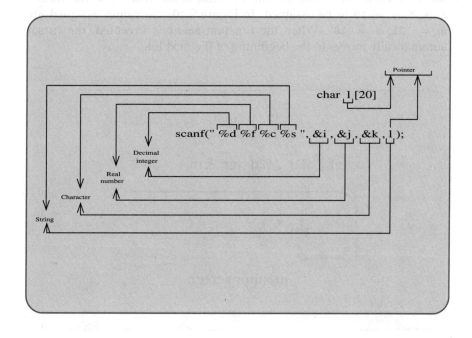

*Figure 2.8*

**Using
the Scanf
Function**

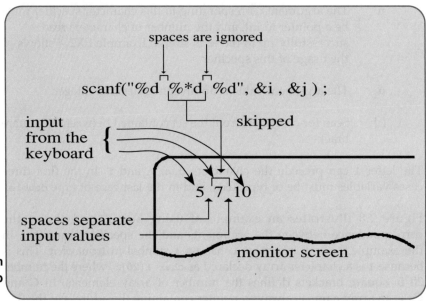

*Figure 2.9*

**Scanf Operation Using * to Skip Input**

Figure 2.9 and Figure 2.10 give further examples of the operation of the function **scanf**. In Figure 2.9, the function **scanf** will cause the values: **i = 5, j = 10** to be assigned. In Figure 2.10, the values assigned are **n = 321, m = 18**. When the function **scanf** is executed, the cursor automatically moves to the beginning of the next line.

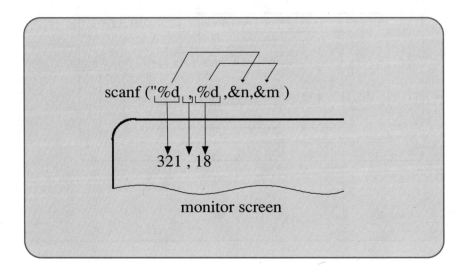

*Figure 2.10*

**The Scanf Operation**

# Input/Output Examples

## Example EX2_2

The first example demonstrates the use of format specifiers:

```
/* example EX2_2 */
#include <stdio.h>
void main(void)
{   char str[40];
    puts("Enter a character string");
    gets(str);
    printf("%50s\n",str);
    printf("%-50s\n",str);
    printf("%50.20s\n",str);
    printf("%-50.20s\n",str);
}
```

Here two new functions **puts** and **gets** are used. The function **puts** outputs the line appearing as an argument in double quotes to the standard output stream which is the screen and moves the cursor to the beginning of the next line. The function **gets** reads characters from the standard input stream, the keyboard, into the character array **str**. It has 40 elements determined by the number 40 in the square brackets in its declaration. Subscripts of the array start from 0, so there are the elements: **str[0]**, **str[1]**, ..., **str[39]**.

The results of the program will be:

> **Enter a character string**
> *Minsk is the capital of  Belorus<Enter>*
> **Minsk is the capital of Belorus**
> **Minsk is the capital of Belorus**
> **Minsk is the capital**
> **Minsk is the capital**

## Example EX2_3

The next example shows the usage of the specifier **%n** which will store the count of the number of characters output so far in the location pointed to by the corresponding input argument:

```
/* example EX2_3 */
#include <stdio.h>
void main(void)
{   int   num1,num2,num3,i,j;
    i = 2;
    j = 12;
    printf("%n%d%d%n   examples%n\n",&num1,i,j,&num2,&num3);
    printf("%i   %i   %i\n",num1,num2,num3);
}
```

The results of program execution will be:

**2 12 examples**
**0 4 13**

In the first **printf** statement we have three **%n** specifiers. The variables which will record the output character count corresponding to each **%n** specifier are **num1**, **num2**, and **num3**. The **%n** specifier requires a pointer to an integer variable as an argument, a pointer being an address as we will see in detail in Chapter 7. The symbol **&** as a prefix to a variable name defines a pointer to that variable. Thus **&num1**, **&num2** and **&num3** which appear as arguments in the first **printf** are pointers to the variables **num1**, **num2** and **num3**.

The first **%n** specifier is at the beginning of the control string which corresponds to the zero position in the input stream. Therefore, the variable **num1** will assume the value 0. The second **%n** specifier appears after the output of the two values **i** and **j** which are separated by a space. If we count the characters up to the second **%n** specifier we will get: 2 is 0, space is 1, 1 is 2, 2 is 3, and **%n** is 4. As a result we'll get **num2** having the value 4. In the same manner we can calculate that **num3** is 13.

## Example EX2_4

Here is an example that demonstrates the specifier %n for the function
**scanf** where it will store the number of character input prior to its
occurrence:

```
/* example EX2_4 */
#include <stdio.h>
void main(void)
{ char str[30];
  int num;
  puts("Enter a string");
  scanf("%29s%n",str,&num);
  printf("Characters entered: %d\n",num);
}
```

If you run the program you should get something like:

> **Enter a string**
> *12345<Enter>*
> **Characters entered: 5**

The pointer corresponding to the %n specifier is **&num**. After execution of
the scanf statement, the variable **num** will contain a count of the number
of characters you enter. In the format specifier **%29s**, the number 29 defines
the maximum number of characters that can be entered.

## Example EX2_5

The following example demonstrates the use of the specifier %[] which defines a search set of characters for acceptable input:

```
/* example EX2_5 */
#include <stdio.h>
void main(void)
{  char str1[30],str2[30];
   int num;
   puts("Enter a string (up to 29 characters)");
   scanf("%[123456789]%s",str1,str2);
   printf("String 1: %s;\nString 2: %s\n",str1,str2);
}
```

The results of executing the program will be:

> **Enter a string (up to 29 characters)**
> *12345abcdef<Enter>*
> **String 1: 12345;**
> **String 2: abcdef**

Here we entered the string "**12345abcdef**". Only the first five characters of the string, "**12345**", are contained within the set of characters enclosed within the square brackets of the corresponding specifier in the **scanf** statement. Therefore, only these five characters will be in the first string **str1**. The specifier %[] continues to read input characters up to the first character which is not in the search set. Thus the remaining characters will be in the second string **str2**. If , instead of the string indicated, you enter:

> *1234a5bcdef<Enter>*

The first variable str1 would contain "1234", and **str2** would contain the remainder of the input string "a5bcdef".

## *Example EX2_6*

In the function printf, the width specifier * requires that the actual width specifier be supplied as input. The last statement shows the use of the character * and also the character # to force 0x in outputting hexadecimal values:

```
/* example EX2_6 */
#include <stdio.h>
void main(void)
{ printf("%*.*f\n",10,3,12.3);
  printf("%#x\n",20);
}
```

The results of this program will be:

**12.300**
**0x14**

Here the number 10, in the first call to the function **printf**, defines the minimum width of an input field and the number 3 defines the number of digits after the decimal point. As a consequence, the output number 12.3 will be shifted to the left in the output field to accommodate three decimal places. The hexadecimal number $14_{16}$, corresponding to $20_{10}$, will be displayed with the prefix 0x by the second call to **printf**.

You will find many more examples using the input/output functions in a variety of ways, in the succeeding chapters of the book.

# CHAPTER 7

# OPERATORS AND EXPRESSIONS

## Variables and Constants

Expressions consist of **operands**, such as variables or constants, connected by **operators,** such as addition, subtraction, or multiplication, which cause some kind of computation to occur. The order of execution among operators, when evaluating expressions, is determined by their priorities.

However, these priorities can be overridden by using round brackets, or parentheses, to enclose sub-expressions. Expressions within the innermost parentheses are evaluated first, with succeeding levels within parentheses being evaluated in sequence from the innermost to the outermost. We can illustrate this by an example. If we write the expression:

```
a+b*c
```

The calculation will first evaluate the products b*c and the result will be added to a. So if a, b, c have the values 1, 2, and 3 respectively, the expression will have the value 7. If we write the expression:

```
(a+b) *c
```

The parentheses force the sum a+b to be evaluated first, the result then being multiplied by c. With the same values assigned to the variables as above, the expression will have the value 9.

All variables must be declared prior to their use. As we have already seen in previous examples, they are declared in a statement which includes a type keyword, followed by a list of variables of that type separated by commas. For example:

```
int   a,b,c,d;
char  X,Y;
```

As we have also seen previously, variables can be declared individually in separate statements if you wish. For example:

```
char  x;
char  y;
```

Along with variables, there are the following types of constants:

1. Floating point, for example 123.456, or 5.61e-8. They can have the suffix **F**, so the examples could be written: 123.456F, 5.61e-8F.

2. Integer, for example 125.

3. Long integer, with the letter **L** appended, for example: 361327L.

4. Unsigned integer, with the letter **U** appended, for example: 62125U.

5. Octal, with a zero leading digit, for example: 071.

6. Hexadecimal, with the characters **0X** as the first two digits, for example: 0X1F2.

7. Character, presented as a single character enclosed between single quotes, for example: 'q', '2', or '!'. The characters that cannot be represented graphically can be written using special combinations of characters, for example, \n which defines the newline character, or \0 which define the end-of- string character, which is a byte with all bits zero. Any bit image of a single byte can be represented as: '\**NNN**', where NNN is one, two, or three octal digits. Hexadecimal representation may also be used, such as '\x2B', or '\x36'.

8. String, a sequence of characters, enclosed between double quotes, for example: **"This is a string constant"**. The quotes are not included in the string but simply confine it. A string is an array of elements, each containing one character, which is terminated by a byte containing the character \0. Thus, the number of bytes necessary for storing the string is one greater than the number of bytes enclosed between the double quotes.

▲9▲ Constant expressions, consisting of only constants and evaluated during compilation of a program, for example, **a = 60 + 30**.

▲10▲ Long double, with the letter **L** as a suffix, for example: 1234567.89L. These are distinguished from long integers by the decimal point.

## C Language Operators

Now take a look at some of the operators in **C**. These operators also apply in **C++**. In the next chapter we'll discuss the new operators that you can only use in **C++**.

| Operator | What it is or does | Associativity |
|---|---|---|
| ()<br>[]<br>.<br>-> | Function Call<br>Array Subscript<br>Direct Component Selector<br>Indirect Component Selector | Left to Right |
| !<br>~<br>-<br>++<br>--<br>&<br>*<br>(type)<br>sizeof | Logical Negation (NOT)<br>Bitwise 1's Complement<br>Unary Minus<br>Pre- or Post-increment<br>Pre- or Post-decrement<br>Address<br>Indirection<br>Type conversion<br>Size of operand, in bytes | Right to Left |
| *<br>/<br>% | Multiply<br>Divide<br>Remainder (Modulus) | Left to Right |
| +<br>- | Addition, Binary Operator<br>Subtraction, Binary Operator | Left to Right |
| <<<br>>> | Shift Left<br>Shift Right | Left to Right |

**TABLE 2.2**

| Operator | What it is or does | Associativity |
|---|---|---|
| <br><= <br>> <br>>= | Less Than <br>Less than or Equal To <br>Greater Than <br>Greater Than or Equal To | Left to Right |
| == <br>!= | Equal To <br>Not Equal To | Left to Right |
| & | Bitwise AND | Left to Right |
| ^ | Bitwise XOR (Exclusive OR) | Left to Right |
| \| | Bitwise OR | Left to Right |
| && | Logical AND | Left to Right |
| \|\| | Logical OR | Left to Right |
| ?: | Conditional Operator <br>(Ternary Operator) | Right to Left |
| = <br>*= /= <br><<= etc | Assignment <br>All of these are <br>Operation then Assignment | Right to Left |
| | Evaluate | Left to Right |

**TABLE 2.2 CONT'D**

Expressions typically contain several operators, executable in a strict sequence. As we have said, this sequence is determined by the relative priorities of the operators. These are shown in Table 2.2, where the **C** operators are listed and divided into priority groups separated by the horizontal lines. Operators within a group are of equal priority.

The groups in the table are in priority sequence with the highest at the top. Operators of the highest priority in an expression are executed first. Operators of equal priority are executed from left to right, or from right to left depending on their group associativity. If an expression contains parentheses, then the contents of each level of parentheses are evaluated in sequence starting with the innermost, through to the outermost.

Let us investigate the basic operators of **C** in a bit more detail. We will first consider the assignment operator (=). The statement:

```
x = y;
```

assigns the value of the variable **y** to the variable **x**. You can also make multiple assignments in a single statement:

```
x = y = z = 100;
```

Here all three variables are assigned a value of 100.

In Table 2.2, we refer to **unary** operator, and **binary** operators. Unary operators have just one operand, whereas binary operators have two. We also have one **ternary** operator which takes three operands. Let's consider the operators falling within the following classifications:

1. Arithmetic operators

2. Logical and relational operators

3. Bitwise operators

Each classification spans several priority groups. The arithmetic operators in Table 2.2 are:

```
+, -, *, /, %
```

The last operator, modulus, computes the remainder when its right operand is divided into its left. It may not be used with floating-point variables or constants. Some sample expressions with these operators are:

```
a=b+c;
x=y-z;
r=t*v;
s=k/1;
p=q%w;
```

The logical and relational operators in Table 2.2 consists of:

```
&&, ||, >, >=, <, <=, ==, !=
```

All these operators result in one of two values; **true**, or **false**. **C** defines these values by the rule that **true** is any non-zero value and **false** is zero. However, expressions employing logical and relational operators normally return 0 for **false** and 1 for **true**. We can show the effects of the logical operators by means of a truth table. Each row in the table defines the results of combining the variables with the values shown, in the expressions indicated in the column headings. The truth table for logical operators is:

| x | y | x && y | x \|\| y | !x |
|---|---|--------|---------|-----|
| 0 | 0 | 0 | 0 | 1 |
| 0 | 1 | 0 | 1 | 1 |
| 1 | 0 | 0 | 1 | 0 |
| 1 | 1 | 1 | 1 | 0 |

A single expression may combine several operators. For example:

```
y = !a && !(b < c) || x > 3;
```

If **a** is 2, **b** is 3, **c** is 4 and **x** is 5, **y** will be assigned the value 1, or **true**. We can arrive at the result by working through the expression. To begin with **(b < c)** is evaluated to **true**. The terms with logical not operators are evaluated next, **!a** being **false** and **!true** from **! (b < c)** also resulting in **false**. Next **x>3** is evaluated because **>** is the highest priority of the operators remaining. The result is **true**. What we now have is the expression:

```
false && false ||true
```

which has the value **true**.

You can apply bitwise operators to variables of type **int**, and **char**, and their modified variants such as **long**. They may not be used with variables of type **float**, **double**, **void**, or more complex types. The bitwise operators are:

```
~, <<, >>, &, ^, |
```

All these operators are defined in Table 2.2. Setting the shift operators aside for a moment, the truth table for the remaining bitwise operators is:

| x | y | ~x | x & y | x \| y | x ^ y |
|---|---|----|-------|--------|-------|
| 0 | 0 | 1 | 0 | 0 | 0 |
| 0 | 1 | 1 | 0 | 1 | 1 |
| 1 | 0 | 0 | 0 | 1 | 1 |
| 1 | 1 | 0 | 1 | 1 | 0 |

Now turn to some examples using shift operators. In the statement:

```
a = b << c;
```

the value of **b** is shifted **c** bits to left. Let us assume that **b** has the value $3_{10}$, which is the same as $0011_2$ and **c** is 2. After execution of the operation, **a** will be $1100_2$, which is the same as $12_{10}$. It is equivalent to 3 multiplied by 2 and then by 2 again. In the statement:

```
a = b >> c;
```

the value of **b** is shifted **c** bits to right . If **b** is $12_{10}$, which is $1100_2$, and **c** is 2, then after execution of the operation **a** will be $0011_2$, which is $3_{10}$.

Suppose we have variables declared as:

```
unsigned char a,b;
```

and further, the variables have values a = $00110011_2$, which is the same as $51_{10}$, and b = $01010101_2$ which is $85_{10}$. Then the results of bitwise operations a && b, a | b, a ^ b, will be:

```
00110011   &&   01010101   =   00010001
00110011   |    01010101   =   01110111
00110011   ^    01010101   =   01100110
```

The results in decimal values are: a & b is $17_{10}$, a | b is $119_{10}$, and a ^ b is $102_{10}$. The unary operator will give the following results:

$$\sim a = 11001100_2 = 204_{10}, \quad \sim b = 10101010_2 = 170_{10}.$$

Two unusual operators in **C** and **C++** are **++**, which is called the **increment** operator and **- -** , which is called the **decrement** operator. They increase or decrease the value of a variable by 1, respectively. You can use them either in front of or behind a variable. When prefixing a variable, such as in **++n** or **- - n** , the value of **n** is incremented or decremented before being used in an expression. Used after a variable, as in **n++** or **n - -**, the value of **n** is incremented or decremented after being used in an expression. Consider the following two lines of a program:

```
a = b + c++;
a1 = b1 + ++c1;
```

Suppose that the initial values are,

$b = b1 = 2$, and $c = c1 = 4$.

Then after executing the statements we will have resulting values as:

$a = 6$, $b = 2$, $c = 5$, $a1 = 7$, $b1 = 2$, and $c1 = 5$.

Another operator that is frequently used, is the conditional operator **?:**, which takes three operands. In the statement:

```
y=x?a:b;
```

**y** is set to **a**, if **x** is not zero and **y** is set to **b** if x equals zero. The statement:

```
y = (a > b) ? a : b;
```

allows you to assign to the variable **y**, the value of the greater of **a** or **b**, i.e. y=max(a,b).

The statement:

```
a=a+5;
```

can also be written as:

```
a += 5;
```

You can use other binary operators besides addition with the equals sign, as indicated in Table 2.2. All the other operators given in Table 2.2 will be reviewed later on.

## Example EX2_7

Coming back to the shift operators using a complete program example:

```c
/* example EX2_7 */
#include <stdio.h>
void main(void)
{  int a;
   unsigned b;
   a = 8;
   printf("shift to right (a=8): %d %d %d\n",a>>1,a>>2,a>>3);
   printf("shift to left (a=8): %d %d %d\n",a<<1,a<<2,a<<3);
   a = -8;
   printf("shift to right (a=-8): %d %d %d\n",a>>1,a>>2,a>>3);
   b = 0xFFFF;
   printf("shift to left (b=0xFFFF): %#x %#x\n",b<<1,b<<2);
}
```

The results of executing the program will be:

> **shift to right (a=8): 4 2 1**
> **shift to left (a=8): 16 32 64**
> **shift to right (a=-8): -4 -2 -1**
> **shift to left (b=0xFFFF): 0xfffe 0xfffc**

The first two calls to **printf** shift a positive number to the right. A shift one place to the right decreases the initial value by a factor of 2 and a shift one place to the left increases the value by a factor of 2. When a negative number is shifted right, as in the third call to the function **printf**, the sign is propagated. Propagating the sign bit when a negative number is shifted right ensures arithmetic consistency with both positive and negative integers. This is because negative integers are represented in your PC in what is called 2's complement form. The 2's complement form for a negative integer can be created very easily from the positive form. Start with the binary representation of +8 as an example which is:

0000 0000 0000 0100

To produce -8 in 2's complement form, first create the 1's complement. You do this simply by flipping all the bits in the binary representation of +8, 0 becomes 1 and 1 becomes 0. You will get:

1111 1111 1111 1011

If you now add one to this the result will be -8 in 2's complement form, which is:

1111 1111 1111 1100

To verify that this is indeed -8, you could add binary +8. You will get the result zero.

If shift right did not propagate the sign bit, a shift right of one on -8 would result in the value:

0111 1111 1111 1110

which is 32,766 in decimal, which would not be a particularly obvious result. So propagating the sign bit is most helpful. Shifting -8 one bit to the right produces the binary representation of -4 in 2's complement form, consistent with the same operation on positive integers.

# *Type Conversion*

When expressions contain operands of different types, the operands are converted to a common type. Each arithmetic operand is converted according to the following sequence of rules:

1. If one of the operators in the expression is of type **long double**, all operators are converted into type **long double**.

2. If one of the operators in the expression is of type **double**, all operators are converted into type **double**.

3. If one of the operators in the expression is of type **float**, all operators are converted into type **float**.

4. If one of the operators in the expression is of type **unsigned long**, all operators are converted into type **unsigned long**.

5. If one of the operators in the expression is of type **long**, all operators are converted into type **long**.

6. If one of the operators in the expression is of type **unsigned**, all operators are converted into type **unsigned**.

7. Otherwise, all operators are converted into type **int**.

The type **char** is converted into type **int** with a sign: the type **unsigned char** is converted into the type **int** with the upper byte being always zero; the type **signed char** is converted into the type **int** with the sign bit inherited from **char**; the type **short** is converted into the type **int** (signed or unsigned).

Suppose we have evaluated the expression in an assignment statement to the right of the assignment operator. To the left of the operator we have a variable and its type differs from the type of the result from the expression. The type conversion rule is easy: the value of the right side of the assignment is converted to the type of the left side. If the size of the result of the expression on the right requires more bytes than are available for the variable on the left, the upper part of the result will be lost.

**C** allows you to explicitly define the type of an expression. A type conversion operator is used for this purpose. It is used in the following general form:

```
(type)  expression
```

You can specify any type that is a valid **C** data type.

Consider an example:

```
int x;
float y,z;
........
z = y + (float) x;
```

Here the integer variable, **x**, is explicitly converted into the type **float**.

## Pointers

**Pointers** are variables that hold the address, or position in memory, of other objects. Using a single pointer you can address different objects at different times in your program. As we shall see in Chapter 8, using pointers can significantly improve the efficiency of execution. They also make many operations, such as string handling for example, much easier to manage and more efficient in the use of memory. The unary operator **&** gives the address of an object. That is why the operation **y=&x;** assigns the address of the variable **x** to the variable **y** as shown in Figure 2.11 (overleaf). The operator **&** may not be used with constants and expressions, so constructions such as **&(x+7)**, or **&28**, are not allowed.

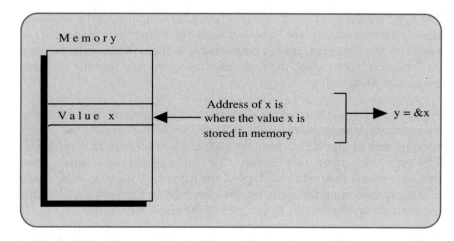

*Figure 2.11*

**An Example
of the
Operand &**

The unary operator **\***, interprets its operand as the address of an object, and uses this address to retrieve the value. Thus the statement:

```
z = *y;
```

assigns the variable **z** the value stored at the address **y**. This is illustrated graphically in Figure 2.12. If we have:

```
y = &x;
z = *y;
```

then, as illustrated in Figure 2.13, **z** will be equal to **x**.

Objects consisting of the symbol **\*** and an address variable, for example, **\*a**, must be declared:

```
int *a *b, *c;
char *d;
```

The declaration **char \*d;** means that the value stored at the address defined by the pointer **d**, is of type **char**.

Pointers may be included in expressions. If **y** is an integer pointer, having been declared as **int \*y;**, then **\*y** may appear anywhere that a variable which is not a pointer can appear. Using **\*y** is the equivalent of using a normal integer variable.

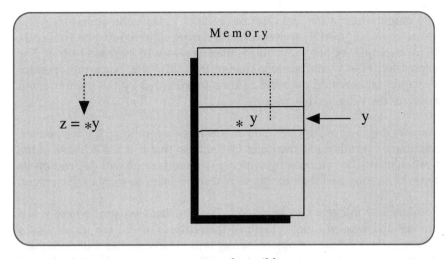

*Figure 2.12*

**An Example
of the
Operand ***

Thus, the following expressions are admissible:

```
*y  =  7;
*x  *=  5;
(*z)++;
```

The first statement stores 7 in the memory cell at the address **y**, the second multiplies the value in the address **x** by 5 , and the third adds 1 to the contents of the memory cell with the address **z**.

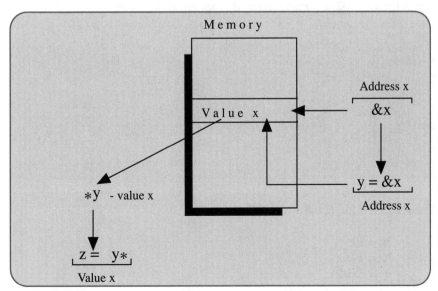

*Figure 2.13*

**The Operation
with Pointers**

The parentheses in the last case are necessary, since the operators * and ++ are of equal priority, and are executed from right to left (see Table 2.2). If, for example, *z has the value 5, then (*z)++ will increase *z to 6. The expression *z++ would simply change the address z, since the operator ++ would be executed over the address represented by the pointer z, but not over the value in this address.

Pointers may be used as operands in arithmetic operations. If y is a pointer, the unary operation y++ increases its value so that it is the address of the next element. The amount by which y is incremented will depend on its type declaration and the number of bytes necessary to store each element.

Pointers and integers can be added. The construction y+n, where y is a pointer and n is an integer, defines the address of the nth object that y points at. This is true for objects of any type. The compiler will determine the appropriate value of the increment of the address from the type defined in the corresponding declaration for the pointer variable.

Any address can be tested for equality (==) or inequality (!=) with a special value, NULL, that enables you to detect an empty pointer that contains no address.

## Example EX2_8

Consider a simple example using the operators & and *:

```
/* example EX2_8 */
#include <stdio.h>
void main(void)
{   int  *a,b;
    b = 10;
    a = &b;
    printf("b   =  %d;\n",b);
    printf("*a  =  %d;\n",*a);
    printf("a   =  %p.\n",a);
}
```

The results of the program will be:

> b  = 10;
> *a = 10;
> a  = FFF4

# Loop Operators

Loops are used to repeat a statement or set of statements n times as shown in Figure 2.14. **C** has three loop operators: `for, while` and `do-while`. The first one can be presented as:

```
for(expression_1;expression_2;expression_3)  loop  body
```

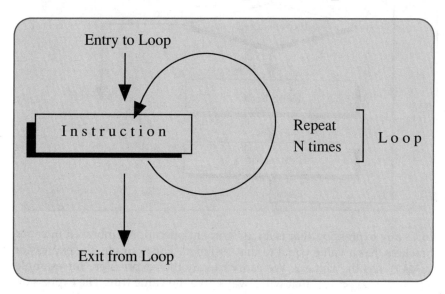

*Figure 2.14*

**Loop Demonstration**

Figure 2.15 (overleaf) gives a block-diagram of the operator `for`. The loop body consists of any number of statements enclosed between braces. The expressions 1, 2 and 3 can have a special variable called a **control variable**. Its values determine the number of repetitions, or the conditions to exit from the loop. The expressions have the following functions:

Expression 1: Initializing the value of a control variable
Expression 2: Checking the conditions for loop continuation
Expression 3: Changing the value of the variable

Any of these three expressions may be omitted in the for-loop statement, but the semicolons are obligatory. Thus

```
for(;;)  {  ...  }
```

is an endless loop that you would need to provide with some other means of exiting.

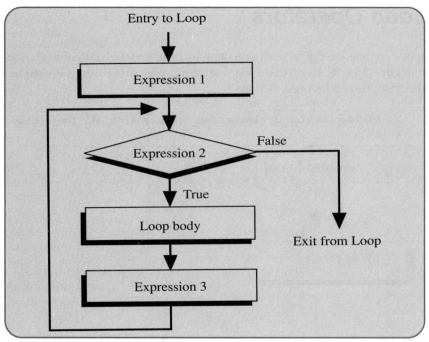

*Figure 3.15*

**A For Loop Demonstration**

In **C**, any expression that is an assignment operation, embraced in round brackets, has a value equal to that assigned. For example, the expression `(a=2+7)` has the value 9. We can write another expression, for example: `((a = 7 + 2) < 10)`, that will always give the value **true**. The expression:

```
((c = getch())  ==  'i')
```

allows you to read in the value of a variable **c**, and be **true** only when the assigned value is the character **i**. In brackets, you can write any number of statements, separated by commas, to construct a complex statement. The commas are known as series operators. The statements will be executed from left to right and the whole expression will assume the value of the last executed statement. For example, if there are two variables of type **char**, the statement:

```
z = (x = y,y = getch());
```

defines the following actions: the variable **x** is assigned the value of the variable **y**; the variable **y** is assigned the value of the character entered from the keyboard; and finally the variable **z** is assigned the value of the variable **y**. The brackets are necessary since the series operator is of a lower priority than the assignment operator following the variable **z** (see Table 2.2). The series operator is extensively used in loop statements. This operator allows you to construct complex expressions that will update the multiple control variable in parallel. You will see applications of this in later examples of programs we will discuss.

The **while** operator can be written as:

```
while(expression)  loop  body
```

Its graphical interpretation is shown in Figure 2.16. The expression in the brackets can assume non-zero (**true**) and zero (**false**) values. If the value is **true**, the loop body is executed and the expression is evaluated again. If it's **false**, the **while** loop ends. The main difference between the **while** loop and   **do-while**, is that the body of the loop in **do-while** is always executed at least once, as the expression is evaluated after executing the loop body. This is not so with the **while** loop, where the conditional expression is evaluated first. The **do-while** operator is written as:

```
do  loop  body  while  (expression)
```

Its graphical interpretation is shown in Figure 2.17 (overleaf). The loop body will be executed unless the expression in brackets is **false**. If it's **false** at the loop entrance, the loop body will be executed once.  All loops may be nested inside one another, so the body of any loop may contain the operators **for, while** and **do-while**.

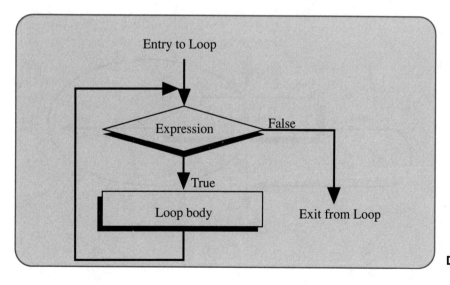

*Figure 2.16*
**While Loop
Demonstration**

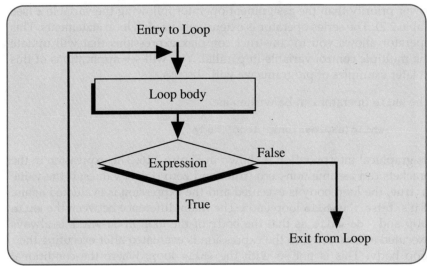

*Figure 2.17*

**Loop Do-while Demonstration**

There are two new operators that may be used in the loop body: **break** and **continue**. **Break** is used to exit unconditionally from a loop. The operator **continue** skips any remaining lines of code to the end of the loop and causes a jump back to the beginning of the loop. Figure 2.18 shows how these operators function.

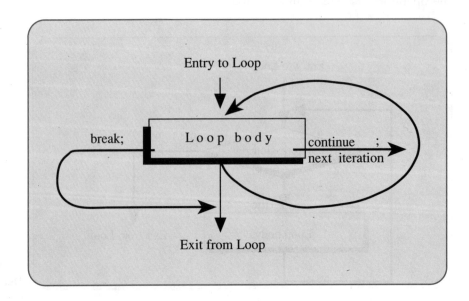

*Figure 2.18*

**Using the Operators Break and Continue**

# *Conditional and Unconditional Operators*

Selection statements `if-else`, `switch` and `goto`, are used in **C** to organize conditional and unconditional jumps in a program. The first statement is written:

```
if (condition_check) statement_1; else statement_2;
```

Figure 2.19 displays possible constructions with `if`. If the condition in the brackets is **true**, then `statement 1` will be executed and if it's **false**, `statement 2` will be executed. If you need to use more than one statement, all of them are enclosed within braces. The operator `if` may be used without the statement `else`. In this case, if the condition in the brackets is **true**, `statement 1` will be executed and if it's **false**, then `statement 1` will be skipped. Thus, `statement 2` will always be executed (see Figure 2.19). If the statement immediately following a keyword `if` or `else` in an `if-else` statement is another `if`, it is referred to as nested. According to the convention adopted in **C**, the keyword `else` belongs to the nearest `if` preceding it.

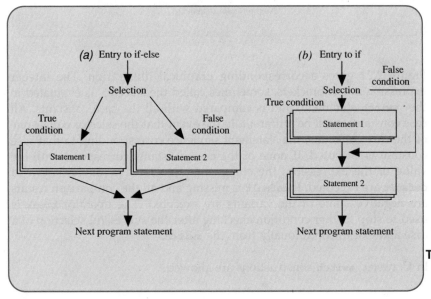

*Figure 2.19*

**Organising Conditional Transitions with else (a) and without it (b)**

The operator **switch** lets you choose any of a number of alternatives, as shown in Figure 2.20.

It's written in the following general form:

```
switch  (expression)
       { case  constant_1:  statement_sequence  break;
         ................................
         case  constant_n-1:  statement_sequence  break;
         default:  statement_sequence    }
```

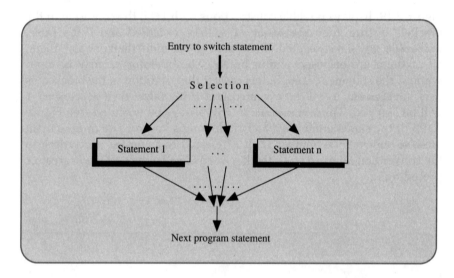

*Figure 2.20*

**Choosing a Variant**

Figure 2.21 gives a corresponding graphical illustration. The integer expression in the brackets, sometimes called the selector, is evaluated in the **switch** statement, and is compared with all the case constants. All case constants must be different. In the event that the selector equals one of the case constants, the statement sequence corresponding to that case constant is executed. If none of the case constants correspond with the value of the expression, the statements associated with the keyword **default** are executed. If **default** is missing and all the comparison results are negative, none of the variants are executed. The operator **break** is used to stop further condition checking after the successful selection of a case and exit unconditionally from the **switch**.

In **C**, nested **switch** constructions are allowed.

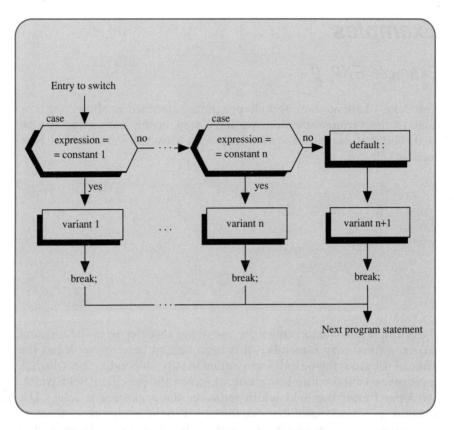

*Figure 2.21*
**The Operator
Switch**

Let's now consider the rules for executing an unconditional jump, which is written as:

```
goto  label;
```

A label is any identifier. The operator **goto** indicates that the execution of the program must restart from the instruction that is preceded by the label. There must be a string in the program containing the label, a colon, and the statement to which the jump is to be executed. The label can precede any statement in the function containing the corresponding **goto**.

# Examples

## Example EX2_9

Now take a look at some sample programs, designed to show you how some of the various operators we have seen in the last section can be used. The first example shows a loop with a control variable **f** of type **double**:

```
/*  example  EX2_9  */
#include  <stdio.h>
void  main(void)
{   double  f;
    for(f=1;   f<1e+10;   f*=100)
    printf("%7lg",f);
    putchar('\n');
}
```

The example also demonstrates the use of the specifier **%g** in the function **printf**. As you may remember, it is used instead of **%f** or **%e**. It has the effect of selecting the output form automatically, depending on which is appropriate to the value being output, given the specified field width. The letter l after the field width indicates the argument is long. The function **putchar** is used to move the cursor to the beginning of the next line on the screen. The results of executing the program will be presented in the form:

    1   100  10000 1e+06 1e+08

## Example EX2_10

The second example shows the use of the **while** loop:

```
/* example EX2_10 */
#include <stdio.h>
#include <conio.h>
void main(void)
{  char c, ESC;
   ESC = 27;
   while((c = getch()) != ESC)
   {  printf("A character entered: %c\n",c);
      puts("Press Esc to terminate the program");
   }
}
```

When we run the program, if we press any key, the corresponding character will be displayed on the screen after the text **A character entered:**. Pressing *Esc*, which corresponds to 27 in the code table, terminates the program. Typical output from the program might be:

> r
> **A character entered: r**
> **Press Esc to terminate the program**
> i
> **A character entered: i**
> **Press Esc to terminate the program**
> **<ESC>**

Here **<ESC>** means that the *Esc* key was pressed.

## *Example EX2_11*

The next program compares two lines of input:

```
/*  example  EX2_11  */
#include  <stdio.h>
#include  <process.h>    /*  for  the  function  exit  */
void  main(void)
{   char  str1[30],  str2[30];
    int  i;
    puts("Enter  the  first  string  (up  to  29  "
                    "characters)");
    gets(str1);
    puts("Enter  the  second  string  (up  to  29  "
                    "characters)");
    gets(str2);
    for(i=0;  str1[i]  ==  str2[i];  i++)
    if(str1[i]==0)
    {   puts("str1  -  str2  =  0");
        exit(1);
    }
    printf("str1  -  str2  =  %d\n",str1[i]  -  str2[i]);
}
```

If the entered lines are equal, you 'll see on the screen:

**str1 - str2 = 0**

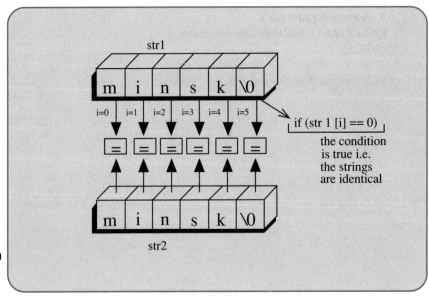

*Figure 2.22*

**Illustration
of the Program
EX2_11 with
Identical Lines**

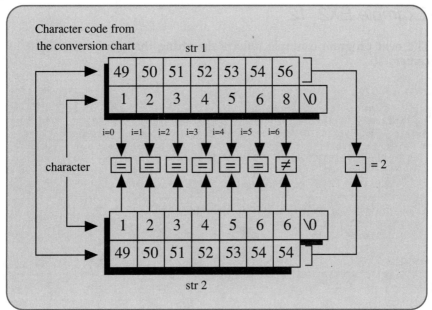

*Figure 2.23*

**Illustration
of the Program
EX2_11 with non
Identical Lines**

Figure 2.22 shows the program operations for this case. The control variable **i** will be changing its value from 0 to 5 while characters in both lines coincide. When **i=5**, the condition **if(str1[5]==0)** is **true** and results in the line mentioned above. The library function **exit** that terminates the program is then executed. This function has the following prototype:

```
void  exit(int  return_code);
```

The value of **return_code** is returned to the calling process, which is usually the operating system. The prototype of the function **exit** is defined in the files **process.h** and **stdlib.h**. Figure 2.23 demonstrates the execution of the program when the lines entered are not identical. When i = 6 the program exits from the loop and jumps to the function **printf** that calculates the difference between the codes 56 and 54. The results of the program can be presented as:

> **Enter the first string (up to 29 characters)**
> *1234568<Enter>*
> **Enter the second string (up to 29 characters)**
> *1234566<Enter>*
> str1 - str2 = 2

## Example EX2_12

The next program example reflects the string that you enter, about its center:

```
/* example EX2_12 */
#include <stdio.h>
#include <string.h>  /* for the functions exit, strlen */
void main(void)
{  char str[30],temp;
   int i,j;
   puts("Enter a string (up to 29 characters)");
   gets(str);
   printf("A string entered: %s\n",str);
   for(i=0,j=strlen(str)-1;  i<j;  i++,j--)
   {  temp = str[i];  str[i] = str[j];
      str[j] = temp;
   }
   printf("Obtained string: %s\n",str);

}
```

The library function **strlen** returns the number of characters in a string, not counting the terminating null character. Its prototype is defined in the file **string.h** and is of the form:

```
int  strlen(char  *s);
```

The results of the program can be presented as:

> **Enter a string (up to 29 characters)**
> *my example<Enter>*
> **A string entered: my example**
> **Obtained string: elpmaxe ym**

Figure 2.24 explains the operation of this example assuming the string entered is "my example".

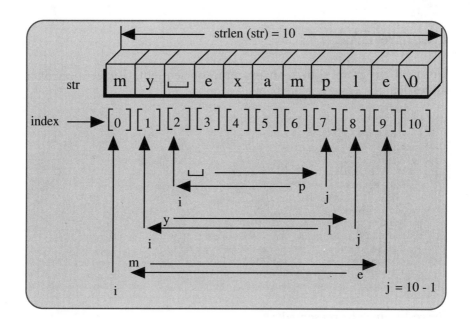

*Figure 2.24*
**Accessing Characters of a String**

## Example EX2_13

Now we come to a program which shows the **for** loop with all three control expressions missing:

```
/* example EX2_13 */
#include <stdio.h>
#include <conio.h>
void main(void)
{  char c, ESC;
   ESC = 27;
   for(;;)
   if((c = getch()) != ESC)
   { printf("A character entered: %c\n",c);
     puts("Press Esc to terminate the program ");
   }
   else break;
}
```

The program works in the same manner as the program EX2_10. The exit from the endless loop is accomplished by the operator **break**, when you press *Esc* . The instruction **if-else** is executed in the **for loop**. If the **if** statement is **true**, then the two output functions in the block, enclosed between braces, are executed. If the condition in the **if** statement is **false**, then the operator **break** exits from the loop after the keyword **else**.

## Example EX2_14

The next program shows an example of sequential execution of a succession of **if-else** statements:

```
/* example EX2_14 */
#include <stdio.h>
void main(void)
{   int a,b,c,d;
    puts("Enter four integers (from -32768 to"
              "32767)");
    scanf("%d%d%d%d",&a,&b,&c,&d);
    if(a<b)  puts("a<b");
    else if(b<c)  puts("a>b and b<c");
        else if(c<d)  puts("a>b>c and c<d");
            else puts("a>b>c>d");
}
```

The results may be presented as:

> **Enter four integers (from -32768 to 32767)**
> *9 6 3 9<Enter>*
> **a>b>c and c<d**

## Example EX2_15

Next we have a program which demonstrates how to use the operator **switch**:

```
/* example EX2_15 */
#include <stdio.h>
void main(void)
{  int z,x,y;
   char sign;
   puts("Enter data as: operand sign operand"
        "\n     (with no spaces between)");
   scanf("%d%c%d",&x,&sign,&y);
   switch (sign)
   {  case '+': printf("%d + %d = %d\n",x,y,x+y);
      break;
      case '-': printf("%d - %d = %d\n",x,y,x-y);
      break;
      case '*': printf("%d * %d = %d\n",x,y,x*y);
      break;
      case '/': printf("%d / %d = %d\n",x,y,x/y);
      break;
      case '%': printf("%d %% %d = %d\n",x,y,x%y);
      break;
      default: puts("wrong operator");
   }
}
```

The results of the program can be presented as:

>**Enter data as: operand sign operand**
> **(with no spaces between)**
> *8\*9<Enter>*
> **8 \* 9 = 72**

As well as the **\*** symbol, you can also enter the operators **+**, **-**, **/** and **%**. Have a look at how the display of the long string by the function **puts** was written in the program.

## Example Ex2_16

Now we come to a program which demonstrates the use of the ternary operator for displaying the integers from 1 to 50. They are organised into a given number of columns specified by an input value:

```
/* example  EX2_16  */
#include  <stdio.h>
void  main(void)
{   int  y,i;
    puts("Enter  an  integer  y");
    scanf("%d",&y);
    for(i=1;i<=50;i++)
    printf("%3.2d%c",i,(i%y==0||i==50)?'\n':'  ');
}
```

Consider the expression in the brackets, **(i%y==0||i==50)**. It is **true** when **i** is exactly divisible by **y** (**i%y==0**), or when the last item is displayed (**i==50**). If the expression is **true**, then the newline character '**\n**' is selected. If it is **false** the character space ' ' is selected.

The characters '**\n**' and ' ', have a conversion specifier **%c**. The result is that each line on the screen displays **y** number of values, except the last line which may have less. The numbers 3 and 2 of the conversion specifier define the format of the output integer **i**. A typical result of program execution might be:

```
14<Enter>
01 02 03 04 05 06 07 08 09 10 11 12 13 14
15 16 17 18 19 20 21 22 23 24 25 26 27 28
29 30 31 32 33 34 35 36 37 38 39 40 41 42
43 44 45 46 47 48 49 50
```

## Example Ex2_17

The last program demonstrates the use of the operators **do-while** and **goto**:

```
/* example EX2_17 */
#include <stdio.h>
#include <conio.h>
#include <dos.h>          /* for the function - delay */
void main(void)
{   char c, ESC;
    ESC = 27;
    again:
    do {  puts("Demonstration of the loop"
            "do-while");
        delay(1000);
    }
    while(!kbhit());
    puts("Exit from the loop do-while");
    if((c=getch())!=ESC)  goto  again;
    puts("Program  termination");
}
```

Two new functions, **delay**, and **kbhit**, are used in the program. The prototype of the first one is defined in the file **dos.h** and is of the form:

> **void  delay(unsigned  milliseconds);**

This function delays the program execution for a specified number of milliseconds. In the example we use 1000 milliseconds which is 1 second. The second function has its prototype in the file **conio.h**. It is of the form:

> **int  kbhit(void);**

The function **kbhit** checks the keystrokes in the keyboard buffer. If a keystroke is available as a consequence of a key having been pressed, **kbhit** returns a nonzero value. If not, it returns 0. This is extremely useful for controlling processes that are to continue until a key is pressed.

The results of the program may be presented as:

> **Demonstration of the loop do-while**
> **Demonstration of the loop do-while**
> **w**
> **Exit from the loop do-while**
> **Demonstration of the loop do-while**
> **<ESC>**
> **Program termination**

Press any key to exit from the **do-while** loop. If it is not the *Esc* key, the statement **goto again;** will cause another entrance to the **do-while** loop. Pressing the *Esc* key terminates the program.

# CHAPTER 8

# STRUCTURED DATA TYPES

## Arrays, Structures and Files

C provides for structured data types in your programs. They are **arrays**, **structures** and **files**.

## Arrays

An **array** is a block of consecutive data items of the same type. The whole array can be accessed by its name. You can also select any element from the array. To do so, you must specify a subscript indicating the relative element position from the beginning of the array.

The number of elements in an array is defined when it is declared and remains constant. Once an array is declared, you can address any of its elements by using the array name followed by the element subscript in square brackets. Arrays are declared in much the same way as variables:

```
int   a[100];
char  b[30];
float  c[42];
```

The first line declares the array **a**, comprising 100 elements of integer type:  **a[0], a[1], ..., a[99]**. All arrays start with the subscript **[0]**. In the second line the elements of the array **b** are of type **char** and in the third line the array **c** is of type **float**.

A two-dimensional array can be thought of as a one-dimensional array, the elements of which are arrays as well. For example, the declaration **char  a[10][20];** specifies such an array consisting of 10 rows of 20 elements. Other dimensions are added by adding another set of square brackets.  The elements of the two-dimensional array are stored row wise in memory, such that the subscript furthest right changes first. For example, addressing the ninth element in the fifth row will be written as `a[4][8]`. Suppose we have a declaration:

```
int  a[2][3];
```

The array elements will be stored in the sequence : `a[0][0]`, `a[0][1]`, `a[0][2]`,  `a[1][0]`, `a[1][1]`, `a[1][2]`. The array name `a` is a constant containing the address of its first element. In our example it is `a[0][0]`. Suppose the address `a` is memory location 1000. Then the address of the element `a[0][1]` address will be 1002, the address of the next element, `a[0][2]`, will be 1004 and so on.

As you may remember, a variable of type `int` requires 2 bytes to accommodate it. But what will happen if you select an element that has no memory allocated for it? Unfortunately, the compiler does not detect that and it will usually result in an error and the program failing to work.

## Pointers and Arrays

In **C**, pointers and arrays are closely related. Any operation involving an array subscript can be executed using pointers and is actually quicker to execute handled in this way. The declaration:

```
int  a[5];
```

defines an array of five elements a[0], a[1], a[2], a[3], a[4].  If the object `*y` is declared as:

```
int  *y;
```

the statement:

```
y=&a[0];
```

assigns the address of the element `a[0]` to the variable `y` (see Figure 2.25). If the variable `y` points to the initial array element `a`, `y + 1` points to the next element. There is automatic correct scaling for the address increment according to the object length, 2 bytes for type `int`, 4 bytes for type `long`, 8 bytes for type `double` and so on. Since the array name is the address of its first element, the statement    `y=&a[0];` can also be written as: `y=a;`.

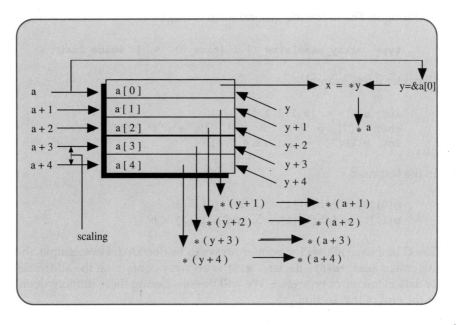

*Figure 2.25*

**The Inter-connection Between Pointers and Arrays**

Further, the element **a[i]** can also be referenced as **\*(a+i)**. In the same way, if **y** is a pointer, **y[i]** and **\*(y+i)** are equivalent.

There is a difference between an array name and a corresponding pointer. A pointer is a variable and therefore statements such as **y=a;** or **y++;** are admissible. An array name is a constant, so similar constructions such as **a=y;**, or **a++;**, are inadmissible, since the constant value of the address **a** cannot be changed. Pointer variables containing addresses can be multilevel and can form a hierarchical structure. So you can have pointers to pointers, where a pointer contains the address of another pointer, pointers to pointers to pointers, and so on to whatever level you are prepared to go to! We will be discussing these in more detail later.

If we have pointers addressing the elements of the same array, they can be compared using the operators: **<, >, ==, !=**, etc. Comparison operations should not be carried out with pointers to different arrays. Though it will not result in compilation errors, it has no sensible interpretation. Any address can be tested for equality or inequality with zero. The difference between pointers to elements of the same array may be calculated by subtracting one from another. The result will be the number of elements placed between the two pointers. **C** allows you to initialize an array while declaring it. The following general form is used:

```
type  array_name[size_1]...[size_n]  =  {  value_list  };
```

Consider a few examples:

```
int  a[5]  =  {0,1,2,3,4};
char  c[7]  =  {'a','b','c','d','e','f','g'};
int  b[2][3]  =  {1,2,3,4,5,6};
```

In the last case:

$b[0][0] = 1$, $b[0][1] = 2$, $b[0][2] = 3$,
$b[1][0] = 4$, $b[1][1] = 5$, and $b[1][2] = 6$.

The **C** language allows for pointer arrays to be declared. For example, the statement **char *m[5];** declares **m[5]** is an array containing the addresses of data elements of type **char**. We will be considering these in more detail at the end of this section.

## Example EX2_18

Let's look at some sample programs demonstrating the use of arrays. The first one shows the interconnection between pointers and arrays:

```
/*  example  EX2_18  */
#include  <stdio.h>
void  main(void)
{   int  a[2][3]  =  {1,2,3,4,5,6},i,j;
    int  *x,*y,**z;
    for(i=0;i<6;i++)  printf("%d ",*(*a+i));          /* 1 */
    putchar('\n');
    for(i=0;i<2;i++)                                  /* 2 */
        for(j=0;j<3;j++)                              /* 2 */
            printf("%d ",a[i][j]);                    /* 2 */
    putchar('\n');
    x = &a[0][0];                                     /* 3 */
    z = &x;                                           /* 3 */
    printf("*x = %d;  **z = %d\n",*x,**z);            /* 3 */
    y = &a[1][0];                                     /* 4 */
    printf("y[-1] = %d; y[0] = %d;"                   /* 4 */
           " y[1] = %d\n",y[-1],y[0],y[1]);           /* 4 */
    for(i=0;i<6;i++)                                  /* 5 */
        printf("*(*z+d) = %d; (*z)[%d] = %d\n",       /* 5 */
               i,*(*z+i),i,(*z)[i]);                  /* 5 */
}
```

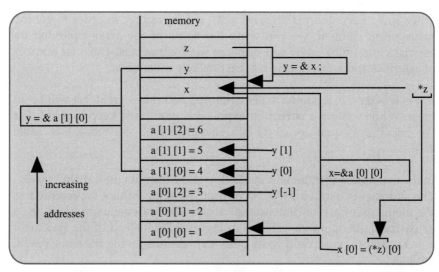

*Figure 2.26*

**Values of Variables**

Consider the two-dimensional array `a[2] [3]`. Figure 2.26 shows its element values after the initialization. As we have discussed, `a` is a constant being the address of the first element of the array. However, the array is two-dimensional and can be considered as made up of rows as in Figure 2.27.

Then `a` is a pointer to the beginning of the array, `a[0]` is a pointer to the first row and `a[1]` is a pointer to the second row. Therefore `*a` and `a[0]`, and also `*a+1` and `a[1]` have identical values. Now `**a` and `*a[0]` both reference the value `a[0][0]`, `*(*a+1)` and `*(a[0]+1)` reference `a[0][1]` and so on as illustrated in Figure 2.27.

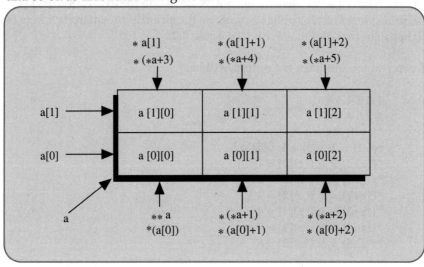

*Figure 2.27*

**Array Element Referencing**

Thus, if we have defined an array with **n** dimensions, in order to get the value of an element, we can write the name of the array preceded by asterisks and followed by subscripts in square brackets. The total number of asterisks and subscripts in square brackets must be **n**.

If it is less than **n**, a pointer will be defined and if it is greater it will be an error. While writing a particular expression, you must keep in mind that the priority of square brackets is higher than that of asterisk (see Table 2.2).

In the example, the statement marked **/* 1 */** outputs the values **\*(\*a+i)**. The statements marked **/* 2 */** output the same values, represented as the elements of a two-dimensional array. The statements marked **/* 3 */** perform the operations shown in Figure 2.26. Instead of the statement **x = &a[0][0];**, you could write other expressions giving the same result, such as:

```
x = *a;
x = a[0];
```

Note that the statement **z = &a[0][0];** would be incorrect, since this would make **z** a pointer to the value **a[0][0]**. We can see from the declaration **int \*\*z;** that **z** is a pointer to a pointer (see Figure 2.26).

The statements marked **/* 4 */** output the values **y[-1]**, **y[0]** and **y[1]**, shown in Figure 2.26. The statements marked **/* 5 */** demonstrate two more variants of array element output. Note that in the expression **(\*z)[i]**, the round brackets are obligatory, since the priority of square brackets is higher than that of the asterisk (see Table 2.2).

If you run the program the output will be:

```
1 2 3 4 5 6
1 2 3 4 5 6
*x = 1; **z = 1
 y[-1] = 3; y[0] = 4; y[1] = 5
*(*z+0) = 1; (*z)[0] = 1
*(*z+1) = 2; (*z)[1] = 2
*(*z+2) = 3; (*z)[2] = 3
*(*z+3) = 4; (*z)[3] = 4
*(*z+4) = 5; (*z)[4] = 5
*(*z+5) = 6; (*z)[5] = 6
```

## *Example EX2_19*

The next example shows the use of the constructions, pointer to pointer to...pointer to pointer to value:

```
/* example EX2_19 */
#include <stdio.h>
void main(void)
{   int  t=10,*x,**y,***z;
    x  = &t;
    y  = &x;
    z  = &y;
    printf("t = %d; *x = %d; **y = %d; ***z = %d\n",
       t,*x,**y,***z);
    printf("z = %p; y = %p; x = %p\n",z,y,x);
}
```

In a declaration, if you write a variable name preceded by an asterisk, the variable becomes a pointer to a value. If you write a variable name preceded by two asterisks, the variable becomes a pointer to a pointer, which in its turn points to a value. If there are three asterisks, you have defined a pointer to a pointer to a pointer to a value. The last case is illustrated by the example. This mechanism is the same for more asterisks. For each additional asterisk, you get another "pointer to..." layer. The results of the program will be:

t = 10; *x = 10; **y = 10; ***z = 10
z = FFF0; y = FFF2; x = FFF4

Figure 2.28 illustrates graphically how the pointers interrelate.

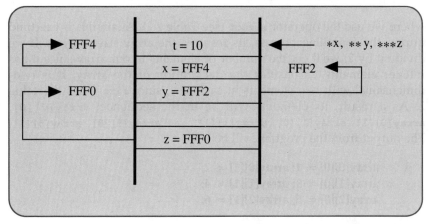

*Figure 2.28*

**Pointer Values**

## Example EX2_20

The last example shows another way to initialize an array:

```
/* example EX2_20 */
#define  size_2  2
#include  <stdio.h>
void  main(void)
{   int  n,i,j;
    int  array[][size_2]  =  {1,2,3,4,5,6,7,8,9,10,11,12};
    n  =  sizeof(array)/2;
    for(i=0;i<n/size_2;i++)
       for(j=0;j<size_2;j++)
          printf("array[%d][%d]  =  %2d  %c",i,j,array[i][j],
                    j==size_2-1?'\n':'  ');
}
```

Here we have used a couple of new facilities. The first of them:

**#define  size_2  2**

is a preprocessor directive which is an instruction to the compilation process. It sets the value of the constant **size_2** as 2. This constant is used at various places in the program. To change its value, for example to make it 3, you only need to change the **define** directive to:

**#define  size_2  3**

The second occurs in the expression:

**n  =  sizeof(array)/2;**

where we use the operator **sizeof** (see Table 2.2). Again this is executed during the compiling process. Its result is the array size in bytes. If we divide it by 2, we'll get the number of elements in our array since it has integer elements.   Consider the declaration of the array. It is two-dimensional with two elements in each row, since **size_2** has the value 2. As a result, its elements will be in the sequence: **array[0][0]**, **array[0][1]**, **array[1][0]**, **array[1][1]**,....,   **array[5][0]**, **array[5][1]**. The output from the program will be:

array[0][0] = 1; array[0][1] = 2;
array[1][0] = 3; array[1][1] = 4;
array[2][0] = 5; array[2][1] = 6;

```
array[3][0] =  7; array[3][1] =  8;
array[4][0] =  9; array[4][1] = 10;
array[5][0] = 11; array[5][1] = 12;
```

Now, if we change the value of **size_2** to 3, the array organization will change as a consequence. The program output will then be:

```
array[0][0] = 1; array[0][1] =  2; array[0][2] =  3;
array[1][0] = 4; array[1][1] =  5; array[1][2] =  6;
array[2][0] = 7; array[2][1] =  8; array[2][2] =  9;
array[3][0] = 10; array[3][1] = 11; array[3][2] = 12;
```

Such operations are very useful when you want the same program to be able to handle arrays of various shapes. Have a look at how the ternary operator is used in the function **printf**.

# Character Strings

The **C** language does not support a separate string data type, but lets you define strings in two different ways. The first method uses a character array, the second uses a pointer to the first location of a region in memory which will hold characters.

The declaration **char a[10];** tells the compiler to reserve space in memory for a maximum of 10 characters. The constant **a** contains the address of the memory cell containing the first of 10 elements of type **char**.

The process for storing a particular string in the array **a**, copies each character of the string to the memory region indicated by the constant **a**, until a null value terminating the string is reached. When a function such as **printf("%s",a);** is executed, it assumes the value of **a** to be the address of the first character of the string. If the first character has a null value, the function **printf** terminates immediately. If not, it displays the first character, adds 1 to the address and starts a null value check again. This process enables strings of any length to be handled within declared dimension limits, of course.

The second method for string declaration uses character pointers. The declaration, **char *b;**, defines a variable **b** that contains the address of an object of type character. However, in this case the compiler does not reserve memory space for character storage and does not initialize the variable **b** with a definite address value.

When the compiler comes across a statement such as **b = "Leningrad";**, it follows a particular process. First, it creates memory space somewhere in the object module, containing the string "Leningrad" followed by the null character. Then, it assigns to the variable **b**, the value of the starting address of the string corresponding to the character L. The function **printf("%s",b);**, would operate in the same way as in the previous case, displaying characters until the terminating null is encountered. An array of pointers can be initialized. That is, you can assign the addresses of defined string constants to its elements in the declaration of the array.

## Example EX2_21

Consider a sample program that uses the ternary operator **?:**. If you enter a value between 1 and 12, you will see the name of the corresponding month displayed on the screen. If you enter any other value you will see the output:

**incorrect month number**

As you can see, all the decision processes necessary to determine what to display, are contained within the **printf** statement.

```
/* example EX2_21 */
#include <stdio.h>
void main(void)
{  int n;
   char *name[] = {
       "incorrect  month  number",
       "January",
       "February",
       "March",
       "April",
       "May",
       "June",
       "July",
       "August",
       "September",
       "October",
       "November",
       "December"  };
   puts("Enter  month  number");
   scanf("%d",&n);
   printf("Month  name:  %s",
       (n<1||n>12)?name[0]:name[n]);
   putchar('\n');
}
```

Typical output from the program will be:

**Enter month number**
*8<Enter>*
**Month name: August**

Note that the dimension of the array of character pointers, `name`, is not specified in the declaration. In this case, the dimension will be automatically determined by the compiler, by calculating the space required to store the strings defined during initialization.

# Structures

**Structures** are groups of one or more objects such as variables, arrays or pointers. Structures are collections of data, similar to an array. The major differences are that you must address its elements by name and different structure elements need not be of the same type.

## Declaring a Structure

You can declare a structure using the keyword `struct` followed by its type name and then the list of its elements enclosed between braces. The general form of the declaration is:

```
struct  type  {element_1_type    element_1_name;
          . . . . . . . . . . . . . .
          element_n_type    element_n_name;  };
```

An element name can be any identifier. You can write any number of identifiers of the same type in one string separated by commas. Consider an example:

```
struct  date  {  int  day;
                 int  month;
                 int  year;  };
```

After the closing brace concluding the list of elements, you can write structure variables of the same type, for example:

```
struct  date  {...}  a,b,c;
```

Here **a**, **b** and **c** will have been defined as structures of type **date** and the necessary memory will have been allocated. The declaration without any list does not allocate memory it simply defines the structure form. A new variable name can be introduced later once the structure form has been declared. For example:

```
struct  date  days;
```

Now the variable **days** is of type **date**. When necessary, structures can be initialized by placing the list of initial elements values after the structure variable declaration. For example:

```
struct  computer  {   int  mem;
                      int  sp;
                      char  model[20];    };
struct  computer  cl  =  {  640,1,"PS/2"   };
```

The first statement declares the form of a structure of type **computer**. The second statement defines an instance of the structure of type **computer** with the name **cl** and initializes it. Structures can also be nested within one another, for example:

```
struct  man  {  char  name[30],  fam[20];
                struct  date  bd;
                int  voz;    };
```

The structure of type **date** that we defined earlier includes three elements: day, month and year containing integers (**int**). The structure **man** includes the elements: **name[30]**, **fam[20]**, **bd** and **voz**. The objects **name[30]** and **fam[20]** are character arrays of 30 and 20 elements respectively. The variable **bd** is a complex element, which is a nested structure, of type **date**. The element **voz** simply contains an integer value. Now we can declare structure variables with the type **man**:

```
struct  man  men[100];
```

Here the array **men** is defined, consisting of 100 elements, each of which is a structure of type **man**. So the C language provides for the use of arrays of structures and, further, those structures can consist of arrays and other structures.

To address an element within a structure, you must specify the structure name, followed by a point and then the element name.

For example:

```
men[i].voz   =   64;
men[j].bd.day   =   22;
men[j].bd.year   =   1976;
```

While working with structures, you must keep in mind that the element type is defined by the corresponding string between braces in the structure declaration. For example, **bd** is of type **date, year** is an integer and so on. Since each structure element belongs to a definite type, its name can appear anywhere where variables or values of that type are allowed. Constructions such as:

```
men[i]   =   men[j];
```

are acceptable when **men[i]** and **men[j]** are objects fitting a uniform structure description. In other words, it is legitimate to assign one structure to another by name as long as they are of the same type.

The unary operator **&** lets you take the address of a structure. Suppose we have the declaration statement:

```
struct date { int d,m,y; } day;
```

Here **day** is a structure of type **date** and includes three elements, **d**, **m** and **y**. Another declaration:

```
struct date *db;
```

states that **db** is a pointer to a structure of type **date**. We can now write the statement:

```
db = &day;
```

Now, to reference the structure elements **d**, **m** and **y**, we can use the constructions, **(*db).d**, **(*db).m** and **(*db).y**. The structure address is **db**, and **\*db** is the structure. The round brackets are mandatory, since a point is of higher priority than an asterisk (see Table 2.2). There is a special operator **->** defined in the language for such operations. It selects the structure element and also lets you present the constructions above in a simpler and much more intelligible way. Using the new operator they become **db->d**, **db->m** and **db->y**.

## *The Typedef Operator*

Consider the structure declaration:

```
struct data { int d,m,y; };
```

As we have seen, we have effectively introduced a new data type specifier, **data**, which can now be used for declaring distinct structure items. For example:

```
struct data a,b,c;
```

**C** also has a special mechanism for assigning new names to data type specifiers. This is an operator **typedef**. The general form of the **typedef** statement is:

```
typedef type name;
```

Here **type** is any acceptable data type and **name** is any legal identifier. Let's look at an example:

```
typedef int INTEGER;
```

Since we have defined the new name, **INTEGER**, for declaring objects of integer type, we can declare:

```
INTEGER a,b;
```

It will operate in exactly the same manner as the usual declaration:

```
int a,b;
```

In other words, **INTEGER** can be used as a synonym of the keyword **int**. You can also make declarations using both:

```
INTEGER a,b;
int c,d;
```

We have declared four variables, **a**, **b**, **c** and **d** of integer type.

## Example EX2_22

Let's consider a complete example of using **typedef** and **struct** which will also test your understanding of pointers:

```
/* example EX2_22 */
#include <stdio.h>
void main(void)
{  typedef int  a[2][3];
   a *my_array;
   int  x=10,y=20,z=30,k=40,p=50,q=60,i,j;        /* 2 */
   int  b[2][3]  =  {1,2,3,4,5,6};                 /* 1 */
   my_array  =  (a*)&b;                            /* 1 */
   for(i=0;i<2;i++)                                /* 1 */
   for(j=0;j<3;j++)                                /* 1 */
   printf("%d;  ",(*my_array)[i][j]);              /* 1 */
   putchar('\n');
   printf("%p;  %p;  %p;  %p;  %p;  %p\n",&x,&y,&z,&k,&p,&q);
   my_array  =  (a*)&q;                            /* 2 */
   for(i=0;i<2;i++)                                /* 2 */
   for(j=0;j<3;j++)                                /* 2 */
   printf("%d;  ",(*my_array)[i][j]);              /* 2 */
   putchar('\n');
}
```

The result of executing the program will be:

> **1; 2; 3; 4; 5; 6;**
> **FFF2; FFF0; FFEE; FFEC; FFEA; FFE8**
> **60; 50; 40; 30; 20; 10;**

Figure 2.29 (overleaf) shows the location of the variables in memory for the current example. In the example, the program statements:

> **typedef  int  a[2][3];**
> **a  *my_array;**

introduce the pointer **my_array** to an object of type **a**. The object is assigned a description in the form of pattern **a[2][3]** defined in the **typedef** statement. Objects of type **a** are not only integer, but are also arrays with the dimensions defined. Therefore, when selecting the elements from memory of such an object, we will use subscripts corresponding to the pattern given. In other words, we can use constructions of the form:

> **(*my_array)[i][j]**.

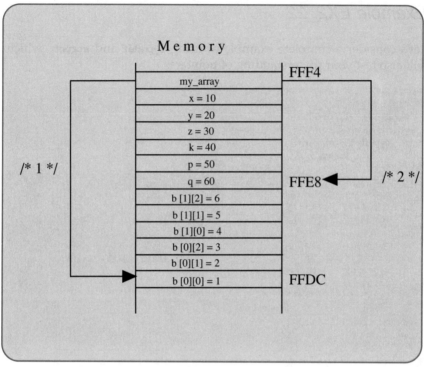

Memory

| | |
|---|---|
| my_array | FFF4 |
| x = 10 | |
| y = 20 | |
| z = 30 | |
| k = 40 | |
| p = 50 | |
| q = 60 | FFE8 |
| b [1][2] = 6 | |
| b [1][1] = 5 | |
| b [1][0] = 4 | |
| b [0][2] = 3 | |
| b [0][1] = 2 | |
| b [0][0] = 1 | FFDC |

/* 1 */     /* 2 */

*Figure 2.29*

**Allocation of the Variables in Memory**

Consider the program statements marked with **/\* 1 \*/**. The first declares and allocates memory for the array **b**. The second assigns the address of the beginning of the array **b**, to the pointer variable **my_array**. Here, **(a\*)** is the type definition operator (see Table 2.2). All operations are illustrated graphically in Figure 2.29. The remaining statements marked **/\* 1 \*/**, output the element values of the array **b** to the screen, using the pointer **my_array**.

Now let's examine the statements marked **/\* 2 \*/**. The statement:

```
my_array  =  (a*)&q;
```

stores a pointer to the variable **q** in the variable **my_array**. The remaining statements output to the screen the values of the variables **q, p, k, z, y** and **x**, through the pointer **my_array**. You will also see that there is a **printf** statement which displays the addresses of those variables, so you can see how they are ordered in memory.

## Example EX2_23

In order to explain the next example, we need to explain a little of the detail of how your display screen works. When a monitor operates in text mode, the computer stores the codes for the displayed characters in a special screen memory area.

Each character occupies two bytes. The even address stores the **ASCII** code of a character and the odd address stores its attribute. An attribute defines the way a character is to be displayed. For a monochrome monitor it can be inverted image, enhanced or normal brightness and so on. For a color monitor an attribute mainly defines the color of the output character.

The screen memory area is located at a fixed address in RAM. For one of the operating modes its initial address is B800 0000. To set this mode you must use a system utility **MODE** and enter the DOS command:

C>MODE co80<Enter>

The program, **MODE**, must be either on your C: drive, or in a directory specified in your **PATH** command. Suppose we have executed the **MODE** command in DOS, then we can consider the following program:

```
/* example EX2_23 */
#include <stdio.h>
typedef unsigned char buf[25][80][2];
buf far *video;
void main(void)
{  struct symbol
   {  int x,y; unsigned char c,attr;  } n;
   video = (buf far*)0xB8000000;
   puts("Enter the coordinates (x,y), a character and "
            "its attribute");
   scanf("%d,%d,%c,%d",&n.x,&n.y,&n.c,&n.attr);
   (*video)[n.y][n.x][0] = n.c;
   (*video)[n.y][n.x][1] = n.attr;
   puts("Enter the coordinates (x,y)");
   scanf("%d,%d",&n.x,&n.y);
   printf("A character: %c; attribute: %d\n",
      (*video)[n.y][n.x][0],(*video)[n.y][n.x][1]);
}
```

The statement:

```
buf far *video;
```

uses a new specifier **far**. It implies that the variable **video** will contain a so-called **far pointer**. Using this pointer you can access any memory cell since it instructs the compiler to use the hardware addressing mode that permits this.

The statement:

```
video = (buf far*)0xB8000000;
```

lets you use the pointer **video** for working with screen memory, by setting the pointer to be the starting address for the screen buffer storage area. Now you can reference screen memory as a three-dimensional array.

The first dimension will select the screen line number for a given character, the second selects the character column number in the line and the third picks the **ASCII** code for the character and its attribute. In the operating mode we have set, the screen has 25 lines and 80 columns. As you can see, the dimensions for **buf** are declared accordingly, the last dimension corresponding to the two variables required for each character position to select the character and its attribute.

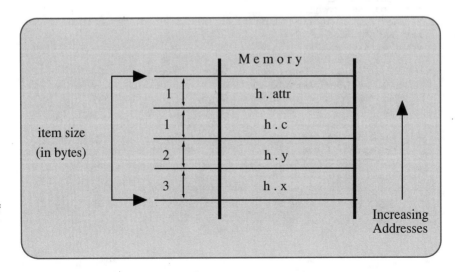

*Figure 2.30*

**Allocation of the Symbol Structure in Memory**

The structure of type **symbol** includes the elements:

| | |
|---|---|
| **x** | - Column number for a character. |
| **y** | - Line number for a character. |
| **c** | - **ASCII**-code for a character. |
| **attr** | - Character attribute. |

The program initially outputs the character, that you define with an attribute, to the specified position on the screen. When you start running it you'll see the prompt:

**Enter the coordinates (x, y), a character and its attribute**

Key in, for example, the following data:

*7,10,R,112<Enter>*

Note, that the values you enter are separated by commas. This is determined by the commas between the conversion specifiers, **%d**, in the function **scanf**. See "Formatted Data Input" (p 73) for a detailed explanation of what's happening here. On entering the specified string, you'll see the character R at the screen position (7,10), and its image will be inverted because of the attribute code 112.

The program then reads a character and its attribute from a defined screen position. You'll see on the screen:

**Enter the coordinates (x,y)**

So now you could enter the following:

*7,10<Enter>*

As a result, you'll see the output:

**A character: R; attribute: 112**

Figure 2.30 illustrates the location of the elements of the structure **symbol** in memory.

## Bit Fields

**Bit fields** are a specific category of structures. A field is a sequence of neighbouring bits inside one integer value. It can be either of type **signed int** or **unsigned int** and occupy from 1 to 16 bits. The fields are located in a hardware word and in sequence from lower to upper bits. For example, the structure:

```
struct prim {int a:2;  unsigned b:3;  int  :5;
             int c:1;  unsigned d:5;  } i,j;
```

defines the memory location shown in Figure 2.31. If the last field was defined by **unsigned d:6;**, it would be located in bits 0-5 of the next word, rather than as shown.

In bit fields of type **signed**, the leftmost bit is interpreted as the sign bit. Thus, a **signed** field 1 bit wide can only store the values -1 or 0, since any nonzero value will be interpreted as -1.

Bit fields are commonly used to pack values of several variables into one hardware word in order to save memory. They can also be very useful in dealing with hardware registers. They cannot be organized into arrays and have no addresses, so you cannot apply the unary operator **&** to them.

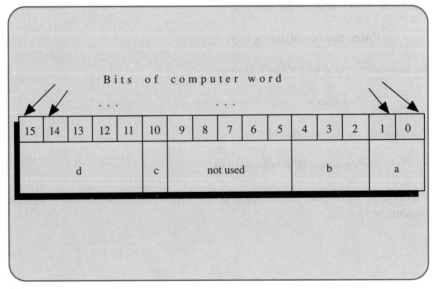

*Figure 2.31*

**Field Structure**

## Example EX2_24

Let's look at some programs using bit fields. The first gets information about the keyboard flag byte. A computer has a special region in the beginning of RAM, where DOS stores a lot of useful information. The cells with addresses 0x417 and 0x418 store information about the status of keys on the keyboard. We can describe the contents of the location with the address 0x417:

> bit 0 - *Shift right*  key state
> bit 1 - *Shift left*  key state
> bit 2 - *Ctrl*  key state
> bit 3 - *Alt*  key state
> bit 4 - *Scroll_Lock*  key state
> bit 5 - *Num_Lock*  key state
> bit 6 - *Caps_Lock*  key state
> bit 7 - *Ins*  key state

The key state can be: 1, pressed; 0, released. A mode is set if the corresponding bit is 1. Here is a program to examine the status of these keys:

```
/* example EX2_24 */
#include <stdio.h>
#include <conio.h>/
typedef struct bios_417
{  unsigned        Rshift:1;
   unsigned        Lshift:1;
   unsigned          Ctrl:1;
   unsigned           Alt:1;
   unsigned   Scroll_Lock:1;
   unsigned      Num_Lock:1;
   unsigned     Caps_Lock:1;
   unsigned           Ins:1;
}   key;

void main(void)
{  key far *sh;
   sh = (key far*)0x417;
   puts("Enter status bits and press any key");
   getch();
   if (sh->Rshift) puts("Rshift key is pressed");
   if (sh->Lshift) puts("Lshift key is pressed");
   if (sh->Ctrl) puts("Ctrl key is pressed");
   if (sh->Alt) puts("Alt key is pressed");
   if (sh->Scroll_Lock) puts("Scroll_Lock mode is set");
   if (sh->Num_Lock) puts("Num_Lock mode is set");
   if (sh->Caps_Lock) puts("Caps_Lock mode is set");
   if (sh->Ins) puts("Ins mode is set");
}
```

Here, the operator **typedef** is used to introduce a new name, **key**, for the data type **struct bios_417 { ... }**. The statement:

```
key far *sh;
```

defines **sh** to be a **far** pointer to objects of type **key**. The next statement:

```
sh = (key far*)0x417;
```

stores the address 0x417 in **sh**. Now, using **sh**, you can analyze the status bits. For example, to analyze the state of the key *Ctrl* you need only check the value of **sh->Ctrl**. If it is 1, the key is pressed, if it's 0, the key is released.

When you run the program, you will first see a prompt appear on the screen:

**Enter status bits and press any key**

Try setting the modes *Scroll_Lock* , *Num_Lock* , and *Caps_Lock* , and press the spacebar. The following lines will appear on the screen:

**Scroll_Lock mode is set**
**Num_Lock mode is set**
**Caps_Lock mode is set**

## Example EX2_25

The second program demonstrates the possibility of combining bit fields and other variables into one structure:

```
/* example EX2_25 */
#include <stdio.h>
#include <conio.h>/
typedef struct bios_413
{   int    vol_mem,test;
    unsigned  Rshift:1;
    unsigned  Lshift:1;
    unsigned        :1;
    unsigned Alt    :1;
}   key;

void main(void)
{   key far *sh;
    unsigned char Alt_key;
    sh = (key far*)0x413;
    puts("Enter status bits and press any key");
    getch();
    if (sh->Rshift) puts("Rshift key is pressed");
    if (sh->Lshift) puts("Lshift key is pressed");
    if (sh->Alt)    puts("Alt key is pressed");
    printf("RAM size: %d Kbytes\n",sh->vol_mem+1);
    printf("Structure size %d bytes\n",sizeof(key));
}
```

The address 0x413 holds two bytes containing the available main memory size in kilobytes. The program uses the integer variable **vol_mem** to obtain the value from the word at this address. An integer variable **test** is introduced to skip the next two bytes at the address 0x415. The status bits then follow at the address 0x417. We use only *Rshift* , *Lshift* and *Alt* . The statement;

> **unsigned**      **:1;**

skips one bit.  The program results can be presented as:

> **Enter status bits and press any key**
> **<press Rshift, Alt and Spacebar>**
> **Rshift key is pressed**
> **Alt key is pressed**
> **RAM size is 640 Kbytes**
> **Structure size is 5 bytes.**

# Unions

A Union is a variable that stores, at various times, objects of different types and sizes. It allows you to use one memory region for manipulating different types of data. A keyword **union** is used to define unions and the syntax is similar to that of structures. Say we have the declaration:

```
union  r  {  int  ir;  float  fr;  chart  cr;  }  z;
```

Here the size of **ir** is 2 bytes, **fr** is 4 bytes and **cr** is 1 byte. The variable **z** will be allocated enough memory to maintain the largest of all three types. Thus, **z** will be 4 bytes. At any particular time, **z** can have a value of only one of the three variables **ir**, **fr** and **cr**.

## Example EX2_26

Let's take a look at an example:

```
/*  example  EX2_26  */
#include  <stdio.h>
void  main(void)
{   union  data_array
        {   struct  data  {  int  d,m,y;  }  my_data;
            char  array[7];
        }  d_a;
    int  i;
    printf("Union  size:  %d\n",sizeof(d_a));
    for(i=0;i<7;i++)
    d_a.array[i]  =  i;
    for(i=0;i<7;i++)
    printf("%d;  ",d_a.array[i]);
    d_a.my_data.d  =  7;  d_a.my_data.m  =  3;
    d_a.my_data.y  =  1950;
    printf("\nday:  %d;  month:  %d;  year:  %d\n",
        d_a.my_data.d,d_a.my_data.m,d_a.my_data.y);
}
```

In the example,the variable **d_a** is a **union** of type **data_array**. It consists of two elements. The first is the structure **my_data** of type **data** and the second is a character array. Only one of them can exist at any one time, and they both occupy the same place in memory (see Figure 2.32). The first function **printf** outputs the space occupied by the union in memory. Its size is determined by the larger of the two elements of the union, **array**.

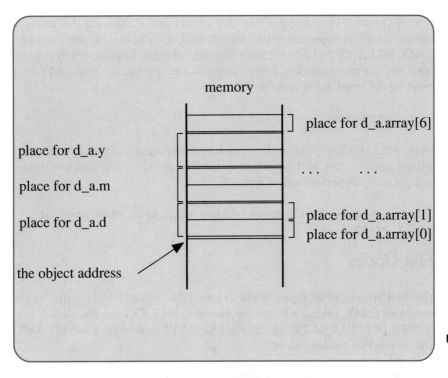

*Figure 2.32*

**Allocation
in Memory
of the Object
Union of Type
Data_array**

When you run the program you will get the output:

> **Union size: 7**
> **0; 1; 2; 3; 4; 5; 6;**
> **day: 7; month: 3; year: 1950**

# *Files*

**Files** hold data intended for long term storage, or data that is too voluminous to be processed entirely within the main memory of your machine. Each file is assigned a unique filename. The **C** language has no statements defined for file manipulation. All operations on files are carried out through the functions included in a standard library, which together form a comprehensive file system.

These functions let you work with a variety of peripherals, such as disks, printers, or communication channels, that may differ greatly from one to another. In addition, the file system makes it possible to deal with them as one abstract logical device called a **stream**. There are two stream types, **text** and **binary**.

Prior to reading or writing a file, you must **open** it. You do this using a library function **fopen**. It takes an external file definition, for example: **C:MY_FILE.TXT** and joins it with its internal logical name which is to be used in your program. The logical name is a pointer to the required file. It must be declared, for example:

```
FILE  *1st;
```

Here, **FILE** is a type name, described in a standard definition contained within **stdio.h**, **1st** is the pointer to the file. A call to the function **fopen** in a program is performed as follows:

```
1st=fopen(pointer_to_string_with_file_name,mode_of
using_file);
```

## File Modes

The first argument of **fopen** is the external file name, which could be for example, **C:MY_FILE.TXT**, for the file **MY_FILE.TXT** on the disk C:, or **A:\MY_DIR\EX2_3.CPP**, for the file **EX2_3.CPP** in directory **A:\MY_DIR**, and so on. File modes can be:

| | | |
|---|---|---|
| **r** | - | open an existing file for read |
| **w** | - | create a new file for write (if the file with the specified filename already exists it will be overwritten) |
| **a** | - | append a file (open an existing file for write, starting from the end of the file, or open a new file if it does not exist) |
| **rb** | - | open a binary file for read |
| **wb** | - | open a binary file for write |
| **ab** | - | append a binary file |
| **rt** | - | open a text file for read |
| **wt** | - | open a text file for write |
| **at** | - | append a text file |
| **r+** | - | open an existing file for read/write |
| **w+** | - | open a new file for read/write |
| **a+** | - | append or open a new file for read/write |
| **r+b** | - | open an existing binary file for read/write |
| **w+b** | - | open a new binary file for read/write |
| **a+b** | - | append a binary file for read/write |
| **w+t** | - | open a text file for read/write |
| **a+t** | - | append a binary file for read/write |

If a mode **t** or **b** is not designated, for example, in the case of **r**, **w** or **a**, it is defined by the value of the global variable **_fmode**. If **_fmode = O_BINARY**, the files are opened in binary mode and if **_fmode = O_TEXT**, the files are opened in text mode. The constants **O_BINARY** and **O_TEXT** are defined in the file **fcntl.h**. The file mode specifiers of the form **r+b** can also be written as **rb+**. If an error occurs while calling the function **fopen**, the function returns a pointer to the constant **NULL**. When you have finished working with a file you must close it. You can do this using the library function **fclose**. It has the following prototype:

```
int fclose(FILE *lst);
```

On successful termination, the function **fclose** returns a zero value. The return value **EOF**, with the value -1, signals an error.

## The Library Functions Used for File Manipulation

Now let's consider the library functions used for file manipulation. They are all defined in the file **stdio.h**:

1. The function **putc** writes a character into a file and has the following prototype:

```
int putc(int c,FILE *lst);
```

Here, **lst** is a pointer to the file returned by the function **fopen**, and **c** is the character to be written. The variable **c** is of type **int**, but only the lower byte is used. At successful completion, the function **putc** returns the written character, otherwise the constant **EOF** is returned. **EOF** is defined in the file **stdio.h**.

2. The function **getc** reads a character from the file and has the prototype:

```
int getc(FILE *lst);
```

As before, **lst** is a pointer to the file returned by the function **fopen**. This function returns the character read from the file. The corresponding value is defined by the type, **int**, but the upper byte is 0. If the end of file is reached the function **getc** returns the value **EOF**.

**3.** The function **feof** tests for the end of a file while reading data and has the prototype:

**int feof(FILE *lst);**

**lst** is a pointer to the file, returned by the function **fopen**. If the end of file has been reached, the function returns a nonzero value, otherwise 0 is returned.

**4.** The function **fputs** writes a character string to a file. It differs from the function **puts** in that it does not write or copy the terminating null character, and **puts** writes to the standard output stream. Consider an example:

```
fputs ("Example",lst);
```

When an error occurs the value **EOF** is returned.

**5.** The function **fgets** reads a character string from a file. It differs from the function **gets** in that it uses a pointer to the file variable as its second parameter. Consider an example:

```
fgets(str,lst);
```

The function returns the pointer to the string **read**, on successful completion. If an end of file is detected, or when an error occurs, it returns the constant **NULL**.

**6.** The function **fprintf** operates in the same way as the function **printf**, but it operates with files. It uses the pointer to the file variable as its first parameter. Consider an example:

```
fprintf(lst,"%x",a);
```

**7.** The function **fscanf** operates in the same way as the function **scanf**, but it operates with files. It uses the pointer to the file variable as its first parameter. An example is:

```
fscanf(lst,"%x",&a);
```

At the end of the file, or if an error occurs, the value **EOF** is returned.

▲8 The function **fseek** lets you read and write with random access and has the prototype:

```
int  fseek(FILE  *lst,long  count,int  access);
```

**lst** is the pointer to the file, returned by the function **fopen**, **count** is a byte number relative to an initial position defined by the variable **access**, from which the execution operation will start. The variable **access** can assume the following values:

> 0 - initial position is the beginning of the file
> 1 - initial position is the current position
> 2 - initial position is the end of the file

On successful completion, a zero value is returned. When an error occurs, a nonzero value is returned.

▲9 The function **ferror** lets you inspect whether the last operation with a file was correct and has the prototype:

```
int  ferror(FILE  *lst);
```

When an error occurs, a nonzero value is returned, otherwise a zero value is returned.

▲10 The function **remove** deletes a file and has the prototype:

```
int  remove(char  *file_name);
```

Here, **file_name** is a pointer to a string with a file specifier. On successful completion, a zero value is returned, otherwise a nonzero value is returned.

▲11 The function **rewind** sets the current line pointer to the beginning of the file and has the prototype:

```
void  rewind(FILE  *lst);
```

## Example EX2_27

Now we can consider some simple programs illustrating operations with files. The first program creates the file **ZNI.F** on the A: drive and writes an integer, 150, into it:

```
/* example EX2_27 */
#include <stdio.h>
#include <process.h>
void main(void)
{   int i =  150;
    FILE *lds;
    if ((lds = (FILE*)fopen("A:ZNI.F","w"))  ==  NULL)
    {  fprintf(stderr," Can't open the file ZNI.F ");
       exit(1);
    }
    else    fprintf(lds,"%d\n",i);
    fclose(lds);
}
```

The **if** statement checks to ensure there are no errors when we use the function **fopen**. C allows you to open five standard files with the following logical names:

> **stdin** - a file for data input from the standard input stream, which is the keyboard by default
>
> **stdout** - a file for data output to the standard output stream, which is the screen by default
>
> **stderr** - a file for error messages output (always connected to the monitor screen)
>
> **stdprn** - a file for data output to a printer
>
> **stdaux** - a file for input/output data to a communication channel

The name **stderr** in the function **fprintf** of the above program is used to display any errors that may have occurred in the operation of the function **fopen**.

Insert a disk into drive A: and execute the program. As a result, a new file **ZNI.F** will appear on disk A:. Figure 2.33 illustrates the operation of the program. The **include** file, **process.h**, contains the description of the function **exit**, which is called to terminate the program.

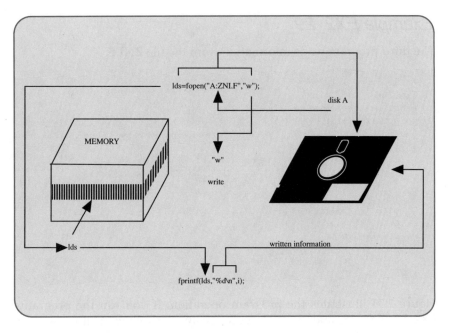

*Figure 2.33*

**Writing Data
to the File on
Disk A:**

## Example EX2_28

The second example illustrates how another integer value of 150 can be
added to the file **ZNI.F**, once it has been created:

```
/* example EX2_28 */
#include <stdio.h>
#include <process.h>
void main(void)
{   int i =   150;
    FILE *lds;
    if ((lds =  (FILE*)fopen("A:ZNI.F","a"))  ==  NULL)
    { fprintf(stderr," Can't open the file  ZNI.F ");
      exit(1);
    }
    else    fprintf(lds,"%d\n",i);
    fclose(lds);
}
```

## *Example EX2_29*

The third program reads information from the file **ZNI.F**:

```
/* example EX2_29 */
#include <stdio.h>
#include <process.h>
void main(void)
{  int   i;
   FILE  *rds;
   if ((rds = (FILE*)fopen("A:ZNI.F","r"))  ==  NULL)
   { fputs("Can't open the file ZNI.F\n",stderr);
     exit(1);
   }
   else while(fscanf(rds,"%d",&i)  != EOF)
   printf("number i =  %d\n",i);
   fclose(rds);
   if (remove("A:ZNI.F"))
   puts("Can't delete file");
}
```

Figure 2.34 illustrates the program operation. If you run the programs EX2_27, EX2_28, and EX2_29 successively, the following lines will be displayed on the screen:

**number i = 150**
**number i = 150**

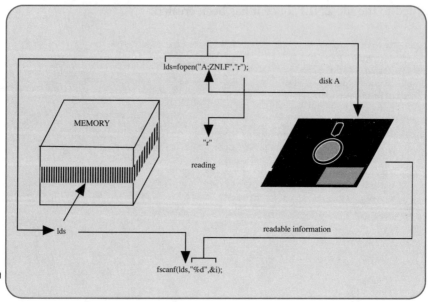

*Figure 2.34*

**Reading Data from the File on Disk A:**

When the program EX2_29 has read the file, the function **remove** deletes the file **ZNI.F** from disk A:.

# *Enumerations*

**Enumerations** are a facility in **C** and **C++**, designed to make it easy for you to describe objects within a defined list of your choice. They are best explained by looking at an example:

```
enum  seasons  {  spring,summer,autumn,winter  };
```

The example contains a new data type **seasons**. Now it is possible to declare a variable of that type:

```
enum  seasons  a,b,c;
```

Each of them, **a, b** and **c**, can assume one of the four meanings or values from the list: **spring, summer, autumn** or **winter**. These could have been declared at once while defining the enumeration, as in the declaration:

```
enum  seasons  {  spring,summer,autumn,winter  }  a,b,c;
```

Consider another declaration:

```
enum  days  {  mon,tues,wed,thur,fri,sat,sun  }  my_week;
```

The names defined in the list of **days** are effectively integer constants, since enumeration data types essentially provide a set of meaningful identifiers for a fixed set of integer values. The first in the list in our example, **mon**, automatically assumes the value 0 and each succeeding item in the list will have a value one greater that its predecessor. So **tues** will be 1, **wed** will be 2 and so on through the list. The constants assigned to items in the list can also be chosen specifically, rather than letting the default values be assumed. For example:

```
enum  days  {  mon=5,tues=8,wed=10,thur,fri,sat,sun  }
my_week;
```

In this case, **mon, tues** and **wed**, will be assigned the integer values we have defined, while the remainder will follow **wed** in sequence. Thus, **thur** will be 11, **fri** will be 12 and **sat** and **sun**, 13 and 14 respectively. You can use **enum** to define the constants **true** = 1 and **false** = 0, together with logical variables that can only assume these values. For example:

```
enum  t_f  {  false,true  }  a,b;
```

# Examples

## Example EX2_30

The first program sorts strings using pointers to arrays:

```
/* example EX2_30 */
#include <stdio.h>
#include <alloc.h>
#include <string.h>
void main(void)
{   int    i=0,j,k;
    char   *m[100],*temp,str[30];
    do {  puts("Enter a string (up to 29 characters)");
          gets(str);
          /*       memory allocation for the next line        */
          if ((m[i] = (char*)malloc(strlen(str)+1)) == NULL)
          puts("Not enough memory");
          strcpy(m[i++],str);
       }
    while (str[0] != 0x30 && i < 100);
    do {  k=0;                                           /* 1 */
          for(j=1;j<i;j++)                               /* 1 */
          if(strcmp(m[j-1],m[j])>0)                      /* 1 */
          {   temp = m[j-1]; m[j-1] = m[j];              /* 1 */
              m[j] = temp; k=1;                          /* 1 */
          }
       }
    while(k);                                            /* 1 */
       puts("Sorted strings");    /* Output of sorted strings
                                   and deallocation of memory   */
    for(j=0;j<i;j++)
    { printf("%s\n",m[j]); free(m[j]);  }
}
```

The function **gets** reads in a string. The function **malloc**, defined in the include file **alloc.h**, dynamically allocates memory for each string when it has been entered. The amount of memory requested is **strlen(str-9)+1** bytes, which corresponds to the string length plus the terminating null.

On successful completion, the function **malloc** returns a pointer to the first byte of allocated memory. The constant **NULL** is returned in case of insufficient memory. Reading a new string and then allocating memory for it continues until you enter a string that has zero as the first character, or 100 strings have been entered. This is determined by the condition, **str[0] != 0x30 && i<100**, controlling the exit from the do-while loop.

The function **strcpy**, defined in the include file **string.h**, copies the entered string to the dynamically allocated memory region. The function **strcmp**, which is also defined in the file **string.h**, compares two strings character by character. If the first string is greater than the second, the returned value will be greater than 0. If the first string is less than the second, the returned value will be less than 0. The function **free** releases dynamically allocated memory for each string. This function is also defined in the file **alloc.h**.

The part of the program that sorts the strings is marked with the comment **/* 1 */**. When the sorting is in process, only the values of pointers **m[j]** change. When the sort has been completed, **m[0]** will indicate the first sorted string, **m[1]** will indicate the second, and so on. The strings' position in memory will not change while sorting. The whole process is completed by manipulating pointers.

Let's now say a few words about the sorting methodology. What happens is that neighboring pairs of strings are compared. When the first is greater than the second the corresponding pointers exchange their values. This is illustrated diagrammatically in Figure 2.35. The sorting process terminates

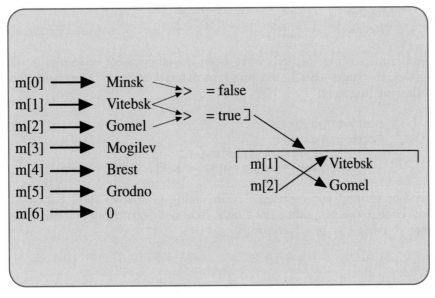

*Figure 2.35*

**An Example
of Sorting**

when, for all neighbouring pairs of strings, the second is greater than the first.

Let's sort the names of all large Belorussian cities. The program output will be as follows:

> **Enter a string (up to 29 characters)**
> *Minsk<Enter>*
> **Enter a string (up to 29 characters)**
> *Vitebsk<Enter>*
> **Enter a string (up to 29 characters)**
> *Gomel<Enter>*
> **Enter a string (up to 29 characters)**
> *Mogilev<Enter>*
> **Enter a string (up to 29 characters)**
> *Brest<Enter>*
> **Enter a string (up to 29 characters)**
> *Grodno<Enter>*
> **Enter a string (up to 29 characters)**
> *0<Enter>*
> **Sorted strings:**
> **0**
> **Brest**
> **Gomel**
> **Grodno**
> **Minsk**
> **Mogilev**
> **Vitebsk**

Numerous sorting methods have been developed. For example, if we replace the statements in the program marked with /* 1 */ with the following fragment:

```
for(j=0;j<i;j++)
for(k=j;k<i;k++)
        if(strcmp(m[j],m[k])>0)
        { temp = m[j]; m[j] = m[k]; m[k] = temp; }
```

another method will be used. Try inventing your own sorting method and change the program accordingly. You will learn from any mistakes that you make, so be adventurous!

## Example EX2_31

This next example shows how to use some of the functions we have discussed for file handling:

```
/* example EX2_31 */
#include <stdio.h>
#include <process.h>
void main(void)
{   int  i;
    FILE *rds;
    if ((rds = (FILE*)fopen("A:ZNI.F","r")) == NULL)
    { fputs("Can't open the file ZNI.F \n",stderr);
        exit(1);
    }
    else if(fseek(rds,-5L,2)) puts("Error fseek");
        else while(fscanf(rds,"%d",&i) != EOF)
            printf("number i = %d\n",i);
    fclose(rds);
}
```

If you run the programs EX2_27, EX2_28, EX2_31 successively, the following line will be displayed on the screen by the last program:

**number i = 150**

Take a closer look at the function **fseek**. It uses the pointer **rds** to the file, opened for reading, as its first parameter. The third parameter value, 2, indicates that the current position pointer must be counted from the end of the file. The second parameter, -5L, requires the file position pointer to be shifted 5 bytes back from the end of the file towards the beginning of the file. The file pointer will now be in the middle. The content of the file **ZNI.F** in hexadecimal code will be:

**3135300D0A3135300D0A**

Here $31_{16}$ is the **ASCII**-code for the digit 1, $35_{16}$ is the **ASCII**-code for the digit 5, and $30_{16}$ is the **ASCII**-code of the digit 0. $0D_{16}$ and $0A_{16}$ are the **ASCII**-codes of carriage return and new line. These come from the control string in the function **fprintf** of the program EX2_27 which is defined as: "**%d\n**". When we countdown five bytes, we get:

**3135300D0A**

As a result, we get the number 150 from the file. The **include** file,

**process.h**, contains the description of the function, **exit**, used for program termination.

## Examples EX2_32 and EX2_33

In the very beginning of this chapter we promised to present the program that would display the **ASCII**-codes of the all the characters on the screen and send them to your printer. Here are two programs. The first writes all the characters of the code table, with decimal code values from 0 to 127, to the file **A:MYFILE.TXT**. The second outputs on the screen, and to a printer if you wish, the decimal and hexadecimal codes of the displayable characters. These correspond to decimal codes from 32 to 126.

```
/* example EX2_32 */
#include <stdio.h>
#include <process.h>
void main(void)
{  int   i;
   char *str;
   FILE *ff;
   str = "A:MYFILE.TXT";
   ff = (FILE*)fopen(str,"w");
   for(i=0;i<128;i++)
      if (putc(i,ff) == EOF)
      { fprintf(stderr,"Writing  error  n");
        exit(1);
      }
   fclose(ff);
}
```

```
/* example EX2_33 */
#include <stdio.h>
#include <process.h>
#include <conio.h>
void main(void)
{  int   i,ch;
   char *str,c;
   FILE *ff;
   str = "A:MYFILE.TXT";
   ff = (FILE*)fopen(str,"r");
   if(fseek(ff,33L,0)) puts("Error  fseek");
   for(i=32;i<127;i++)                           /* 1 */
      if ((ch = getc(ff)) != EOF)                /* 1 */
      printf("%3x  (%3d)  -  %c;%c",             /* 1 */
         ch,ch,ch,(i-31)%5?' ':'\n');            /* 1 */
   puts("Output  to  a  printer?  (Y/N)");
   c = getch();
   if(c == 'Y' || c == 'y')
```

```
{  if(fseek(ff,33L,0))  puts("Error  fseek");
   for(i=32;i<127;i++)                               /* 2 */
   if ((ch = getc(ff)) != EOF)                       /* 2 */
   fprintf(stdprn,"%3x    (%3d)  -  %c;%c",           /* 2 */
      ch,ch,ch,(i-31)%5?'  ':'\n');                   /* 2 */
   }
   fclose(ff);
   }
```

Run the first program. It will create the file **MYFILE.TXT** on your disk A:. Then run the second program. A table will appear on the screen with entries in the format:

```
decimal_code  (hexadecimal_code)  -  character;
```

Each line output on the screen will consist of five entries. Then you'll see a prompt:

### Output to printer? (Y/N)

If you type **Y** or **y**, exactly the same table will be printed. In the program EX2_33, the comments **/* 1 */** mark the statements that output the table to the screen and **/* 2 */** mark those that output to your printer. Remember, that **stdprn** is a standard open file for data output to a printer. For the table format, a ternary operation is used in the function **fprintf**.

Both programs use a pointer to the string **str** as their first parameter of the function **fopen**, that was previously defined by the statement **str = "A:MYFILE.TXT";**. It is done this way, simply in order to show different variants of parameter transfer.

# CHAPTER 9

# FUNCTIONS

## Introducing C Functions

As we discussed in Chapter 1, **C** programs typically consist of a great number of separate **functions**. Functions are sometimes also referred to as sub-programs. These functions are normally small in size and are stored either in a single file or in multiple files. All functions are global.

In **C,** the form of a function can be declared several times in a program. There can be only one definition of a function. A function declaration can be made using a function prototype declaration which defines the function name, its argument types and the type of the return value. Of course, the function prototype declaration must match the definition of a function. In **C++,** a function prototype is mandatory. While it is optional in **C,** it is a good idea to always include one. It makes your programs more readable and less error–prone. The general form of a function prototype is:

```
function_type  function_name(argument_list)
```

The `function_type` preceeding the name defines the type of the value returned from a function. As we saw in Chapter 1, both the `function_type` and `argument_list` can be specified as **void** indicating either no return value or no arguments.

As we have already seen in the examples the definition of a function is of the form:

```
function_type  function_name(argument_list)
{
     Body of function
}
```

It is essentially a function declaration with a body. The body of the function contains the statements to be executed when the function is called. The **C** language prohibits the definition of a function inside another function.

The connection between functions is accomplished through arguments when calling a function, through return values when returning from a function and external variables generally. A called function transfers its value to a calling function through a statement containing a **return expression** following the keyword **return**. It can be written in the general form:

```
return  return_expression;
```

When there is more than one return expression in a function, each of them can fix the corresponding exit point if the return values are specifically differentiated. The calling function may ignore the return value, if you so wish. If nothing follows the word **return** then no value is returned to the calling function. Execution control switches back to the calling function on executing a return statement. This also happens in the case of an "end" exit, by falling through the concluding brace in the called function.

In **C**, function arguments are transferred by value. Transferring arguments by value means that the called function receives its own local copy of each argument value, but has no access to the memory location containing the original value. As a consequence, the called function cannot change the original argument in the calling program. It will be shown later how you can overcome this restriction. However, if a function uses an array name as its argument, the starting address of the array is transferred and the elements are not copied. Therefore, the function can change the array elements, since it has access to its address.

There is a correspondence of parameters between a function call and a function list. Clearly the argument type must be the same. Other than that, the matching of arguments is determined by their sequence. For example, the third argument in a function call will correspond to the third argument in the function definition. The argument names used in the definition of a function are local to that function. The names used in a function call do not need to correspond. They can be anything you like. Suppose a calling program calls a function as follows:

```
a = fun(b,c);
```

Here **b** and **c** are arguments whose values are transferred to the called program. If the function description starts with:

```
int fun(int b,int c)
```

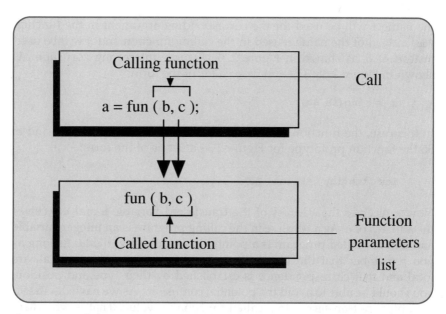

*Figure 2.36*
**Setting the
Correlation
Between the
Parameters in
the Function
Call**

the names of the arguments transferred in the call and the program **fun**,
will be identical, as is illustrated in Figure 2.36. On the other hand, if the
function starts with the statement:

```
int  fun(int  i, int  j);
```

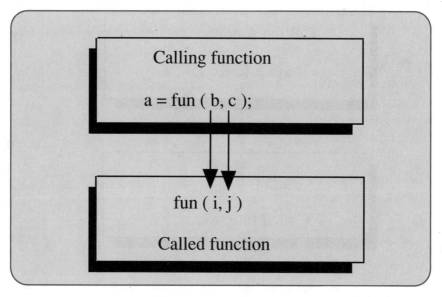

*Figure 2.37*
**Setting the
Correlation
Between the
Parameters in
the Function
Call**

the name **i** will be used for the corresponding argument in the function **fun**, instead of the name **b** used in the calling function and **j** will be used instead of **c**, as shown in Figure 2.37. A more interesting correlation is shown in Figure 2.38. The function call is of the form:

```
a  =  fun(&b,&c);
```

In this case, the function receives the addresses of the variables **b** and **c**. So the function prototype for Figure 2.38 must be of the form:

```
int  fun(int  *k,int  *c)
```

Now **k** receives the address of the transferred variable **b** and **c** receives the address of **c**. As a result, **c** in the calling program is an integer variable and **c** in the called program is a pointer to an integer variable. As long as you remember that the names of the parameters in a function call are local and that correspondence is established by their type and position, you should be able to avoid the potential confusion. As we have discussed, variables are transferred to a called function by value. That is why there is no direct means of changing a variable in the called function that has been defined in the calling function. However, as is now evident, it is easy to arrange for this to be possible. You simply transfer pointers to variables in the called function, instead of the variables themselves.

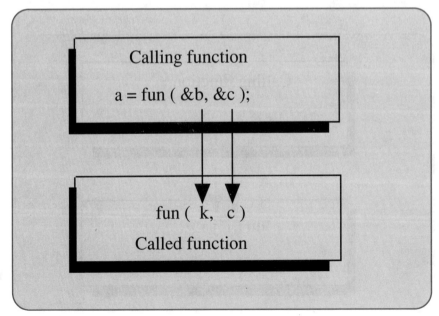

*Figure 2.38*

**Setting the
Correlation
Between the
Parameters in
the Function
Call**

Circumstances may arise where you need a function to deal with a variable number of parameters. **Printf** is an example of a library function which accepts a variable number of arguments. To declare a function having a variable number of arguments you simply add an ellipses( ... ) to the end of the argument list. For example the declaration:

```
int  func(int  a,char  c,...);
```

declares the function func with two specific arguments  **a** and **b**, followed by a variable number of additional arguments. Clearly the specific number and type of arguments have to be determined for each call of the function at execution time. There is no way to know in advance how many there are, other than that there are at least two in this case. The library **stdarg.h** will provide you with the facilities for handling such situations. Look up **va_arg**, **va_start** and **va_end** in your **Turbo C++** library reference manual for details.

## Example EX2_34

Consider the following program containing a call to a function **izm**:

```
/*  example  EX2_34  */
#include  <stdio.h>
void  izm(int  *a,int  *b)
{   int  temp;
    temp = *a;  *a = *b;  *b = temp;
}
void  main(void)
{   int  a,b;
    puts("Enter  values  a,b");
    scanf("%d%d",&a,&b);
    printf("a  =  %d,  b  =  %d\n",a,b);
    izm(&a,&b);
    printf("Changed  values:  a  =  %d,  b  =  %d\n",a,b);
}
```

This program illustrates the use of pointers as arguments of the function **izm**. It obtains the values of variables **a** and **b** and exchanges them. We should note that, if **a** and **b** are the variables in **main**, in **izm** they will be addresses.

The values in these addresses will be **\*a** and **\*b**, respectively. The function **izm** gets a copy of the addresses of the variables **a** and **b** and exchanges the values stored at these addresses. The copies of the addresses obtained as parameters are deleted when control passes back to the main program. The addresses **&a** and **&b** do not change in the main program, but the values that they point to are exchanged. If you run the program, typical results will be as follows:

> **Enter values a,b**
> *100 200<Enter>*
> **a = 100, b = 200**
> **Changed values: a = 200, b = 100**

## Using Arrays as Parameters

Now we shall look at how to transfer an array in the form of a parameter to a function. There are three possible ways of doing this:

 A parameter is defined as an array. For example:

> **int m[100];**

 A parameter is defined as an array with unspecified size. For example:

> **int m[];**

 A parameter is defined as a pointer. For example:

> **int *m**

The third method of those listed is most frequently used. Regardless of the method, the function receives a pointer to the beginning of the array, as shown in Figure 2.39.

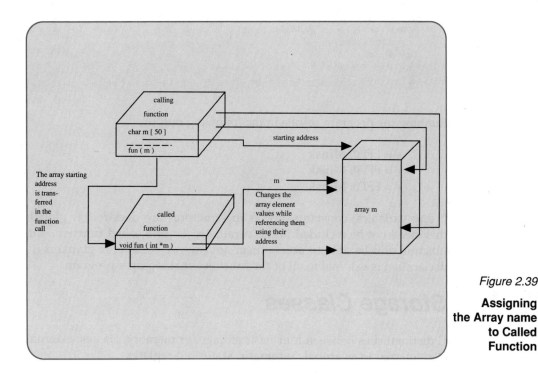

*Figure 2.39*

**Assigning
the Array name
to Called
Function**

## Example EX2_35

Now let's look at a program illustrating the use of all the variations we
have mentioned:

```
/*  example  EX2_35  */
#include  <stdio.h>
void  my_func1(char  s[6])
{  printf("s  =  %p;  ",s);
   puts(s);
}
void  my_func2(char  s[])
{  printf("s  =  %p;  ",s);
   puts(s);
}
void  my_func3(char  *s)
{  printf("s  =  %p;  ",s);
   puts(s);
}
void  main(void)
```

```
{   char str[6]  =  "Minsk";
    my_func1(str);
    my_func2(str);
    my_func3(str);
}
```

Running the program results in the following output:

> **s = FFF0; Minsk**
> **s = FFF0; Minsk**
> **s = FFF0; Minsk**

If any variables, constants, arrays or structures are declared as **global**, they need not be included in the parameter list of a called function. The function will be able to access them anyway. A variable is **global** if its declaration is external to all of the functions making up a program.

## Storage Classes

C distinguishes between four basic storage, or memory, classes: **external** also referred to as **global**, **automatic**, **static** and **register**.

### External Variables

**External variables** are defined outside functions and, hence, are accessible to any of them. They can be declared only once. As you may remember,

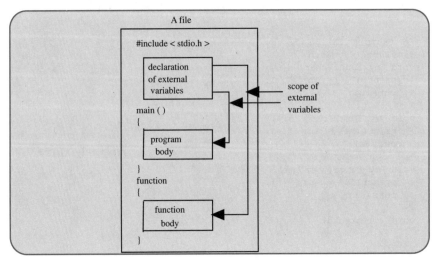

*Figure 2.40*

**The Scope of External Variables for the Functions in one File**

functions are always global. **C** prohibits the declaration of functions inside other functions. The scope of an external variable ranges from the point in a source file where it's declared, to the end of file. If you need to refer to an external variable prior to its declaration, or it is defined in another source file, the **extern** keyword comes into its own. Figure 2.40 shows the declaration and scope of external variables if the **main** program and called function are in the same file.

Figure 2.41 illustrates differences occurring when **main** and any called functions are held in different files.

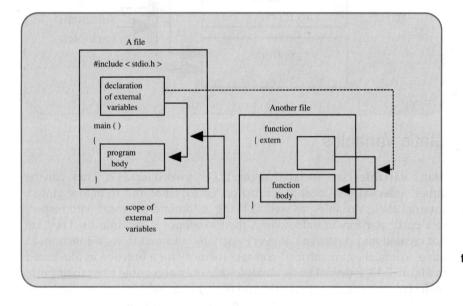

*Figure 2.41*

**The Scope of External Variables for the Functions in Different Files**

## Automatic Variables

**Automatic variables** are internal and local to a function. They start their existence at the beginning of a function and are destroyed on exit. Figure 2.42 shows the declaration of automatic variables. A keyword **auto** may be used to declare them.

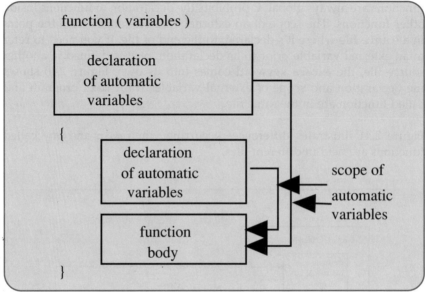

*Figure 2.42*

**Declaration and
Scope of
Automatic
Variables Using
Static Variables**

## Static Variables

**Static variables** are declared using the keyword **static**. They can be
either **internal** and local to a function, or **external** and therefore global.
Internal static variables, as well as being automatic, are local with respect
to a particular function. However, their existence is continuous. They are
not created and destroyed at every entry to, and exit from, a function. In
other words, they are intrinsic constant memory for a function as illustrated
in Figure 2.43. External static variables are only accessible from their point
of declaration within a file, to the end of the file in which they are declared.
They are unknown in other files. In particular, this lets you hide data
defined in one file, from another file.

## *Register Variables*

**Register variables** belong to the last storage class. A keyword **register**
indicates that the variable in question will be intensively used. Where
possible, the values of these variables are stored in internal microprocessor
registers by the compiler, making your program faster and shorter. The
address of register variables cannot be obtained and they can only be
automatic of types **int** and **char**.

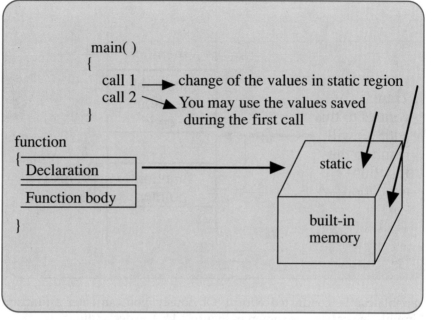

*Figure 2.43*
**Using
Static Variables**

Thus, we have four storage class type specifiers for use in declaring objects: **extern**, **auto**, **static**, and **register**. They are used in statements of the general form:

```
storage_specifier  type  var_list;
```

We have already mentioned **initialization**, which is the assignment of initial values to objects when declaring them. If explicit initialization is absent, external and static variables are guaranteed to be of zero value, whereas automatic and register variables have no definite value.

## *Pointers to Functions*

In **C**, a function cannot be the value of a variable, but you can define **a pointer to a function**. This pointer can be used as a variable. You can transfer it to other functions, put it into an array and so on. The code for a function occupies physical memory in your PC. There is an entry point address in this memory, at which execution starts when you enter the function. A pointer to a function contains the address of this entry point. It can be treated as an ordinary variable and all operations typical of a

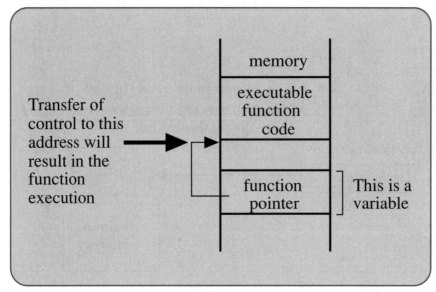

*Figure 2.44*
**An Illustration
of Function
Pointers**

variable can be conducted with it. Obviously, you can enter a function through this pointer, as shown in Figure 2.44. The declaration:

```
int  (*f) ();
```

defines **f** as a pointer to a function returning an integer value. The first pair of brackets is obligatory, since without them, **int *f();** would mean that **f** is a function returning a pointer to an integer value. Once a pointer to a function is declared, you can use it in your program: **\*f** is the function, and **f** is the pointer to the function. A similarity with arrays can be observed. The name of any function, without brackets and arguments, is a pointer to the function.

## *Example EX2_36*

Let's consider some examples of using pointers to functions. The first program shows how to transfer a pointer to a function, the form of an argument to another function:

```
/*  example  EX2_36  */
#include  <stdio.h>
void  my_func(void)
{  puts("Pointer  to  function  demonstration");}
void  func(void  (*a)(void))
{  puts("Function  func");
   a();
}
void  main(void)
{  func(my_func);
}
```

In the expression **void func(void (*a)(void))**, the function **func** has a parameter which is a pointer to the function **a**. The statement **a();**, calls the function transferred as a parameter. The program results will be:

**Function func**
**Pointer to function demonstration**

When **func(my_func);** is called, control passes to the function **func**. First it displays the message:

**Function func**

which is created by the output function **puts**. Then the identifier **a** is substituted in the call **a();**, by **my_func**. It invokes the function **my_func** and a further message is displayed:

**Pointer to function demonstration**

## Example EX2_37

The next program illustrates calling a function through an interrupt:

```
/* example EX2_37 */
#include <stdio.h>
#include <dos.h>
#include <conio.h>
void interrupt handler(...)
{  static int count;
   printf("Interrupt handler(call - %d)\n",count++);
}
int main(void)
{  setvect(200,handler);
   puts("PRESS ESC TO TERMINATE THE PROGRAM");
   while(getch() != 27) geninterrupt(200);
}
```

The lower region of memory in your PC holds what are known as
**interrupt vectors**. Each vector occupies 4 bytes, and contains the address
of an entry point to a particular program. There are specific functions to
enable you to run a program corresponding to vector number N within
the table of interrupt vectors. The function **geninterrupt** is one of those.
It is defined in the include file **dos.h**. Its prototype is of the form:

**void geninterrupt(interrupt_number);**

There are 256 interrupt vectors in total, but many of them are employed
by the operating system. The execution of DOS service functions is carried
out by means of calling system service interrupts. Virtually all basic
interaction with DOS on a lower level is accomplished through the
interrupt vectors. However, many vectors are usable. You can write your
own program, match it with an unused vector and make it an interrupt
handling program. The example EX2_37 does this. When writing your
own interrupt handler, you must obey the rules applicable to this sort of
program.

An interrupt handling function must be defined with the specifier **interrupt**. This is one more keyword used in **C**. Consider the program statement:

```
void  interrupt  handler(...)
```

Here, **handler** is an interrupt handling function.

To place an address in a vector, you may use the function **setvect**, defined in the file **dos.h**. It has the following prototype:

```
void  setvect(int  N,void  interrupt(*F)(...));
```

Here **N** is the number of the vector calling the function, **F** is the function to be called through the vector **N**.

The program statement:

```
setvect(200,handler);
```

sets an entry point to our program **handler** in the vector **200**. Now it will be called through the while-loop, where the function **geninterrupt** **(200);** is called to initiate the interrupt. To terminate the program, press *Esc*. The program results can be as follows:

**PRESS ESC TO TERMINATE THE PROGRAM.**
**0**
**Interrupt handler (call - 0)**
**A**
**Interrupt handler (call - 1)**
**<ESC>**

By pressing *Esc*, you terminate the program. The characters entered will not be displayed on the screen.

## Example EX2_38

The last program allows you to call various functions through a pointer:

```
/* example EX2_38 */
#include <stdio.h>
long add(int a,int b)
{ puts("Adding:");
  return ((long)(a + b));
}
long sub(int a,int b)
{ puts("Subtraction:");
  return ((long)(a - b));
}
long mul(int a,int b)
{ puts("Multiplying:");
  return ((long)(a * b));
}
void my_func(int a,int b,long (*calc)(int a,int b))
{ printf("a = %d; b = %d; the result :"
        "%ld\n",a,b,(*calc)(a,b));
}
int main(void)
{ my_func(10,20,add);
  my_func(10,20,sub);
  my_func(10,20,mul);
}
```

The first function call, **my_func(10,10,add);**, replaces the identifier **calc** by **add**. The second function call uses **sub** and the third employs **mul**. Thus, by changing the call parameters, you can evaluate different functions. The program results will be:

Adding:
a = 10; b = 20; the result: 30
Subtraction:
a = 10; b = 20; the result: -10
Multiplying:
a = 10; b = 20; the result: 200

# *External Arguments of the Function Main*

The **C** language allows you to convey certain arguments into a program. When **main** is called initially, it receives three parameters. The first defines the number of arguments applicable while calling the program. The second is a pointer array to character strings containing these arguments, where each string holds one argument. The third is also a pointer array to character strings with other information. All of the arguments are in the form of a character string with a terminating null. The last line is identified by two terminating nulls.

We can reference the arguments of the function **main** as **argc**, **argv** and **env**, in sequence, although other names are also possible. The following definitions for **main** are admissible:

```
main()
main(int  argc)
main(int  argc,  char  *argv[])
main(int  argc,  char  *argv[],  char  *env[])
```

Suppose, there is a program **PROG.EXE** on disk B: and suppose further, that we execute it in the following way:

    *B>PROG Birmingham London Minsk<Enter>*

Then **argv[0]** is the pointer to **PROG**, **argv[1]** is the pointer to the string **Birmingham**, **argv[2]** to **London**, and **argv[3]** to **Minsk**. The first actual argument is pointed to by **argv[1]**, and the last one by **argv[3]**. If **argc=1**, then there are no parameters in the command line after the program name. In our example **argc=4** (see Figure 2.45).

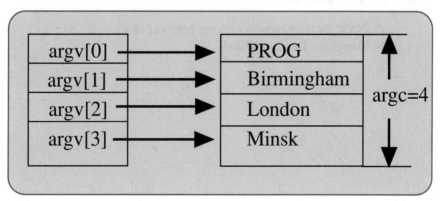

*Figure 2.45*

**Arguments to Main ()**

## Example EX2_39

The program below, outputs all arguments from the command line:

```
/* example EX2_39 */
#include <stdio.h>
void main(int argc,char *argv[])
{  while(--argc>0)
    printf((argc>1) ? "%s " : "%s\n",*++argv);
}
```

In the while-loop, the value **argc**, obtained from the command line, is decremented by 1, using **--argc**, until it reaches zero. The call to the function **printf** demonstrates that the format argument can be an expression. As long as **argc** is greater than 1, the line **\*++argv** is evaluated according to **%s**. Otherwise, a newline operation, due to the **\n**, is carried out in addition. This occurs when the last line is displayed on the screen. Recalling our discussion of pointers and arrays from Chapter 8, you will see that the expression **\*++argv** ensures that the pointer **argv** is incremented by the appropriate value to pick up the address for the next string.

Before running the program in the **Turbo C++ IDE**, you must assign some arguments to it. To do so, choose the command **Arguments** in the Run menu and type in the window the necessary arguments, for example, Birmingham, London, Minsk, - although you could put whatever you like.

The program execution and the results with the arguments we have suggested, will be as follows:

C:>*EX2_39 Birmingham London Minsk<Enter>*
**Birmingham London Minsk**

## Example EX2_40

The second program expands the first and illustrates the use of the third argument in the function **main**.

```
/* example EX2_40 */
#include <stdio.h>
void main(int argc,char *argv[],char *env[])
{  int   i;
   while(-argc>0)
   printf((argc>1)  ?  "%s  "  :  "%s\n",*++argv);
   for(i=0;*env[i]  !=  0;i++)
   puts(env[i]);
}
```

As a result of its execution, the DOS environment contents will appear on the screen, for example:

**COMSPEC=C:\COMMAND.COM**
**PROMPT=$p$g**

The first shows where the processor instruction was taken from. The second defines the current form of the DOS prompt. This is the information stored in the strings pointed to by the third argument to **main**.

# *Recursion*

**Recursion** describes the process of a function calling itself. You need to think very carefully about the termination conditions when writing a recursive program. It is very easy to make a mistake that will force the function to successively call itself an unlimited number of times.

Evaluating the **factorial** of an integer is a simple, traditional example of recursion. Remember, that the factorial of 5 equals 1 * 2 * 3 * 4 * 5 =120.

## Example EX2_41

A program to evaluate factorials is given below:

```
/*  example EX2_41  */
#include  <stdio.h>
long  fact(int  N)
{   if(N  ==  1)  return    1L;
return((long)(fact(N-1)*N));
}
void  main(void)
{   long  num;
    puts("Enter  number");
    scanf("%ld",&num);
    printf("Factorial  of  number:  %ld\n",fact(num));
}
```

Here the function **fact** calls itself. If the number entered has the value 1, **fact** returns the value 1. If it is 2, the function is multiplied by the value returned by **fact(1)**, which is 1. Then the value 2 is returned to **main**. If the number entered is 3, the following succession of function calls to **fact** will occur:

      **fact(3)**        **fact(2)**        **fact(1)**

Then **fact(1)** returns the value 1 to **fact(2)**, **fact(2)** returns 2 to **fact(3)**, and   **fact(3)** returns 6 to **main**.

Typical results of executing the program can be presented as:

      **Enter number**
      *5 <ENTER>*
      **Factorial of number: 120**

## Example EX2_42

The second recursive program calculates the highest common factor of two positive integers:

```c
/* example EX2_42 */
#include <stdio.h>
int nod(int a,int b)
{ int c;
   if (b > a) c = nod(b,a);
   else if(b <= 0) c = a;
      else c = nod(b,a%b);
   return(c);
}
void main(void)
{ int a,b;
   puts("Enter first and second number");
   scanf("%d%d",&a,&b);
   printf("Highest common factor: %d\n",nod(a,b));
}
```

Typical program results will be:

**Enter first and second number:**
*44 164 <ENTER>*
**Highest common factor :4**

Remember that the highest common factor is the largest integer, by which the two numbers can be divided with no remainder.

In the example, the function **nod** is recursive as it contains calls **nod(b, a)** and **nod(b, a%b)**. The first **if** statement in the function **nod** interchanges its arguments where necessary, to ensure that the first is larger than the second. Then for the values entered, there will be the following succession of calls:

    nod(44,164)   nod(164,44)   nod(44,32)   nod(32,12)
    nod(12,8)     nod(8,4)      nod(4,0)

Finally, the value 4, the first parameter, will return to the function **main** through all called functions.

# Library Functions

In **C** programming systems, subprograms are grouped into libraries for the purpose of solving problems that are likely to be met frequently. They will typically include for example, the evaluation of mathematical functions, data input/output, string handling, interaction with the operating systems, and a number of other groups. We have already met some of them. By using library functions, you release yourself from the necessity of developing such functions yourself and they provide a very wide range of facilities.

Library functions are typically supplied together with the **C** program development system and compiler. They are declared in files with names **\*.h**. Therefore, programs using library functions must have appropriate statements at the beginning for the library functions used, of the form:

```
#include  <include_file_type_h>
```

There are also facilities for expanding and creating new libraries, containing your own programs.

# Examples

Let's consider two rather more complicated programs. Should any problems arise, or you find the going a bit difficult for the moment, you can skip this part of the book with no damage to your understanding of the remaining material.

## Example EX2_43

The first program is designed to illustrate how to use structures with pointers to themselves. It initially reads in a sequence of words. The program sorts them and displays on the screen the sorted list of words.

The words are placed in order using an arrangement called a **binary tree**. Different words will match different branch points within the tree. Each branch point in the program given below is a structure of type **der**, which consists of: an array **w** holding any word from the list; the number **c** of word entries; a pointer **l** to the next branch point (structure) in the tree to the left; and a pointer **r** to the next branch point (structure) to the right. All of the branch points are structures of the same type. None of the branch points can have more than two next branch points, but they can have less, either one or none at all.

The tree is built up such that, from each branch point, the next left branch point contains a word less than the current one and the right contains a word greater. Figure 2.46 illustrates building the tree providing the words entered were as follows and in the following sequence:

     1. Minsk;
     2. Grodno;
     3. Brest;
     4. Vitebsk;
     5. Mogilev;
     6. Gomel;
     7. Brest.

Since the word Brest was entered twice, in the corresponding structure the field **c** will have the value 2. On entering a new word, the eighth after those defined above, for example **zzz**, a new structure will be built (see Figure 2.46). To build another structure we must dynamically allocate a memory block of the required size.

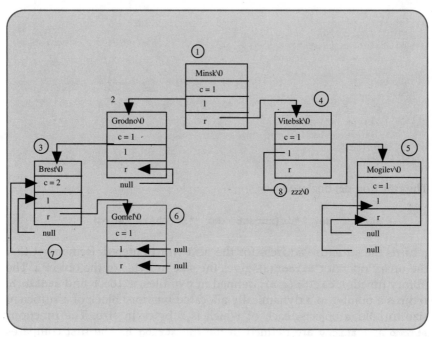

*Figure 2.46*

**An Example of a Binary Tree**

The program is as follows:

```
/* example EX2_43 */
#include <string.h>
#include <alloc.h>
#include <stdio.h>
struct der { char w[21]; int  c; struct  der  *l,*r;  };
struct  der  *dr(struct  der  *kr,char  *word)
{  int   sr;
   if(kr  ==  NULL)
   {  kr  =  (struct  der  *)calloc(1,sizeof(struct  der));
      strcpy(kr->w,word);
      kr->c = 1;
      kr->l  =  kr->r  =  NULL;
   }
   else  if(!(sr  =  strcmp(word,kr->w)))kr->c++;
      else  if(sr<0)  kr->l  =  dr(kr->l,word);
         else  kr->r  =  dr(kr->r,word);
   return(kr);
}
void  drpr(struct  der  *kr)
{  if(kr  !=  NULL)
   {  drpr(kr->l);
      printf("Word  -  %20s,  Repeat  value  -  %2d\n",
                        kr->w,kr->c);
      drpr(kr->r);
   }
}
void  main(void)
{  struct  der   *kr;
   char  word[21];
   kr  =  NULL;
   do
   {  puts("Enter  next  word");
      scanf("%20s",word);
      kr  =  dr(kr,word);
   }  while  (word[0]  !=  '0');
   drpr(kr);
}
```

The function **dr**, declared as:

```
struct  der  *dr(struct  der  *kr,char  *word)
```

returns the structure address for the next word entered. Remember that
the unary operator **sizeof(a)** gives the size in bytes of the object **a**. The
library function **calloc(a,b)**, defined in two files, **alloc.h** and **stdlib.h**,
returns a pointer to a dynamically allocated memory block of a sufficient
size to hold **a** objects, each of which is **b** bytes in size. The functions
**strcmp** and **strcpy** are defined in the file **string.h**. The first compares

two strings, with pointers to the strings as arguments. It returns the following integer values:

<0 if the first string is smaller than the second
=0 if the strings are equal
>0 if the first string is greater than the second

The function **strcpy** copies a string pointed to by the second argument, to the string pointed to by the first argument.

The function **drpr** uses the binary tree to output the sorted list to the screen. It is shown in Figure 2.47. You would need to add similar recursive calls in the illustration, after multiple points, to show the output of the words Vitebsk and Mogilev.

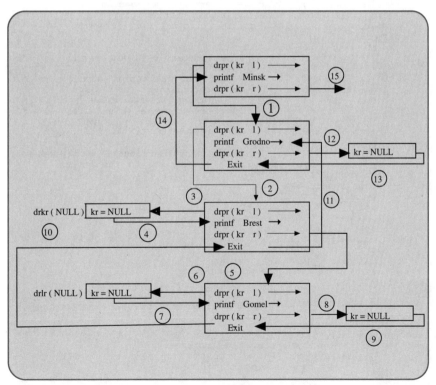

*Figure 2.47*

**Recursive Calls of theFunction drpr and Executable Operations**

## Example EX2_44

The second example is a memory resident program displaying the current
time in the top right corner of the screen.

```
/*  example  EX2_44  */
   #include  <dos.h>
   #include  <stdlib.h>
   #include  <string.h>
   typedef  unsigned  char  disp[25][80][2];
       /*  disp  -  is  3-dimensional  array  for  screen  memory:       */
       /*     25  -  number  of  lines;  80  -  number  of  columns;      */
       /*      2  -  character  and  attribute                            */
   disp  far  *video;
       /*  video  -  is  far  pointer  to  start  of  array  disp         */
   void  interrupt  (*old)(...);   /*  old  -  pointer  to  function      */
   void  interrupt  pre28(...)
       /*  this  function  is  called  by  28th  interrupt               */
   {  int   m,h;            /*  m  —  minutes;  h  —  hours               */
      char   str[20],rax,rcx,rdx;
      static  char  ct;     /*  ct  —  interrupts  per  second  count     */
      void  print_it(int  x,int  y,int  at,char  s[]);
      (*old)();             /*   calling  original  DOS    program        */
      if(ct++  ==  18)
      {  ct  =  0;  rax=_AX;    rcx=_CX;    rdx=_DX;
         /*  information  about  time  updates  once  per  second        */
         /*(first  MP  registers  used  are  saved)                      */
         _AX  =  0x0200;          /*  getting  information  about  time   */
         geninterrupt(26);  /*  calling  interrupt  26                    */
         m  =  _CL;               /*  m  —  current  minutes  value       */
         h  =  _CH;               /*  h  —  current  hours  value         */
            /*** S E C O N D S   ***/
         itoa(_DH,str,16);
         print_it(78,0,112," ");  ·
                                  /*  information  output  from  the      */
         print_it(78,0,112,str); /*  string  str  to  the  screen        */
            /*** M I N U T E S ***/
         itoa(m,str,16);
         print_it(75,0,112,"    :");
         print_it(75,0,112,str);
            /*** H O U R S ***/
         itoa(h,str,16);
         print_it(72,0,112,"    :");
         print_it(72,0,112,str);
         _AX=rax;  _CX=rcx;  _DX=rdx;
         /*    resetting  the  MP  registers                             */
      }
   }
   void  print_it(int  x,int  y,int  attr,char  *str)
   {  int  i;
      for(i=0;i<strlen(str);i++)
      {  (*video)[y][x+i][0]  =  str[i];
         /*    even  byte  stores  a  character                          */
         (*video)[y][x+i][1]  =  attr;
         /*    odd  byte  stores  attribute                              */
      }
   }
   void  main(void)
```

```
{   video  =  (disp  far  *)0xB8000000;
    /*     setting  the  pointer  video,                        */
    /*     to  the  beginning  of  screen  memory  area         */
    old  =  getvect(28);
    /*     the  variable  old  saves  the  entry  point         */
    /*        to  original  DOS  program                        */
    setvect(28,pre28);
    /*     interrupt  28  to  call  the  program  pre28         */
    keep(0,4000);
    /*     program  termination  and  making  it  resident      */
}
```

You will need to execute this example after exiting the IDE. You will also need to reboot your machine in order to stop its execution and remove it from memory.The program uses some new functions. We will now take a look at them.

The function **geninterrupt** (see also "Pointers to Functions" p. 165) allows you to call an interrupt handling program with the interrupt number specified as an argument. The majority of such programs are included in the operating system to enable you to access service functions. In the example we called an interrupt handling program number 26.

This program executes a number of functions and one of them, initiated with the number 0x200 in the **_AX** register before the interrupt, returns the current time. The program results are stored in internal registers of the microprocessor which we will discuss later.

For the moment, it is sufficient to note that the results are returned in three registers, **CL**, **CH** and **DH**. They all are 8-bits long. The registers are accessed using special variables **_CL**, **_CH** and **_DH**. The value of seconds is returned to the register **DH**, the value of minutes to **CL** and hours to **CH**. The variables **m** and **h** are used to save the values of minutes (**m**) and hours (**h**), since the microprocessor registers are used very intensively in most programs and can be changed.

The function **itoa** provides conversion of an integer, defined by the first argument, into a character string stored at the location specified in the second argument, which is a string pointer. The conversion is implemented in a number system defined by the third argument which is of integer type, which can have values from 2 to 36.  The program is made resident by the function **keep**, which is discussed below. Our program stays permanently in memory and must be activated through a timer interrupt. So we use the **vector 28**. The computer hardware addresses this vector every 55 ms, which is approximately 18.2 times a second.

Figure 2.48 illustrates the use of the library functions **getvect** and **setvect** (see also "Pointers to functions" p. 165). The first, **getvect**, saves the system vector number 28 in the variable **old**. This variable must be a pointer to a function, andis declared as such. The function **setvect** then writes the entry point to our program, **pre28**, into the vector 28. Now, at approximately 55ms intervals, the program **pre28** will be called. The statement:

```
if(ct++ == 18) { output time to monitor screen)
```

causes the time display to be updated at approximately one second intervals.

The function **keep** allows you to save the program **pre28** in memory as resident. Its first argument value is a termination code, returned to the parent process, usually the operating system. The resident program size, in 16-byte paragraphs, is transmitted as the second argument. We will omit discussion of how to calculate it for the time being.

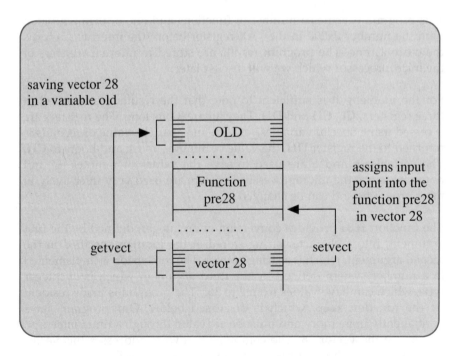

*Figure 2.48*

**The Library Functions getvect and setvect**

The function **print_it** displays the line on the screen starting from set point. It has the parameters:

| | |
|---|---|
| starting column number | - **x**; |
| starting line number | - **y**; |
| line characters attribute | - **attr**; |
| pointer to string | - **str**. |

When the program is running, the current time will appear in the top right corner of the screen. It will continue to be displayed whilst any other program is running. Obviously, the explanation here of the program operation is not comprehensive, since some aspects are dependent on a detailed knowledge of how the operating system works. Unfortunately, this is beyond the scope of this book, but we hope that the example EX2_44 gives you a glimpse of how to write and use interrupt service routines.

# CHAPTER 10

# OTHER FEATURES OF C

## The Preprocessor

The **C** compiler incorporates a device called a **preprocessor**, which greatly expands its capabilities. It provides substitutions for macro calls, joins defined files and executes other useful operations. The preprocessor is invoked by program statements which begin with the character **#**. Each statement may contain only one preprocessor directive.

The directive:

```
#define  identifier  substitute
```

invokes the replacement of the named identifier by the substitute in the following program code. It is important to note the absence of a semicolon at the end of the statement. If the directive is of the form:

```
#define  identifier(identifier,...,identifier)
substitute_string
```

with no space between the first identifier and the opening parenthesis, this is a definition of a macro substitution with arguments. We will look at how this is used in some later examples. When a substitute has a long definition requiring several lines of text, the character \ (backslash), is used as a continuation character at the end of each line to be continued.

There are some other preprocessor directives. The first, **include**, was discussed earlier. It can be used in two forms:

```
#include  "file  name"
#include  <file  name>
```

Both directives include the file with the specified **name** into a program. The first one loads the file either from the current directory, or a directory specified as a prefix. The second searches for the file in standard directories defined in the programming system (see the command Directories in the Options menu in the **Turbo C++ IDE**).

If the file name, written in double quotes in the first form of the directive, is not found in the specified directory, the search will be continued in the directories specified for the second form of the statement **#include <...>**. However, if you explicitly define the directory with the file name, this is the only directory that will be searched. The **#include** directives can be nested.  The directive **#error** is written in the form:

```
#error  error_message
```

If this statement is encountered in the program code, the compilation terminates and an error message is displayed on the screen. This instruction is mainly used while debugging within a preprocessor conditional statement, which is discussed in the next group of directives. Note that the error message need not be enclosed between double quotes.

The next group of directives allows you to selectively compile parts of your program. The process is called **conditional compilation**. The group comprises the directives **#if**, **#else**, **#elif**, **#endif**, **#ifdef** and **#ifndef**. The basic form of the **#if** conditional directive is:

```
#if  constant_expression
statement_sequence
#endif
```

The value of the constant expression is checked here. If it is **true**, the following statement sequence is compiled. Should it be **false**, the statement sequence is skipped.

The directive **#else** operates in a way similar to the instruction **else** in **C**, for example:

```
#if  constant_expression
statement_sequence_1
#else
statement_sequence_2
#endif
```

If the constant expression is **true, statement_sequence_1** is compiled, if it is false, then **statement_sequence_2** is compiled instead. The directive

**#elif** means an action of the type **else if**. It is mainly used as:

```
#if  constant_expression
statement_sequence
#elif  constant_expression_1
statement_sequence_1
.  .  .  .  .  .  .  .  .  .  .  .  .  .
#elif  constant_expression_n
statement_sequence_n
#endif
```

This is similar to the **C** construction: **if...else if...else if...**
The directive:

```
#ifdef  identifier
```

determines whether a specified identifier has been defined through a previous **#define** statement. The statement of the form:

```
#ifndef  identifier
```

checks that the specified identifier has not been defined by a previous **#define** directive. These directives can be followed by any number of lines of code, potentially containing the statement **#else** and ending with the string **#endif**, but **#elif** may not be used. If the condition being checked is **true**, all statements between **#else** and **#endif** are ignored. If the condition is **false**, the statements between the check and **#else**, or the check and **#endif** if **#else** is missing, are ignored. The statements, **#if**, **#ifdef** and **#ifndef** can be nested within one another.

The directive:

```
#undef identifier
```

makes a specified identifier undefined by nullifying any previous **#define** directive, so it is not to be replaced.

The directive **#line** is used to change the values of the variables **__LINE__** and **__FILE__**, defined in the **C** programming system. The variable **__LINE__** contains the number of the currently executable program statement. The identifier **__FILE__** is a pointer to the compiled program name string. The general form of the directive **#line** is presented as:

```
#line  number  "filename"
```

Here **number** is any positive integer assigned to the variable __LINE__.
Filename is an optional parameter that redefines the value __FILE__.

You can include in macro definitions two objects separated by the
characters  **##**, for example:

```
#define  pr(x,y)   (x##y)
```

Following this directive, **pr(a,3)** will invoke a substitute **a3**. The character
**#**, preceding a macro substitution argument, indicates it is to be converted
into a string, for example, after the directive:

```
#define  prim(var)  printf(#var"=%d",var)
```

The following program code:

```
year=1991;
prim(year);
```

is converted as:

```
year=1991;
printf("year""=%d",year);
```

The directive **#pragma** gives commands to the compiler. For example, the
statement:

```
#pragma  inline
```

tells the compiler that the C program contains inline statements in
assembler language.

Consider some global identifiers or **macro-names**. Five names are
predefined: __LINE__, __FILE__, __DATE__, __TIME__, and __STDC__.
Two of them, __LINE__ and __FILE__, have already been discussed.
The identifier __DATE__ defines a string that contains the date of compiling
the source file to object code. The identifier __TIME__ defines the string
that contains the time of compiling the source file to object code. The
macro __STDC__ has the value 1, if you compile with the **ANSI**
compatibility flag on. Otherwise, this variable will not be defined.

Consider some examples. The directive:

```
#define  begin  {
```

makes it possible to replace the opening bracket ({) for the word **begin** in the program code.

When we include in our program the statement:

```
#define  read(valr)   scanf("%d",&valr)
```

the instruction **read(i);** is understood as **scanf("%d",&i);**. Here **valr** is an argument and macro substitution has been carried out.

Three other directives:

```
#ifdef  write
#undef  write
#endif
```

check whether the identifier **write** has been defined within a directive of the form **#define  write** .... If it has been, the name **write** is set undefined and will not be replaced. The directives:

```
#ifndef write
#define write fprintf
#endif
```

check whether the identifier **write** has been defined. If it has been, the identifier **write** is now defined to be replaced by the name **fprintf**.

## Example EX2_45

The following program demonstrates the use of predefined macro names:

```
/*  example  EX2_45  */
#include  <stdio.h>
void  main(void)
{  int   j;
   j = __LINE__;
   printf("j  =  %d;  __LINE__  =  %d\n",j,__LINE__);
   printf("%d  %s\n",__LINE__,__FILE__);
   printf("%d  %s\n",__LINE__,__DATE__);
   printf("%d  %s\n",__LINE__,__TIME__);
}
```

The program results can be presented as:

> j = 5; __LINE__ = 6
> 7 ex2_45.cpp
> 8 Mar 14 1992
> 9 23:29:59

The value of __LINE__ varies depending on the line number in which it appears. In the fifth statement j is assigned the value 5. In the next statement which is the sixth in the program, we print the value of j which is 5 and the current value of __LINE__ which is now 6. __DATE__ and __TIME__ will have values corresponding to the instant of their use.

# Using Microprocessor Program Accessible Elements

Figure 2.49 gives all the program accessible registers of the Intel 8086 microprocessor (MP). The addressable memory extent of the microprocessor is 1 Mb and hence the address format is 20 bits. Despite the 20-bit code generation, the MP operates with logical addresses containing a 16-bit segment (base) address and a 16-bit offset within a

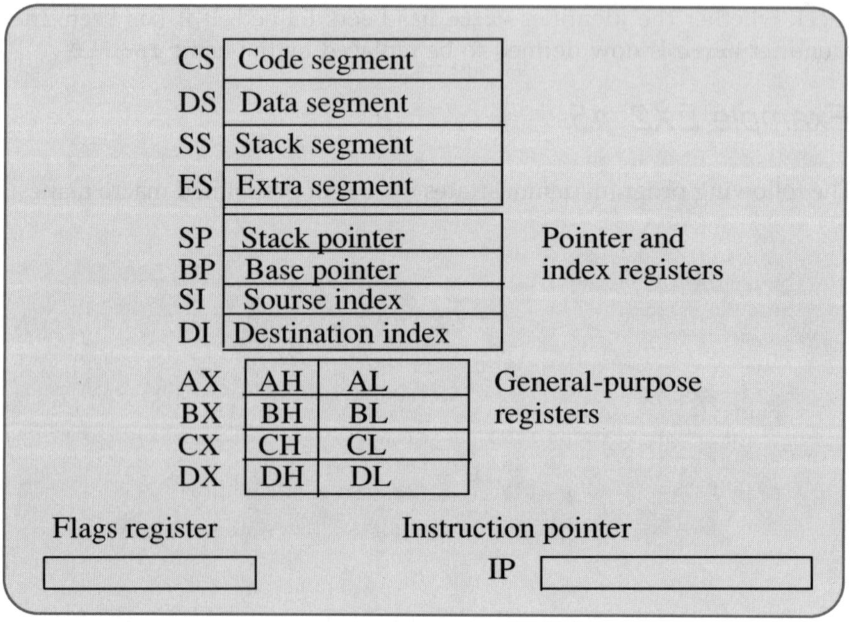

*Figure 2.49*
**8086 CPU Registers**

segment. The segmentation mechanism assumes that all the addressable area is divided into regions (segments) of 64 Kbytes each. The starting address of a segment, which is 20 bits, has zeros in its four lower bits so it appears as $XXXX0_{16}$. X represents any hexadecimal digit from 0 to F. Thus, segments can only start on a 16 byte block boundary. A 16 byte block boundary is called a **paragraph** boundary.

The segment starting address is stored in a 16-bit segment register and memory cells inside the segment are addressed using a 16-bit offset. If the segment address is 0, the physical address equals the offset. The majority of the MP instructions operate with 16-bit offsets, and segment addresses are stored in one of the four registers: **CS** - code; **DS** - data; **SS** - stack; **ES** - extra data. The block of general purpose registers comprises four 16-bit elements, **AX**, **BX**, **CX**, and **DX**, allowing for independent addressing of higher (**H**) and lower (**L**) parts. All registers of the block participate in the execution of arithmetic and logical operations, in presenting operands and storing the result. There are also numerous instructions that specify some registers (see Figure 2.49).

Four 16-bit pointer and index registers, **SP**, **BP**, **SI**, and **DI**, are used to store offsets within a segment. These registers are also used in arithmetic and logical operations with two-byte words. The registers **SP** (stack), and **BP** (base), are used to access data in the current stack segment, and **SI** and **DI** in the current data segment. Some MP commands specify these four registers.

Figure 2.50 illustrates these registers, and shows the memory area address organization.

**C** incorporates special objects called **pseudovariables**. They are used to address the resources of the **Intel 8086** microprocessor. The full list of pseudovariables includes 21 elements: **_AX**, **_BX**, **_CX**, **_DX**, **_CS**, **_DS**, **_SS**, **_ES**, **_SP**, **_BP**, **_DI**, **_SI**, **_AL**, **_AH**, **_BL**, **_BH**, **_CL**, **_CH**, **_DL**, **_DH**, **_FLAGS**. The first twelve and the last one, are of type **unsigned int**, and the rest are of type **unsigned char**. They are connected in a special way with the MP registers given in Figure 2.49.

Their names are built from the register names prefixed with the character _. Thus the variable **_FLAGS** is connected with the flag register. Assigning a value to any variable, for example, **_AX**, stores this value into the register **AX**. Evaluating a variable, for example **_BX**, is equal to evaluating the register **BX**. Thus, the pseudovariables are a set of identifiers

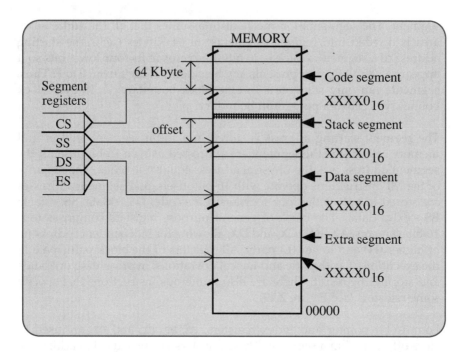

*Figure 2.50*
**The 8086 Memory Addressing Mechanism**

corresponding to the given registers. They can be considered global objects of the appropriate defined type.

## Example EX2_46

This is a program using pseudovariables:

```
/*  example  EX2_46  */
#include  <stdio.h>
void  main(void)
{   _AX  =  _BX  =  _CX  =  _DX  =  1;
    _AX  =  _BX  =  _CX  =  _DX  =  4;
    _AX  =  _BX  =  _CX  =  _DX  =  9;
}
```

We can execute it step by step in a debugging session. First, make the **R**egister window active in the **W**indow menu. It will contain the values of all the registers of your microprocessor that we have discussed. Executing the program step by step, which you achieve by pressing the *F8* key, will let you see in the **R**egister window how the registers **AX**, **BX**, **CX** and **DX** change as the execution progresses.

# SECTION THREE

## Programming in C++

# SECTION THREE

# CHAPTER 11

# *AN INTRODUCTION TO C++*

## *Object Oriented Programming*

The idea of Object Oriented Programming (**OOP**) was implemented for the first time in the Smalltalk language. **OOP** introduces the concept of **an object**, and defines techniques that provide for:

1. Describing an object structure, or class.

2. Describing methods or functions for the manipulation of objects, using unique object inheritance principles.

3. Protecting object class members, and defining object accessing rules.

4. Passing messages between objects.

**OOP** was envisaged as a tool for creating complex programs by means of simple methods. **OOP** inherits all the beneficial features of structured programming and combines them with several new approaches. We will first characterize in outline the basic concepts of **OOP**, and introduce some of the unique notions it incorporates. It is a good idea to try to get a feeling for the basic concepts without worrying about the details. In later chapters in this section, we will be defining them much more precisely.

## *Classes*

For describing object class members, **C++** implements constructions similar to **struct** and **union** in C. Such a construction is a **class**. Both **struct** and **union** in **C** are effectively special cases of a class in C++. Class members can be of two types, **data** and **methods**. The latter are also referred to as **functions**. So a class is essentially a user defined data type, and the class name becomes the specifier for objects of the new type.

## An Example of Using Classes

Consider a simple example. Let us suppose we wish to create a class **Point**, which is to comprise instances of the obvious entities, geometric points. These will be defined in terms of their coordinates and a function or method that will display a point on the screen. We could make the following description:

```
Class  Point
Integer members x and y
If an object of type Point is defined with two parameters
x and y, display on the screen a point with coordinates
x and y.
```

Of course, the description is greatly simplified. An important characteristic is that, as with data types **struct** and **union** in **C**, a class type defines a particular pattern. However, it determines two subsets of members - **data** and **functions**. So **x** and **y** are just the data members of the class. Thus, an object of class **Point** is a particular instance of the members of the class. Later on we will see that some members can be hidden, thus preventing their use outside the class. Now we have a class definition for **Point**, class **objects** can be defined which will consist of coordinate pairs, x and y.

On the basis of the Class **Point** that we have just defined, we could create another class, for example **Rectangle**. Let it have two members of type **Point** to describe the objects of the class, and some action–specifying functions such as **move, copy** and so on. Once we have defined our class **Rectangle**, using objects of the class **Point**, we could describe a program that would handle the objects of type **Point** and **Rectangle** for creating graphic images. This is illustrated in Figure 3.1.

## The Key Concepts of *OOP*

Object Oriented Programming is based on three key concepts:

    ▲1    **Encapsulation**

    ▲2    **Inheritance**

    ▲3    **Polymorphism**

We will quickly look at what these involve.

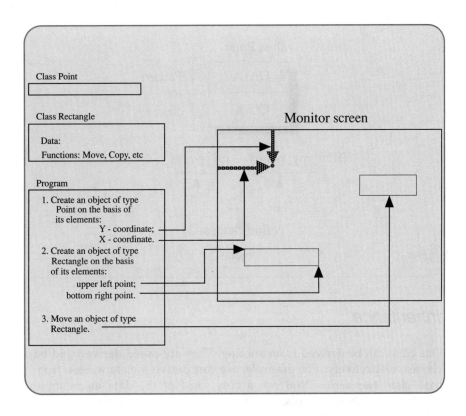

*Figure 3.1*
**An Example
of Using
Classes**

## Encapsulation

A class includes data and code that handles this data. This is illustrated in Figure 3.2. The executable code comprises the programmer–defined functions included in a particular class for processing class data members. Part of the data and code can be protected from any influence outside the class if desired. This enclosure of code or data within the class is called **encapsulation**. Encapsulation can apply to structured data within a class, or to functions defining possible actions for manipulating data and setting data access rules.

Once a class has been defined you can declare its specific members. For example, variables **my_point1** and **my_point2** shown in Figure 3.2 are particular objects of the class **Point** and, as we have said, the described class is a new data type.

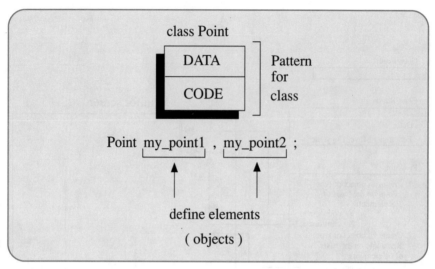

*Figure 3.2*
**Elements of a Class**

## Inheritance

One class can be derived from another. They are called **derived** and **base** classes, respectively. For example, we can derive a class **Window** from a base class **Rectangle**. You can access some of the data elements and functions which are members of a base class from a derived class. Thus, **inheritance** is the possibility to assign to a new class some of the features of another class from which it is derived.

Consider the example of inheritance shown in Figure 3.3. Let us suppose we have defined a class **Point**. It includes the functions that can display a point at any position on the screen. Now we can create three more classes, **Line**, **Text** and **Rectangle**. The functions of these classes enable you to operate with such elements as lines, text and rectangles. Prior to displaying any element on the screen, you must define its base coordinates in terms of a point on the screen, which will be a screen pixel position. Since we need a point to fix the position of any element to be displayed, it is natural to derive classes **Line**, **Text** and **Rectangle** from the class **Point** as a base class, as shown in Figure 3.3.

Now create one more class, **Window**, with rectangles, lines and text as its elements. They are all essential elements to defining a window, since these objects are used to create a **Window** object. So the class **Window** is derived from the base classes **Line**, **Text** and **Rectangle**. Figure 3.3 shows that each derived class inherits specific features from its base classes.

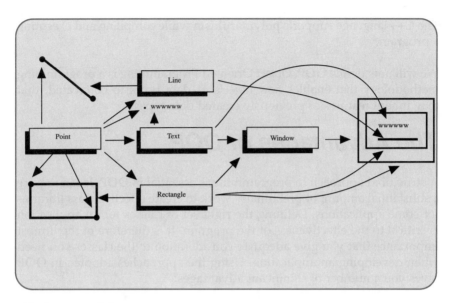

*Figure 3.3*
**Class
Inheritance**

## Polymorphism

**Polymorphism** refers to the use of the same name for a number of slightly different program functions. For example, you could define a function that will accept arguments of either type **int** or type **float**, by writing a function corresponding to each argument type and giving them the same name. When the function is called, the type of its arguments is analyzed by the compiler and the appropriate version of the function is executed. This is illustrated in Figure 3.4.

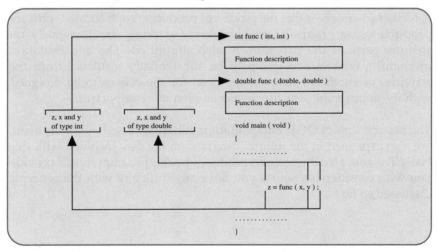

*Figure 3.4*
**Function
Overloading**

The **C++** language supports **polymorphism** while compiling and executing a program.

We will now define **OOP**. Object Oriented Programming is a programming methodology that enables new objects or data types to be created, that may inherit features of previously created data types.

## *The Advantages of OOP*

A structured approach to programming is essential in **OOP**. It can require a substantial amount of preliminary work to create effective class libraries for some applications. Defining the right set of classes for an application is critical to the effectiveness of the program. It is therefore of the utmost importance that you give adequate consideration to the classes you need when developing an application. Using the approaches adopted in **OOP** gives you a number of significant advantages:

1. You can create very complicated programs with a greatly simplified programming process.

2. The reliability of programs is considerably enhanced.

3. The style of programming makes programs easier to understand and simplifies their modification.

4. The process of finding errors in your program is simplified.

A further advantage is that the process of producing sophisticated software products using groups of programmers, working simultaneously on various parts of the program, is also simplified. The encapsulation mechanism enables one group to be substantially insulated from the activities of another. However, the need for the classes to be designed with the appropriate structure becomes even more important.

The key concepts of **OOP**, **encapsulation**, **inheritance** and **polymorphism**, are also explained in the tutorial program on the disk included with this book. The animated illustrations produced by this program should provide you with considerable help if you have any difficulty with the concepts discussed so far.

## A Conceptual Example of a Program

Consider an example of designing a program using **OOP** technology, which will show some of the new approaches to programming and some of the advantages to be gained. Suppose we have to design a simple graphic editor capable of drawing lines, rectangles and circles at arbitrary positions on the monitor screen. The first step in designing such a program is to determine all of the classes of object we will have to deal with. We will need to introduce the following types of objects:

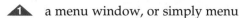 a menu window, or simply menu

 a cursor

3. a diagram

We must describe each of these objects.

The menu window has the options: Quit, Load, Save, and Clear screen. You can choose any option by moving the cursor on the monitor screen to your choice using the arrow keys. Once you have positioned the cursor on the required option you press <*Enter*> to activate it. You can also click on your choice with the mouse. To simplify the programming problem, let us suppose that the graphic file always has the same name defined by the editor. It is always saved on the current drive and loaded from it. These restrictions are imposed for the sake of simplicity and may be easily removed.

Suppose, the cursor is to be one of two forms: + or_. It is to be moved on the screen by means of the arrow keys. To fix the cursor's position you must press <*Enter*>. All the functions for the cursor operation belong to the object **cursor**.

The object **diagram** will contain the components required for drawing graphical entities, which are lines, rectangles and circles. It receives a message from the object **menu**, which defines the type of entity required, either line, rectangle or circle. From this message it chooses the appropriate object, either a line, rectangle or circle. Initially, the object **diagram** receives from the object **cursor** the reference points of the corresponding figure, for instance, the coordinates of the beginning and end of the line. These are then transferred to the chosen object. This figure will be drawn with the help of the **C++** library functions line, rectangle or circle.

On the basis of the characteristics of each of the objects, we can define the functions they must carry out and the messages that need to be passed between them. This is all illustrated in Figure 3.5.

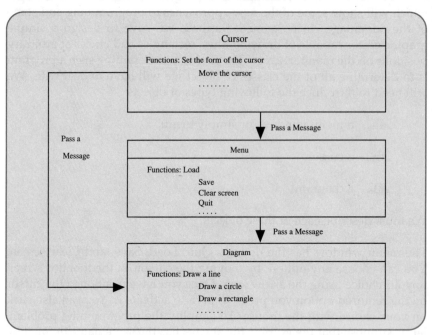

*Figure 3.5*
**Classes and Message Passing**

## The Program Structure

We could represent the structure of the program we need to write as:

Description of the classes (these are shown in Figure 3.5):
The class **menu**
  description of the data for the class **menu**
  description of the functions  for the class **menu**
The class **cursor**
  description of the data for the class **cursor**
  description of the functions for the class **cursor**
The class **diagram**
  description of the data for the class **diagram**
  description of the functions for the class **diagram**

The program designed in terms of the defined classes
  declare the object of type **menu** with defined coordinates
  display the menu on the monitor screen

declare the objects of type **cursor**

declare the objects of type **diagram**

**1.** Call the function which will set the cursor form. Then, depending on the user's choice, which is selected by pressing *F1* or *F2* , the cursor will be of the form + or _.

**2.** Call the cursor movement function. If it returns an action value corresponding to a menu choice, then pass control back to the main program.

**3.** Analyze the returned action value. If it corresponds to the keys Quit, Load, Save or Clear screen, call the corresponding function of the class **Menu** and pass the coordinates to it. If the returned action value corresponds to the options line, rectangle or circle, call the corresponding function of the class **Menu** and pass the coordinates to it.

**4.** Execute the corresponding function of the class **Menu** which, depending on the coordinates received, will carry out one of the following operations: save the screen in a file, load the screen from a file, clear the screen, or exit to DOS.

**5.** Return to the initial program step(1).

**6.** Execute the corresponding function of the class **Diagram** which, depending on the coordinates received, will carry out one of the following operations: draw a line, draw a rectangle or draw a circle.

**7.** Return to the beginning of the program (1).

End of program.

This conceptual program operates with new type definitions which are rather more complicated in structure than those in **C**. Each such definition is defined as an **object class**. The object class definition is very close to the structure definition in **C**. So close in fact, that, as we have said at the beginning of this chapter, **struct** is effectively a special case of a class.

The major difference is that the general class definition includes not only data, but also functions, which can manipulate this data in various ways. The program design is now expressed in terms of objects rather than elementary variables and is much simpler as a consequence. The objects are now considered to be the basic program elements. The programmer must know how to use the functions that manipulate the objects within each class, but not necessarily understand the operating mechanism in detail.

The object classes in the program have names that reference the objects they define and manipulate. For instance, the class named **cursor**, operates with the cursor on the monitor screen. To move the cursor you simply call the function of the object class **cursor** that does this, without going into any of the detailed operations of the function.

The idea of an interface  now becomes predominant and you can regard the object class as a "black box" with which you communicate in a precisely defined set of ways. You can only interact with the class members through the interface defined by the class definition. One of the most important features of **OOP** languages is the possibility of creating libraries of classes which can be used for designing a whole range of programs.

These class libraries include not only the object data descriptions, but all of the functions necessary to manipulate or operate on the objects. If the class libraries are well designed, then the functions they include can be reused again and again in different programs, with substantial gains in programming productivity.

## Unique Features of C++

C++ extends the existing **C** language.  Since **C** is a subset, programs written in **C** can be compiled and executed in the **C++** environment. Obviously, the converse is not true!  As we have just discussed, the major advantages of programming in **C++** are gained by using the **Object Orientated Programming** features.  There are also new capabilities in **C++** that are not specifically in this area. We shall come back to object oriented methods later. We will first introduce some of the unique features of **C++** not found in **C**.

As we saw in Chapter 6, **C++** provides an additional method for including comments in a program.  Anything appearing on a line following a pair of slashes is treated as a comment by the compiler and ignored.  For example:

```
//This is a comment
```

You can still use the **C** form of comments as well:

```
/*This is also a comment*/
```

Since the **C** form enables you to show things in a way that the **C++** form does not, you will probably want to use both.

A further facility unique to **C++** is stream input/output. We have already met an example of this in Chapter 1. We can extend our knowledge of stream input/output by means of the next example.

## Example EX3_1

```
/* example EX3_1 */
#include <iostream.h>
void main(void)
{   unsigned i;
    unsigned char my_str[80] = "An example of output in C++\n";
    // possible output in C++
    cout << my_str;
    cout << "Input an integer:   ";
    // possible input in C++
    cin >> i;
    cout << "Input number:   " << i << "\n";
    cout << "enter a string:   ";
    cin >> my_str;
    cout << "input string:   " << my_str;
}
```

This example uses the **stream** input/output facilities that are not available in **C**. Of course, you can still use the functions available in **C** if you wish. You can even use both in the same program. However, you will find the new facilities very much easier to use. The include file, **iostream.h**, defines the functions that provide support for the facilities we are using. The program statement:

```
cout <<   my_str;
```

will output to the screen

**An example of output in C++**

and the cursor will move to the beginning of the next line, since the text terminates with the character **\n**. The screen is the default output stream. Note how simple the statement is. Formatting is automatic without the need for you to supply any additional description or format codes. They are all predefined in **iostream.h**. The output data can be single characters, strings and numbers. Numbers can be integers or floating points.

The next statement:

```
cin >> i;
```

receives input from the keyboard as the default input stream and stores it in the integer variable **i**. Again, formatting is automatic. The input data can also be single characters, strings and decimal numbers.
The next statement:

```
cout <<"input number: " << i << "\n";
```

is another output to the screen. In this instance it outputs the character string, **input number:** , followed by the value of the variable **i**, and finally positions the cursor at the beginning of the next line. The symbol << can be used any number of times to output multiple data items. This also applies to the symbol >> for input.

Of course, in other contexts, the symbols << and >> still define **shift** operations. There is clearly no possibility of confusing the two functions since the context completely determines which is meant to be executed.

We shall come back to stream input/output again in Chapter 14 . It has some important capabilities in relation to classes. As you will see, it provides an open-ended set of functions that you can extend very easily yourself to handle any new types that you may define. It has the potential to provide automatic input/output for almost anything.

## *Defining Classes*

We discussed at the beginning of this section the most important distinguishing feature of **C++**, which is the introduction of new data types, called **classes**. A key word, **class**, enables you to create new data types which are similar to **struct** and **union** in **C**, but which can include both data and functions as members. The members of a class can be assigned attributes which may be **private**, **public** and **protected**. These define the accessibility of a class member. For the moment we shall consider only the first two attributes.

As a default, all class members are assigned the attribute **private**. Compare this with members of a **struct** which are **public** by default. Members of a **struct** can also have alternative attributes assigned using the keywords **private** or **protected**. Members of a union are **public** by default and cannot be assigned alternative attributes.

In general, apart from some specific exceptions described below, members of a class with the default **private** attribute, will not be accessible outside the class in which they are defined. The default attribute is changed by using the appropriate keyword followed by a colon, for instance **public:**, preceding the data or functions within the class whose accessibility is to be changed. The **public** members are accessible in any part of a program. A typical class declaration would be as follows:

```
class  class_name
{    data and functions with default private attribute
public:
        data and functions with public attribute
}    the list of class objects;
```

The list of class objects can be empty, in which case the class definition is simply a pattern that may be used elsewhere in the program to define a specific class object/specific class objects as required.

## Example EX3_2

Now consider a sample program that will illustrate various aspects of class definition and help us in further discussion:

```
/* example EX3_2 */
#include <iostream.h>
#define dim 50
/*******************************************/
/* Defining a pattern for class list_int */
/*******************************************/
class list_int
   { int my_list[dim]; // these are members of class
     int count;        // list_int with attribute private
     public:           // all other members have the attribute
                                                     public
         void init(void);
         void add(int); // these are function-members
         void del(int); // of class list_int
```

```
          void  get_int(void);
   };
/*******************************************************/
/* Defining  function-member   init  of  class  list_int */
/*                (list initialization)                */
/*******************************************************/
void  list_int::init(void)
   {  count  =  0;  }
/*******************************************************/
/* Defining  function-member   add  of  class  list_int  */
/*          (adding integer member to the list)       */
/*******************************************************/
void  list_int::add(int  new_el)
   {  if(count  ==  dim)
         {  cout  <<  "list  is  full\n";
            return;
         }
      for(int  i=0;  i<count;  i++)
      if(my_list[i]  ==  new_el)return;
      my_list[count++]  =  new_el;
   }
/*******************************************************/
/* Defining  function-member   ins  of  class  list_int  */
/*       (deleting an  integer  member from the list)   */
/*******************************************************/
void  list_int::del(int  del_el)
{  for(int  i=0;  i<count;  i++)
   if(my_list[i]  ==  del_el)
   {  for(int  j=i;  j<count;  j++)
my_list[i]  =  my_list[i+1];
count--;
      return;
   }
}
/*******************************************************/
/* Defining  function-member   get_int  of  class  list_int  */
/*       (output to the  screen of the list members)   */
/*******************************************************/
void  list_int::get_int(void)
{  for(int  i=0;  i<count;  i++)
   cout  <<  my_list[i]  <<  "  ";
   cout  <<  "\n";
}
void  main(void)
{  list_int m_l;      // declaring member  m_l of class list_int
   m_l.init();        //  list  initialization
   m_l.add(10);       //  adding number  10  to  the  list
   m_l.add(20);       //  adding number  20  to  the  list
   m_l.add(30);       //  adding number  30  to  the  list
   m_l.get_int();     //  output to the screen of the list members
   m_l.del(20);       //  deleting number 20 from the list
   m_l.get_int();     //  output to the screen of the list members
}
```

It should be emphasised that **C++** does not accept the rather relaxed approach to function declaration used in **C**. In every case you must define a specific function **prototype**. You should keep in mind that, not only must the data type for the return value be defined, but also all the function argument types must be declared.

Example EX3_2 defined a single class named **list_int**. First you should note that the object **list** is empty, since the closing **}** is followed immediately by a semicolon. The four class members **init, add, ins, get_int** are functions and they each must have program code defined. The function code can be specified immediately after the appearance of the function name within the class definition. For example, for the first function **init**, after the attribute specifier **public**, we could have written the following statement to define the function code:

```
void init(void) { count = 0; }
```

In our example EX3_2 above we have chosen the alternative approach, which is to define the function code separately from the definition of the function as a class member. In this case we have used the following statements:

```
void list_int::init(void)
{ count = 0; }
```

The symbol : : is called the **scope resolution operator**. It tells the compiler that this version of the function **init**, as there could be others, belongs to the class **list_int**. Different classes may use different functions with the same name. We shall see later how this is managed.

The object **m_1** of the class **list_int** is declared in the function **main**. The members of this class can be accessed using the notation used for **struct** and **union** components:

```
object_name.member_name
```

For example, **m_1.init()** references the function **init**. Remember that to declare an object, you should only use the class name. You must not use the keyword **class**. The members **my_list** and **count**, of the class **list_int**, are by default **private** and thus are local to that class and cannot be referenced externally. Thus, attempted references using **m_1.count** or **m_1.my_list[i]** will result in an error.

Consider the definition of a class member that is a function, for example **add**. Since it is a class member it can access any other members of the same class, including those that are **private**, for example **count**. Reference to any other member of the same class can be made simply by using the member name. Prefixing the class name to the member name is not necessary. Of course, if reference is to be made to a **public** member of a separate class, then the name prefix as in the example above, is essential.

A further feature of **C++** is the ability to declare a variable and its type anywhere in a function, and not just at the beginning as in **C**. For example, in the function **add**, the variable **i** is declared as an integer in the loop statement:

```
for(int  i=0;i<count;i++)
```

Figure 3.6 shows the operations that can be carried out in the example. The preceding program, EX3_2, puts three integers into a list, displays the list, then deletes the second element from the list and finally displays the resultant list. The maximum number of elements is 50 as defined in the **#define** statement and can be changed simply by altering the value in this statement. You could try changing **main()** to manipulate a longer list.

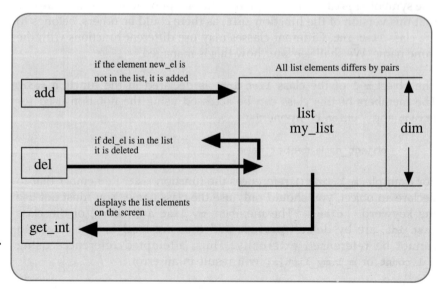

*Figure 3.6*
**Class Member Functions in Ex3_2**

# The Concept of Overloading

We can now look at the facility in **C++** which allows two or more different functions to have the same name and number of arguments, and differ only in their argument types and return values. This is called **function overloading**. The following program illustrates how such functions may be defined and how they are subsequently used.

## Example EX3_3

```
/* example EX3_3 */
#include <iostream.h>
/*******************************************/
/* The function my_mul can be overloaded */
/*******************************************/
// first definition of my_mul
int my_mul(int i,int j,int k)
{  cout << "Function operates with integers\n";
   return i * j * k;
}
// second definition of my_mul
double my_mul(double i,double j,double k)
{  cout << "Function operates with floats\n";
   return i * j * k;
}
void main(void)
{  // multiplication of integers using my_mul
   cout << "5 * 6 * 7 = " << my_mul(5,6,7) << "\n";
   // multiplication of floats using my_mul
   cout << "5.2 * 6.3 * 7.4 = " << my_mul(5.2,6.3,7.4) << "\n";
}
```

There are two functions defined providing rather similar but distinct calculations, both referenced by the name **my_mul**. The first definition of **my_mul** multiplies three integers together and the second multiplies three double precision floating point numbers. The **C++** compiler determines which of the two versions of **my_mul** to use in any particular instance by analyzing the argument types being used.

The value of overloading can be appreciated by considering the C library functions **itoa**, **ltoa** and **ultoa**. They provide functions which convert integers, long or unsigned long variables to a character string, depending on which one you use. Despite the fact that they provide identical operations but on different variable types their names are different. **C++**

allows us to use one name for all three functions. This reduces the number of library function names you have to be aware of and makes programs using this function much more readable.

Polymorphism affects other **C++** facilities as well. A further feature of **C++** is **operator overloading**. This refers to the notion of a single operator being assigned multiple functions, the actual function used in any particular case determined by context. We have already seen an example of this with the stream input/output functions in **C++** and the shift operators. If you overload a given operator with a new function it still retains its original definition.

## *Example EX3_4*

Consider an example:

```
/* example EX3_4 */
#include <iostream.h>
#include <string.h>
/************************/
/* Defining class String */
/************************/
class String
{ char str[20];              // local member
  public:                    // global members follow below
    void init(char *s);      // initialization function
    int operator - (String s_new);
} my_string1, my_string2;
    // two objects have been declared,
    // my_string1 and my_string2 of class String
/****************************************************/
/*        Function init copies an argument-string s */
/*        to member-string (str) of class String    */
/****************************************************/
void String::init(char *s)
    { strcpy(str,s); }
/*****************************************************/
/*   using operator (-) for subtraction of two strings */
/*****************************************************/
int String::operator - (String s_new)
{ for(int i=0; str[i] == s_new.str[i]; i++)
    if (str[i] == 0) return 0;
    return str[i] - s_new.str[i];
}
```

```
void  main(void)
{  char  s1[20],  s2[20];
   cout << "Enter  the  first  string  (up  to  19  characters):  ";
   cin >> s1;
   cout << "\nEnter  the  second  string  (up  to  19  characters):  ";
   cin >> s2;
   my_string1.init(s1);      // initializing  object  my_string1
   my_string2.init(s2);      // initializing  object  my_string2
   // output  to  the  screen  the  difference  of  two  strings
   cout << "\nString 1   -   String 2   =   ";
   cout <<   my_string1 - my_string2 << "\n";
}
```

The operator is used to subtract two strings. The result of the subtraction operation is the numerical difference between the **ASCII-codes** of the first two characters that do not coincide. So, in the two strings **Minsk** and **Minsk_MREI**, the second is longer than the first. The first five characters coincide and the sixth character in the word **Minsk_MREI**, which is an underline, is bigger than the terminating null in the word **Minsk**.

The following statement from our example:

**int  String::operator  -  (String  s_new)**

indicates that the operator, -, is within the scope resolution of the class **String** and its result is integer. The word **operator** in the statement is a keyword, which, when followed by an operator symbol, forms what is called the **operator function name**. This is being used in the same way as a normal function name when defining a new overloaded function for the operator.

Since the operator is a member of the class **String**, its first operand must always be an object of the class **String**, which means it must have been declared to be of type **String**. The identification of the type of the first operand is implicit. In other words, if the expression **A-B** is defined, the variable **A** must be a member of the class **String**. The type of the second operand is specified within the parentheses and, in the example above, is also of type **String**.

The variable **str**, in the subsequent statements defining the overloaded function -, implicitly references the member of the class **String** corresponding to the first operand and **s_new.str** is the member corresponding to the second operand.

The objects **my_string1** and **my_string2** are defined as specific instances or objects of the class **String**, immediately following the definition of the class and they are global in scope. In **main()** they are initialized to the string values entered as input using the **init** function that is a member of the class **String**. Thus, the expression **my_string1 - my_string2** uses the overloaded version of the operator -.

In the previous examples we met with the **initialization** of class members, i.e. assigning initial values to the object members. For this purpose we used an explicit member function **init**. C++ provides the means for automatic initialization while you are creating an object. These operations are executed by a particular function called the **constructor**. This function has the name of the class in which it's defined. For instance, instead of the function **init** in the example EX3_2, we could write:

```
String(char *s) { strcpy(str,s); }
```

You need to keep in mind that **the constructor** is a little different from other functions in that it never returns the value. It is always called when you declare a specific object of a class, that is, when you are creating an object. The converse actions to **constructors** are performed by functions called **destructors**. They destroy objects. When invoked, **the constructor** allocates memory for an object, whereas **the destructor** deallocates it. **The destructor** has the same name as **the constructor**, but its name is preceded by the tilde, or logical 'not' symbol, ~.

## Example EX3_5

Consider an example using constructors and destructors. Note that some operators, for example the output operator, have been introduced into the example simply to explicitly demonstrate how the constructors and destructors actually work. It does not necessarily represent the best way to write the program.

```
/* example EX3_5 */
#include <iostream.h>
#include <string.h>
class String
 {  int i;
    public:
       String(int  j);        //  constructor
       ~String(void);         //  destructor
       void  show_i(void);
 };
```

```
String::String(int  j)
{   i = j;  cout << "constructor  operates\n";   }
void String::show_i(void) { cout << "i = " << i << '\n'; }
String::~String(void)
{   cout << "destructor  operates\n";   }
void main(void)
{   String  my_ob1(10);          //  initializing  object  my_ob1
    String  my_ob2(20);          //  initializing  object  my_ob2
    my_ob1.show_i();
    my_ob2.show_i();
}
```

When you execute this program you should get results as follows:

> **constructor operates**
> **constructor operates**
> **i = 10**
> **i = 20**
> **destructor operates**
> **destructor operates**

The constructor operates as we create specific objects of the class in **main()** and the destructor operates automatically at the end of **main()** to destroy the objects we have created. Since we create two objects of type **string**, the constructor of that class is invoked twice. On exit from the program the two objects are destroyed by the automatic calling of the destructor for the class. Thus, the output message from the destructor occurs twice.

# Using Objects

## Object Declaration

As we have seen we can define classes of a particular kind using the keywords **struct** and **union**, where the members are **public** by default. If we create a class using the keyword **class**, the members are **private** by default. Also in the case of **class** and **struct**, we can alter the default attributes of members by using appropriate keywords.

## Example EX3_6

Consider an example:

```
/* example EX3_6 */
#include <iostream.h>
// structure members have an attribute public by default
struct for_example
{   void print(void) { cout << "using structure\n";   }
    private:
        int x;          // x will have an attribute private
    public:           // other members have an attribute   public
        for_example(int X) { x = X; }              // constructor
        void put_x(void) { cout << "x = " << x << "\n"; }
};
void main(void)
// declaring an object of type for_example
{   for_example    ex1(10);
    ex1.print();
    ex1.put_x();
}
```

In **main()** we first create an object of the structure **ex1** with an initial
value of 10. The initialization is defined in the constructor. We have also
declared the variable **x** in the structure **for_example** to be **private**. The
remaining members have been explicitly declared as **public**, although
we could have arranged that they have this attribute by default. If you
run the program the results will be:

> **using structure**
> x = 10

## Example EX3_7

Members of a **union** are always **public**. As we saw in Section 1, a **union** is like a **struct** that stores all its data-components in one place. Consider a simple example:

```
/* example EX3_7 */
#include <iostream.h>
#include <string.h>
// union members have an attribute public
union my_union
{   char    str[21];
    struct str1_2
    {   char    str1[10];
        char  str2[11];
    }   my_s;
    my_union(char *s); // constructor
    void print(void);
};
my_union::my_union(char *s)
{ strcpy(str,s); }    // copying the string s to the string str
void  my_union::print(void)
{   cout << my_s.str2 << '\n';
    my_s.str2[0] = 0;
    cout << my_s.str1 << '\n';
}
void main(void)
{   my_union    ob("abcdefghij0123456789");
    ob.print();
}
```

Here we have a structure containing two strings and sharing space within a union with another string. Figure 3.7 (overleaf) illustrates the allocation of memory to the objects. The numbers 1 and 2 denote the sequence of the two output operations in the function **print**.

The program results will be:

**0123456789**
**abcdefghij**

The function **print** first outputs the bytes from the string **my_s.str2**. This string will contain **0123456789\0**. Then the terminating null is written into the zero byte of **my_s.str2** and the output of the string **my_s.str1** will continue up to this byte.

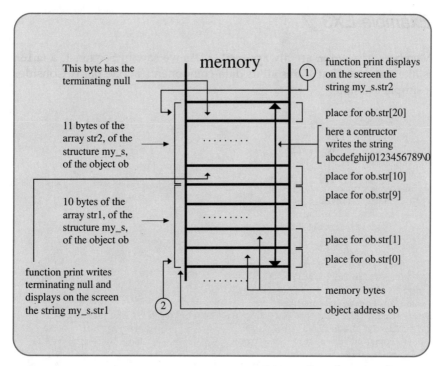

*Figure 3.7*
**Memory Allocation in EX 3_7**

# Operations with Objects

Operations with objects are mainly the same as with other data types. For example, an object can be assigned to a function as a parameter. So the following statements are legitimate:

```
class my_ob { ... }
. . . . . . . . . .
void function(my_ob p) { ... }
```

You can create pointers to objects of type **my_ob**. If we declare:

```
my_ob a, *b;
b = &a;
```

**b** will be a pointer to **a**. In this instance the reference to its members can be carried out using the symbol **->** that we have discussed as a means of referencing structure elements. If **k** is a member of the class **a**, then you can refer to it as: **b -> k**. We have already discussed previously that incrementing or decrementing the value of a pointer by 1 will automatically lead to adding or subtracting the correct value to point to the next element, taking into account the size of appropriate data type. This is equally valid for operations with classes. For example, if **b** is a pointer to a member of an array of objects, **b+1** is the pointer to the next member.

## Example EX3_8

Consider an example:

```
/* example EX3_8 */
#include <iostream.h>
class My
{   int   i;
    public:
        My() { i = 0; }          // constructor
        void put_i(void) { cout << "i = " << i << "\n"; }
        void set_i(int Y) { i = Y; }
};
// function receives an object x of type My
void function(My x)
{  My *y;           // y - pointer to object of type  My
   y = &x;          // now y is pointer to object x of type My
   x.put_i();       // reference to object by name
   y -> put_i();    // reference to object through pointer
};
void main(void)
{  My mas[4],*p;    // declaring an array mas of four objects
                    // and pointer p to the object array
   mas[0].set_i(10); // assigning values to member i
   mas[1].set_i(20); // of objects mas[0], mas[1] and mas[2]
   mas[2].set_i(30);
   p = &mas[1];      //now p is a pointer to mas[1]
   p -> put_i();     //output of value   20
   (p+1)  -> put_i(); //output of value   30
   (p-1)  -> put_i(); //output of value   10
   function(mas[1]); //calling function & assigning it object
                     //mas[1] as parameter, outputs 20 and 20
   function(mas[3]); //calling function and assigning object
                     //mas[3] as parameter, outputs 0 and 0

}
```

The function **function** accepts an object of the class **My** as an argument. It uses the class member function **put_i** to access and output the value of the object received as a parameter directly and also by means of a pointer. In **main()** the first three elements of the object array **mas** are initialized through the pointer p. The last element, **mas[3]**, remains with its initialized value zero.

The program results will be as follows:

```
i = 20
i = 30
i = 10
i = 20
i = 20
i = 0
i = 0
```

# INHERITANCE AND PROTECTION

## Base and Derived Classes

As discussed in Chapter 11, **C++** has a feature called  **inheritance**, where the properties of one class may be inherited from another class which has been used as the basis for its definition. The class that serves as the basis for creating another class is called **the base class** and the created class is called **the derived class**.

In Chapter 11 we also outlined the idea of a class **Point**, in which an object was definied by an x,y coordinate pair and included a function for displaying a point on the screen. With the class **Point** as a base, we could then derive a class **Rectangle**, where a **Rectangle** object was defined in terms of two **Point** objects. Therefore the creation of a **Rectangle** object would involve the creation of two **Point** objects using a constructor for the class **point**. This is possible because the class **Rectangle** would inherit the members of the class **Point** including its functions. The declaration of the class **Rectangle** as a derived class is achieved by referencing the class **Point** as a base class.

The declaration syntax for a derived class is:

```
class derived_class_name:optional_attribute base_class_name_list
    { derived_class_body } derived_class_object_list;
```

This is almost the same as the class declaration syntax we have already seen.  The colon following the class name, followed by the list of base classes are the only additions.  As is indicated by the syntax definition, there can be multiple base classes and they each may have an attribute. The elements in the object list are separated by commas. The object list may also be empty.

Consider an example of a declaration:

```
class Rectangle : public Point { ... };
```

The class **Point** is the base class with the attribute **public**. We will come to the importance of the attribute in a moment. The class **Rectangle** is the derived class. The object **list** is empty, as the closing brace is followed immediately by a semicolon so no **Rectangle** objects are defined. They can be declared separately using **Rectangle** as the type keyword. We have omitted the definition of the body of the class **Rectangle** that would normally appear between the braces for the sake of simplicity.

The class attribute where it is included, is defined by using the keyword **private**, or the keyword **public** as in our previous example. Where it is omitted, the attribute is assigned by default, **private** for classes and **public** in the case of structures. Note that **unions** cannot be base or derived classes. The attribute of a base class does not alter the access attributes of its members, but it can affect the accessibility of its members from the derived class.

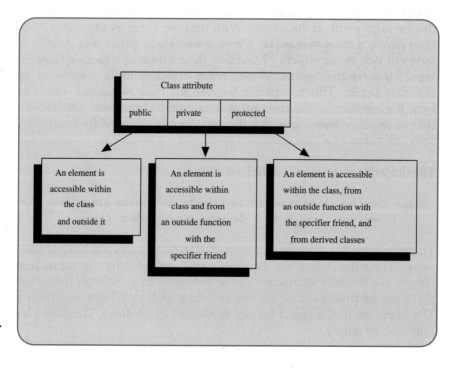

*Figure 3.8*
**The Effects of
Class Member
Attributes**

## *The Effects of Class Member Attributes*

A derived class inherits all the members of a base class. We need to consider how they can be accessed. Suppose that the member **x** of a base class has the attribute **public**. It can be accessed in a derived class by using the name **x** directly. The prefix of the name of the base class and a decimal point which are normally required external to a class are not necessary in this case. Let us briefly re-examine the protection possibilities offered by **C++** to members of classes.

Take a look at Figure 3.8. It illustrates how the attributes **public, private** and **protected**, when applied to members of a class, affect the member access procedures. The appropriate member becomes global and can be accessed anywhere. The attribute **private** allows you to access a member only from the component functions of that class. There is an exception, which is the case of external functions defined with the attribute **friend**. We shall come to those a little later. The attribute **protected** extends access beyond **private**, by allowing the possibility of referencing from component functions of derived classes. Note, that the attribute in Figure 3.8 is a member attribute written within the class pattern, that is, in a statement enclosed within the braces bounding the class definition. Do not confuse it with the base class attribute which we will take a look at next.

Consider Figure 3.9 (overleaf). This shows how the attribute of a base class in the declaration of a derived class determines the attributes and accessibility of the inherited base class members within the derived class. Members of the base class with the attribute **private** remain inaccessible from the derived class functions, regardless of the class attribute. They are accessible only from the original base class functions. Public members of a public base class remain public in the derived class, so they are accessible anywhere within your program. Protected members of a public base class become protected members of the derived class. You can also modify the attribute of an accessible inherited member of a base class by declaring its attribute explicitly within the body of the derived class. To do this you must use the qualified name in the public or protected declarations of the derived class. The qualified name of member **x** of the class **Point** is **Point::x**.

The keywords **public**, **private**, and **protected**, can appear anywhere in any order and any number of times in the class pattern or structure. You will probably find that grouping members with common attributes and

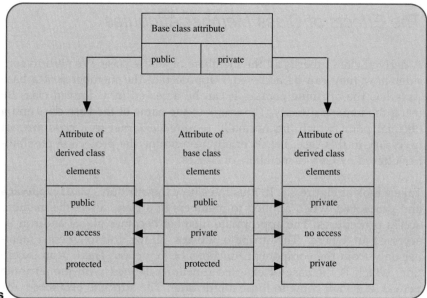

*Figure 3.9*
**The Effects of
Base Class
Attributes in
Derived Classes**

adopting a standard sequence will make your programs more readable.

## Example EX3_9

Consider an example:

```
/* example EX3_9 */
#include <iostream.h>
#include <graphics.h>
#include <conio.h>
class Location
{  protected:
     int  x,y;            // these members will be accessible in
                          // a derived class
   public:
     Location(int  InitX,int  InitY);
     void set(int a,int b) { x = a; y = b; }
     int getx() { cout << "x = " << x << "\n"; return x;  }
     int gety() { cout << "y = " << y << "\n"; return y;  }
};
/**********************************************************/
/* Class Point is derived from a base class Location   */
/**********************************************************/
class Point : public Location
{  int   color;
   public:
     Point(int InitX,int InitY,int InitC);
```

```
        void putpixel() { ::putpixel(x,y,color); }
};
Location::Location(int InitX,int InitY)
{  x = InitX; y =  InitY;
   cout << "Location constructor operates\n";
}
Point::Point(int InitX,int InitY,intInitC):Location(InitX,InitY)
{  color  =  InitC;
   cout <<  "Point constructor operates\n";
}
void main(void)
{  int gd = DETECT,  gm;
   initgraph(&gd,&gm,"");         // initializing graphic system
   Point my_point(200,100,3);
   my_point.putpixel();
   my_point.getx();   // calling the function getx of base class
   my_point.gety();   // calling the function getx of base class
   getch();           // suspension until any key pressed
   closegraph();      //  closing graphic system
}
```

Here we have the simplest case of inheritance, with one base class
**Location** and a derived class **Point**. Although this is a short and simple
example, we can use it to examine aspects of operations with derived
classes, the operation of constructors and introduce the use of **Turbo C++**
graphics library functions. We will look at each of these in turn.

Since the base class has the attribute public in the declaration of the class
**Point**, all members of the class **Point** inherited from the class **Location**
will have the same attributes in the derived class as they had in the base
class. The members **x** and **y** of the class **Location** will have the attribute
**protected** in the class **Point** and other members of the class **Location** will
have the attribute **public**. Since the base class has no private members,
all its members are accessible in the function **putpixel()** of the class
**Point**. We will come back to the function **putpixel()** when we discuss
graphics function usage in this example.

On execution, the example first creates a **Point** object **my_point**. This
object is then displayed on the screen and the coordinates are output in
turn through the base class functions. Finally, the program will wait
until you press a key to terminate. If you run the program the results will
be as follows :

> **Location constructor operates**
> **Point constructor operates**
> **x = 200**
> **y = 100**

On the screen you will see a point positioned according to the specified coordinates (200,100). If the program does not run as indicated, have a look at the discussion on the use of graphics drivers for this example for the probable source of the problem.

Suppose you started the definition of the class **Point** with a different statement:

```
class Point : private Location
```

Alternatively, you could write it with a default base class attribute of **private**:

```
class Point : Location
```

Now all members of the class **Location** will have the attribute **private** in the derived class **Point**. In this case, the program will not work since we could not call the functions **getx()** and **gety()** in **main()**. The compiler would flag the call statements as an error and indicate that the functions are inaccessible.

An illustration of how data in the classes **Location** and **Point** may be accessed for the example written, is provided in Figure 3.10. It shows that, since the data members of the base class have the attribute **protected**, they

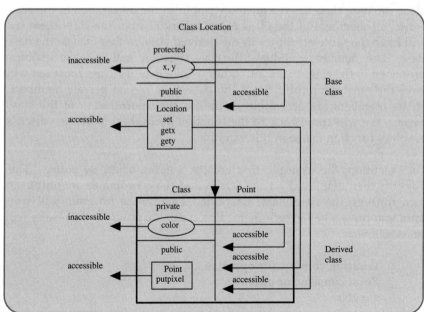

*Figure 3.10*
**Data Access in Classes Location and Point**

can only be accessed by the functions of the base class and the derived class. The functions of the base class are **public** and are therefore accessible everywhere, as is the function **putpixel()** which is specific to the derived class and is also **public**. The data member **color** of the derived class has the attribute **private** and is only accessible from the function **putpixel()** in the derived class.

## Constructors in Example EX3_9

First, note that if a base class has a constructor defined explicitly with one or more arguments, any derived class must have a constructor as well. In the example a constructor for the class **Location** is defined as:

```
Location(int  InitX,int  InitY)
          { x = InitX, y = InitY;
               cout << "Location  constructor  operates\n";}
```

It has two integer arguments **InitX** and **InitY**. Now we can declare an object of this class in the function **main**, or any other function for that matter, as:

```
Location  my_1(10,20);
```

As a result, the members **x** and **y** of the class **Location** will be assigned the values 10 and 20 and the line:

**Location constructor operates**

will be displayed on the screen. The derived class **Point** must also have a constructor. In the example it is defined as:

```
Point::Point(int  InitX,int  InitY,int  InitC)  :
Location(InitX,  InitY)
{       color  =  InitC;
        cout  <<  "Point  constructor  operates\n";
}
```

The definition of this constructor includes the reference to the class name **Point** preceding the scope resolution operator and the constructor name. The constructor name is followed by its constructor argument list in parentheses. The reference to the constructor from the base class following the colon causes the base class constructor we have defined to be called first. If we had omitted this, the default base class constructor with no arguments would have been called instead. The argument values **InitX** and **InitY** are interpreted as horizontal and vertical coordinates of a point and **InitC** as its screen color.

As we have said, **C++** allows you to derive a class from several base classes and we shall discuss this in detail a little later. However, the constructor definition needs to take account of this, so the general syntax for defining a constructor of the derived class is:

```
derived_class_constructor_name(arguments_list_for_derived_class):
     base_class_1_name (arguments_list_for_base_class_1),...,
     base_class_N_name (arguments_list_for_base_class_N);
```

The argument list for the base classes may include constants, global parameters and parameters from the constructors list of the derived class. If a base class does not have an explicitly defined constructor with arguments then the default constructor will be called automatically.

## Graphics in Example EX3_9

The example EX3_9 uses library functions that output graphic elements to the screen, they are all defined in the include file **graphics.h**.

The function **initgraph** initializes the graphics system by loading a graphics driver from disk and putting the system into graphics mode. Graphic drivers are held in files with names of the form **\*.BGI**. The first parameter of the function **initgraph** is a pointer to the integer variable **gd**. The value of this variable lets you choose an appropriate graphics driver for your PC. If you define **gd = DETECT** (**DETECT** is a zero constant), the correct driver will be selected automatically. The second parameter to **initgraph** is also a pointer, corresponding to the integer variable **gm**. This variable defines the graphic mode. If we define **gd = DETECT**, then **gm** will define the maximum resolution mode for the automatically selected driver. The third **initgraph** argument is a pointer to the first character in a string specifying the path and file name of a graphic driver. If the line is defined as ``″, the current directory will be searched for the appropriate driver. You need to ensure that the appropriate driver, which will be a file with an extension **BGI**, is in the current directory. In most instances the file **EGAVGA.BGI** will be appropriate. If the example fails with a graphics related error, try copying **EGAVGA.BGI** into your current directory.

The function **closegraph** shuts down the graphics system. This will be called after waiting in the **getch** function for you to press a key.

The function **putpixel** outputs the point to the screen and has three integer parameters. The first two define the horizontal and vertical coordinates of the point and the third defines its color.

We can have a look at another function in this example:

```
void putpixel() { ::putpixel(x,y,color); }
```

Note that this function is a member of the class **Point** and has the same name as the library function **putpixel** which it references. In such cases, to avoid recursive calls or errors in the program, you must write the scope resolution operator :: before the library function name this indicates it is not a class member but a global function that our **putpixel** function was calling. It could be a call to itself or to the library function with the same name. The prefix :: eliminates the ambiguity.

Now examine another use for the operator ::. Consider an example:

```
int a;   // it's a global variable a
. . . . . . . . . . . . . . . . . .
void my_func(void)
{ int a;   // it's a local variable a
  a=10; // local variable a is assigned the value 10
  ::a=20;// global variable a is assigned the value 20
  cout << a << " " << ::a << "\n";// the values 10 and 20
              // are output
. . . . . . . . . . . . . .
}
```

Here the operator :: allows you to access the global element when local and global elements have the same name.

# *Multiple Inheritance*

Now we can turn to the question of **multiple inheritance**, which occurs
when a new class is derived from several base classes. We outlined an
example back in Chapter 11 where Figure 3.3 shows a class **Window**, derived
from the three classes: **Line**, **Text** and **Rectangle**. Take a look at the slightly
simpler example in Figure 3.11. It illustrates how the members of the
derived class **Derive** can be inherited from the two base classes **Base_1**
and **Base_2**, with the attributes **public** and **private**, respectively.

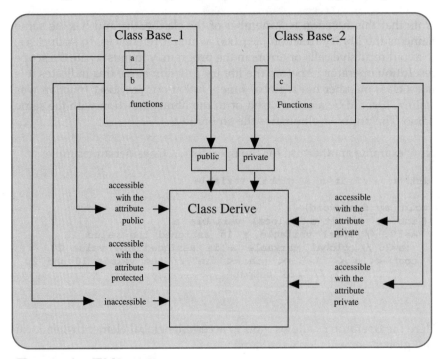

*Figure 3.11*
**Multiple**
**Inheritance**

## *Example EX3_10*

Consider the following program:

```
/* example EX3_10 */
#include <iostream.h>
class Base_1
{   int  a;
    protected:
        int b;
    public:
```

```
        Base_1(int  x,int  y);
        ~Base_1();
        void  show1(void)
        {  cout << "a = " << a << "; b = " << b;}
};
class  Base_2
{  protected:
        int  c;
    public:
        Base_2(int  x);
        ~Base_2();
        void  show2(void)
        {  cout << "; c = " << c << "\n";}
};
class  Derive  :  public  Base_1,  private  Base_2
{  int  p;
    public:
        Derive(int  X,int  Y,int  Z);
        ~Derive();
        void  show3(void)
        {  cout << "a + b + c = " << p+b+c;}
};
Base_1::Base_1(int  x,int  y)
{  a=x;  b=y;
    cout  << "\nconstructor  Base_1";
}
Base_1::~Base_1()
{  cout  << "\ndestructor  Base_1";}
Base_2::Base_2(int  x)
{  c=x;
    cout  << "\nconstructor  Base_2";
}
Base_2::~Base_2()
{  cout  << "\ndestructor  Base_2";}
Derive::Derive(int  X,int  Y,int  Z)  :  Base_1(X,Y),  Base_2(Z)
{  p=X;  cout  << "\nconstructor  Derive\n";}
Derive::~Derive()
{  cout  << "\ndestructor  Derive";}
void  main(void)
{  Derive    my_d(10,20,30);
    my_d.show1();
    my_d.show2();
    my_d.show3();
}
```

Each of the classes **Base_1** and **Base_2** have their own constructors defined
with one and two arguments, respectively. The derived class also contains
an explicitly defined constructor. Figure 3.11 gives the inherited attributes
of the functions and data members **a, b** and **c**. An object **my_d** is declared
in the function main through the statement **Derive my_d(10,20,30);**. It
will call the constructors of the base classes. Consider the initial statement

of the derived class constructor:

```
Derive(int  X,int  Yint  Z)  :  Base_1(X,Y),  Base_2(Z)
```

According to the rule adopted in **C++** for derived class constructors, the base class constructors are called first, in the same sequence as their appearance in the list. In the example, the constructor **Base_1** will be called first, then the constructor **Base_2**. When all the base class constructors in the list have been called, the constructor for the derived class is called. Destructors are executed in the reverse order, as illustrated in Figure 3.12. The circled numbers in the figure indicate the sequence of events.The results from executing the program will be:

> **constructor Base_1**
> **constructor Base_2**
> **constructor Derive**
> **a = 10; b = 20; c = 30**
> **a+b+c = 60**
> **destructor Derive**
> **destructor Base_2**
> **destructor Base_1**

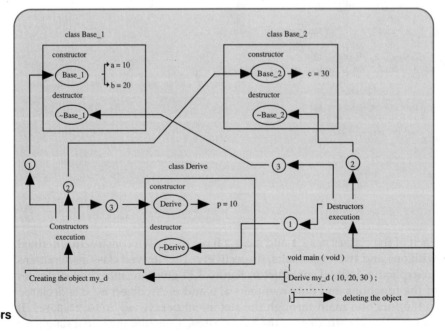

*Figure 3.12*
**Operation of Constructors and Destructors**

The values for **a** and **b** are displayed by the function **show1()** inherited by the class **Derive** from the class **Base_1**. The value of **c** is displayed by the function **show2()** inherited from the class **Base_2**. Then the sum of all three variables are displayed by the function **show3()** which is specific to the class **Derive**. Finally, the destructors for the classes are called automatically on exiting **main()** in the reverse order to that of the corresponding constructors.

## *The Effects of Attributes on Inheritance*

## *Example EX3_11*

Now consider a more complicated example containing multi-level inheritance rather than multiple inheritance. Suppose, that from a base class that we will name **h_level**, we derive a subsidiary class that we name **m_level** and then from that class we derive a further class we name **l_level**. So we have the top level class **h_level** whose members are inherited by **m_level**, whose members in turn are inherited by the lowest level class **l_level**.

We can write a sample program using this class structure as follows:

```
/* example EX3_11 */
#include <iostream.h>
class h_level
{ int  x;
   public:
      void hinit(int X) { x = X; }
      void hshow(void) { cout << "x = " << x << '\n'; }
};
class m_level : public h_level         // if private - errors 3
{ public:
      void mshow(void)
      { cout << "\tupper level: "; hinit(1); hshow(); }
};
class l_level : public m_level         // if private - errors 2
{ public:
      void lshow(void)
      { cout << "middle level: "; mshow();
        cout << "upper level: "; hinit(10);       // 3
        hshow();                                  // 3
      }                                           // 3
};
```

```
void main(void)
{   l_level   my_ob;
    my_ob.hinit(100);                    // 3          // 2
    my_ob.hshow();                       // 3          // 2
    my_ob.mshow();                                     // 2
    my_ob.lshow();
}
```

To understand the effects of attributes on inheritance, we can try three variants of the program, using different attributes of the base class while deriving a new class. The first version is the example given above. In the second version we define the class **l_level** as:

> **class  l_level  :  private  m_level  {  ...  };**

You just need to change the base class attribute in the declaration of **l_level** in the example from **public** to **private**. In this case, at the compilation stage, the statements marked with **// 2** will cause errors. The potential errors are noted in the comment in the original of the statement we have just altered. We can change the statement back to the original version and consider the third version, in which the class **m_level** is defined as:

> **class  m_level  :  private  h_level  {  ...  };**

Again, you just change the base class attribute from **public** to **private**. In this case, errors will be caused by the statements marked with **// 3**, as indicated in the original class definition statement. In order to correctly understand the nature of the errors, we can take a look at Figure 3.9 earlier in this chapter. It shows how the base class attribute changes the attributes of its members in a derived class. Additional illustrations are given in Figure 3.13 where all three versions are presented.

In the first variant, making the attribute of the base class **m_level** private in the declaration of the class **l_level** makes the functions inherited from **m_level** and **h_level** in **l_level** inaccessible to **main()**. As a consequence we get errors from the statements marked **// 2** in **main()**.

In the second variant, the **private** attribute of the base class **h_level** makes the functions inherited by **m_level** private and therefore inaccessible in **l_level** and **main()**. As a consequence we get errors in both of these.

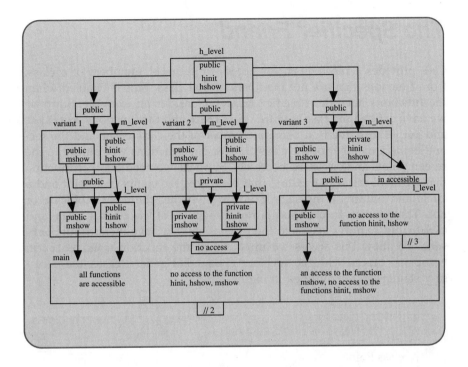

*Figure 3.13*
**Multilevel
Class
Inheritance**

As we said initially, the previous sample program is not an example of multiple inheritance. It simply demonstrates the situations that can arise when there are more than two levels of inheritance. The program results for the first version are as follows:

> x = 100
> upper level: x = 1
> middle level:   upper level: x = 1
> upper level: x = 10

In the function **mshow** of class **m_level**, the function **hinit** is called with the argument set to 1. The function **lshow** in the class **l_level** calls the function **mshow**, then calls the function **hinit** with the argument set to 10. In the function **main**, **hinit** is called with the argument set to 100. If you follow the function calls through you will see how we get the results above.

# *The Specifier Friend*

C++ provides a mechanism for access to **private** members of a class, from functions that are not members of that class. This is enabled when the functions have the specifier **friend**. Consider an example. Suppose we have defined the classes **Point** and **Circle** and the functions **putpixel** and **put_circle**, the first being a member of the class **Point** and the second being a member of the class **Circle**. The functions will output to the screen points and circles respectively. Suppose we need another function that we shall call **equal_color**, that compares the colors of a point and a circle and outputs a message indicating whether the colors coincide or not. The function in question is not a member of the classes **Point** and **Circle**, but requires access to their members that have the attribute **private**. To allow this access we must define the function **equal_color** in **Point** and **Circle** with the specifier **friend**. For general cases, the necessary statements are outlined in Figure 3.14.

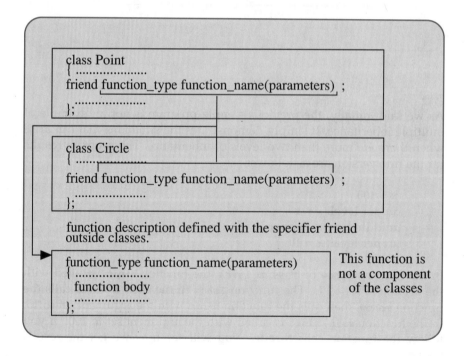

*Figure 3.14*
**Friend Functions**

## Example EX3_12

Consider a complete example using the function **equal_color**, as we have just discussed:

```
/* example EX3_12 */
#include <iostream.h>
#include <graphics.h>
#include <conio.h>
class Circle;
class Location
{ protected:
    int x,y;
  public:
    Location(int InitX,int InitY) { x = InitX; y = InitY; }
    void set(int a,int b) { x = a; y = b; }
    int getx() { cout << "x = " << x << "\n"; return x; }
    int gety() { cout << "y = " << y << "\n"; return y; }
};
class Point : public Location
{ int color;
  public:
    Point(int InitX,int InitY,int InitC);
    void putpixel() { ::putpixel(x,y,color); }
    // defining function with the specifier friend
    friend void equal_color(Point p,Circle c);
};
class Circle : public Location
{ int color,temp,radius;
  public:
    Circle(int InitX,int InitY,int InitC,int InitR);
    void put_circle()
        { temp = getcolor();
          setcolor(color);
          circle(x,y,radius);
          setcolor(temp);
        }
    // defining function with the specifier friend
    friend void equal_color(Point p,Circle c);
};
// constructor for class Point
Point::Point(int InitX,int InitY,int InitC) :
    Location(InitX,InitY) { color = InitC; }
// constructor for class Circle
Circle::Circle(int InitX,int InitY,int InitC,int InitR) :
    Location(InitX,InitY)
        { color = InitC;
          radius = InitR;
        }
```

```
/***********************************************************/
/*Function equal_color compares colors of pixel and circle */
/*(it is not a member of classes Point and Circle)         */
/***********************************************************/
void equal_color(Point p,Circle c)
{ if(p.color == c.color) cout << "\ncolors coincide\n";
  else cout << "\ncolors do not coincide\n";
}
void main(void)
{ int gd = DETECT, gm;
  initgraph(&gd,&gm,"");        // initializing graphic system
  Point my_point(200,100,3);
  Circle my_circle1(400,200,3,100);
  Circle my_circle2(200,200,1,50);
  my_point.putpixel();
  my_circle1.put_circle();
  my_circle2.put_circle();
  equal_color(my_point,my_circle1);
  equal_color(my_point,my_circle2);
  getch();                      // suspension until any key pressed
  closegraph();                 //    closing graphic system
}
```

This example is an extended version of the example EX3_9. At the beginning of the program you can see an empty declaration:

**class Circle;**

This is obligatory since there is a reference to an undefined class **Circle**, (**equal_color(Point p, Circle c);**), in the definition of the class **Point**. That is why we must indicate to the compiler at the beginning of the program, that **Circle** is a class that will be defined later. If we don't do this we will get an error message. Such definitions are only necessary in cases with functions having the specifier **friend**. In the example, the class **Location** is the base for two derived classes, **Point** and **Circle**. The program will output to the screen a point and two circles. It will then display two messages. The first is:

**colors coincide**

for the point and the first circle and the second is:

**colors do not coincide**

for the point and the second circle.

As you can see in the program, because it is a **friend** function for both the **Point** and the **Circle** classes, the function **equal_color** can access any of their members. The variables **color** for the point **p** and the circle **c** are accessed simply by using the appropriate qualified name. Figure 3.15 shows the access to local date by the function **equal_color**.

The program uses three graphic library functions we have not seen before. The function **getcolor** returns an integer value that corresponds to the number of the color you have currently set for displaying graphical entities. Unless it is changed, it will be used to display subsequent graphic entities.

The function **setcolor** sets the current color to that corresponding to the integer parameter value. The function **circle** displays a circle on the screen and has three integer parameters. The first two define the horizontal and vertical coordinates of the centre of the circle and the third defines its radius.

The program statements:

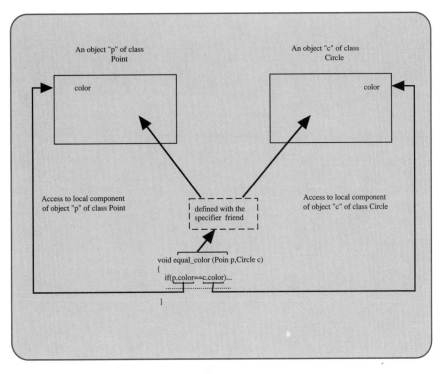

*Figure 3.15*
**Class Member
Access from
Friend
Functions**

```
temp = getcolor();
setcolor(color);
circle(x,y,radius);
setcolor(temp);
```

save the current color in the variable **temp**, change the color to a new value, display a circle and finally reset the color back to the initial value from the variable **temp**.

# CHAPTER
## 13

# PROGRAMMING WITH CLASSES

## Overloading Functions and Operators

### Overloading at the Compilation and Execution Stages

As we have already discussed, **C++** allows overloading of both **functions** and **operators**. In this chapter, we would like to examine these in rather more detail.

### Early Binding and Late Binding

In Object Oriented Programming the terms **early binding** and **late binding** are frequently used. The former term refers to the case where overloaded operations are resolved at the compilation stage, whereas the latter refers to when they are resolved at the stage of program execution. By resolving an overloaded operation, we mean the determination of the correct function or operation to be invoked.

Early binding takes place when standard functions are called and also applies to overloaded functions and operators. The advantages of such an approach are high program execution speed and small storage requirements. The disadvantage is that there is a loss of flexibility in programming for some problems. Late binding is realised by using **virtual functions** which we will come to later. It offers greater programming flexibility, but at the cost of reduced execution speed. In many cases, programmers combine the two approaches.

# *Overloading Functions*

## *Example EX3_13*

Some aspects of function overloading have already been discussed in Chapter 11 (see example EX3_3). Therefore, we shall confine ourselves to considering only one additional example:

```
/* example EX3_13 */
#include <iostream.h>
#include <stdlib.h>
char *toa(int num, char *s, int r)
    { return itoa(num,s,r);}
char *toa(long num, char *s, int r)
    { return ltoa(num,s,r);}
char *toa(unsigned long num, char *s, int r)
    { return ultoa(num,s,r);}
void main(void)
{   char str[80];
    int r;
    cout << "Define the number system from 2 to 36" << '\n';
    cin >> r;
    cout << "int = " << toa(789,str,r) << '\n';
    cout << "long = " << toa(123456L,str,r) << '\n';
    cout << "unsigned long = " << toa(4000000000UL,str,r) <<'\n';
}
```

In this program, three **C++** library functions **itoa**, **ltoa** and **utoa**, are replaced with one function **toa**. The prototypes of the library functions are represented as:

```
char *itoa(int  num,char  *str,int  radix);
char *ltoa(long  num,char  *str,int  radix);
char *ultoa(unsigned  long  num,char  *str,int  radix);
```

All the prototypes are described in the include file **stdlib.h**. Each of the functions converts a number **num** to a string defined by **str**. Conversion is performed in the number system **radix**, where **radix** can be from 2 to 36. The number, **num**, is an integer for the function **itoa**, a long integer for the function **ltoa**, or an unsigned long integer for the function **utoa**. All of the functions return a pointer to the resultant character string.

The results of program execution can be presented in the form:

> **Define the number system from 2 to 36**
> 10 *<Enter>*
> **int = 789**
> **long = 123456**
> **unsigned long = 4000000000**

# *Overloading Constructors*

## *Example EX3_14*

A constructor is also a function and hence it can be overloaded. Let us consider an example:

```
/* example EX3_14 */
#include <iostream.h>
class Over
{ int i;
  char *str;
  public:
    // 1st constructor
    Over() { str = "1st constructor\n"; i = 0; }
    // 2nd constructor
    Over(char *S) { str = S; i = 50; }
    // 3rd constructor
    Over(char *S,int X) { str = S; i = X; }
    // 4th constructor
    Over(int *Y) { str = "4th constructor\n"; i = *Y; }
    void print(void) { cout << "i = " << i << "; str = " << str;}
};
void main(void)
{ int a = 10,*b;
  b = &a;
  // declaring four objects: my_over, my_over1 and my_over2
  Over my_over,
  my_over1("for one-parameter constructor\n"),
  my_over2("for two-parameter constructor\n",100),
  my_over3(b);
  my_over.print(); // constructor Over() is active
  my_over1.print();// constructor Over(char *S) is active
  my_over2.print();// constructor Over(char *S,int X) is active
  my_over3.print();// constructor Over(int *Y) is active
}
```

There are four constructors in this example: the first is without parameters **over()**, the second has one parameter, **over(char *s)**, the third has two parameters, **over(char \*s, int_x)** and the fourth has one parameter, **over(int_\*y)**. Declaration of **my_over** causes execution of the first constructor, declaration of **my_over1** leads to executing the second constructor, declaration of **my_over2** invokes the third constructor, and declaration of **my_over3** calls the fourth constructor. The results of program execution are presented as follows:

> i=0; str=1st constructor
> i=50; str=for one-parameter constructor
> i=100; str=for two-parameter constructor
> i=10; str=4th constructor

# Dynamic Initialization

In **C++**, local and global variables can be initialized during program execution. The process is sometimes called **dynamic initialization**. We mentioned before that declaration of local variables in **C++** can occur in any position within the corresponding function body and not just, as is the case in **C**, at the beginning. In **C++** a typical example of such declarations would be:

```
int  j  =  strlen(str);
```

The initial value of the integer **j** will be the result of executing the function to calculate the length of the string **str**. Here, the = sign could equally well be followed by other expressions evaluated as a result of program execution.

## Example EX3_15

Let us consider an example:

```
/* example EX3_15 */
#include <iostream.h>
#include <string.h>
void main(void)
{   int  i,j;
    i = 4;
    char str[] = "1 2 3 4 5 6 7 8 9";
    cout << "An example of dynamic initialization\n";
    cout << "str = " << str << "\n";
    int z = strlen(str)-1;
    for(int  k=i,l=z;k<=l;k++,l--)
        {   j=str[k];  str[k]=str[l];  str[l]=j;}
    cout << "str = " << str << "\n";
}
```

As is shown in the example, declarations can appear in any position within the program body. Consider the declaration for **z**:

> **int  z=strlen(str)-1;**

At the compilation stage, the value of **strlen(str)** is unknown because a library function, **strlen**, is used to calculate the string length and this function is not appended until the linkage stage and still needs to be executed to generate a value. As a result, initialization of the variable **z** will be performed only during execution of the program. In the loop, the expression:

> **int  k=i,l=z**

defines integer variables **k** and **l** and assigns the values *i* and **z** to them.

The result of program execution will be as follows:

> **An example of dynamic initialization**
> str=1 2 3 4 5 6 7 8 9
> str=1 2 9 8 7 6 5 4 3

## Example EX3_16

Dynamic initialization mechanisms can also be applied to constructors. We can modify the example EX3_14:

```
/* example EX3_16 */
#include <iostream.h>
class Over
{ int i;
  char *str;
  public:
    Over() { str = "1st constructor\n"; i = 0; }
                                    // 1st  constructor
    Over(char *S) { str = S; i = 50; }// 2nd constructor
    Over(char *S,int X) { str = S; i = X; }// 3rd constructor
    Over(int *Y) { str = "4th constructor\n"; i = *Y; }
                                    // 4th  constructor
    void print(void) { cout << "i = " << i << "; str = " << str;}
};
void main(void)
{ int a = 10,*b;
  b = &a;
  // declaring four objects: my_over, my_over1 ¿ my_over2
  Over my_over,
  my_over1("for  one-parameter  constructor\n"),
  my_over2("for  two-parameter  constructor\n",100),
  my_over3(b);
  my_over.print();   // constructor Over() is active
  my_over1.print();  // constructor Over(char *S) is active
  my_over2.print();  // constructor Over(char *S,int X) is active
  my_over3.print();  // constructor Over(int *Y) is active
  /*************** Appendix to the program **************/
  char my_str[100];
  cout << "Enter  a  string\n";
  cin >> my_str;  // string my_str entered
  Over my_over4(my_str);  // declaring the object my_over4
  my_over4.print();  // one-parameter constructor is active
}
```

Declaration and initialization of the object **my_over4** are performed during program execution. The typical results of execution are:

> i=0; str=1st constructor
> i=50; str=for one-parameter constructor
> i=100; str=for two-parameter constructor
> i=10; str=4th constructor
> Enter a string:
> *123456789<Enter>*
> i = 50; str = 123456789

# The Pointer "this"

Any class member function to be executed is given a pointer to the corresponding object on which it operates. For instance, in the example EX3_16 for the string **my_over3.print()**;, the function **print()** is given a pointer to the object **my_over3**. In the member function **print()** the object is accessible through a keyword **this**.

Consider the illustration in Figure 3.16. The class pattern **my_class** is described, in which there is a function **f**. We will ignore the other members of the class. It is assumed that **f** does not return a value and takes no arguments. In the current context this is of no importance. The function **f** contains the pointer **this**. Suppose the function **main**, or any other function for that matter, declares an object **X** of the class **my_class**. This results in the instance shown in Figure 3.16. Let the function **f** have an attribute **public** and be called by **X.f()**;. Then **this** will point to the object **X** of the class **my_class**.

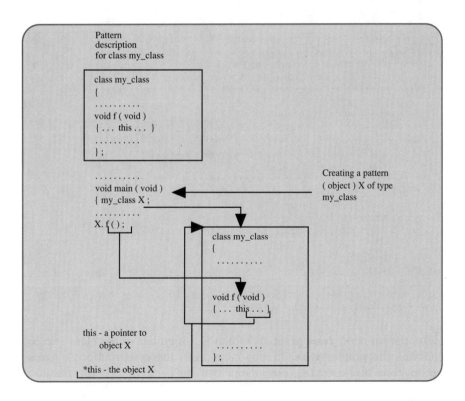

*Figure 3.16*
**The Pointer 'This'**

## Example EX3_17

Consider an example:

```
/* example EX3_17 */
#include <stdio.h>
#include <string.h>
class String
{ char str[100];
  int k;
  int *r;
  public:
  String() { k=123; r=&k; }
  void read() { gets(str); }
  void print() { puts(str); }
  void read_print();
};
void String::read_print()
{ char c;
  printf("k = %d\n",this->k);
  printf("*r = %d\n",*(this->r));
  puts("Enter a string");
/******************************************************/
/* The keyword this contains a hidden pointer to      */
/* the class in question (i.e. the class String). That's */
/* why the constructor this->read selects (via the pointer) */
/*          the function read of that class           */
/******************************************************/
  this->read();
  puts("Entered string");
  this->print();// analogous construction for the function print
/******************************************************/
/*   In the for loop, the characters are reversed     */
/*       about the string centre                      */
/******************************************************/
  for(int i=0,j=strlen(str)-1;i<j;i++,j--)
    { c=str[i]; str[i]=str[j]; str[j]=c;}
  puts("Changed string");
  (*this).print(); // this construction is also possible
}
void main()
{ String s;
  s.read_print();  // calling the function read_print
}
```

Here, the function **read_print()**, which is a member of the class **string**, contains the pointer **this**. In this case, both the constructions **this->component** and **(*this).component** can be used to call the member

**component** of the class **string**. The result of execution will be as follows:

> **k=123**
> ***r=123**
> **Enter a string**
> *1234567890<Enter>*
> **Entered string**
> **1234567890**
> **Changed string**
> **0987654321**

## Examples EX3_18 and EX3_19

Let us consider two more examples in which use is made of member functions of the class **string**, returning an object in the first program and of an object pointer in the second program:

```
/* example EX3_18 */
#include <stdio.h>
#include <string.h>
//
class String                                        //
  public:                                           //
    char *str;                                      //
    String() { str = "MREI - Minsk"; }              //
    String  rout_string();                          //
};                                                  //
// function rout_string returns an object           //
String  string::rout_string()                       //
{ int k;                                            //
  for(int  i=0,l=strlen(str)-1;i<l;i++,l--)          //
  { k=str[i]; str[i]=str[l]; str[l]=k; }             //
  return *this;         // this will point to the object
                        // with changed value of str
                        // *this is the object

}
void  main()
{ String my_string;      // declaring the object my_string
  puts(my_string.str);   // displays field str of object my_string
  puts(my_string.rout_string().str);
                         // displays the component str
                         // of the object returned by function
                                                rout_string.
// the function is applied to the object my_string, which returns
// another object of the class from which the member str is
                                                selected
}
```

```
/* example EX3_19 */
#include <stdio.h>
#include <string.h>
//
class String                                              //
{ public:                                                 //
    char *str;                                            //
    String() { str = "MREI - Minsk"; }                    //
    String *rout_string();                                //
};                                                        //
// function rout_string returns a pointer to an object
String* String::rout_string()                             //
{ int k;                                                  //
  for(int i=0,l=strlen(str)-1;i<l;i++,l-)                 //
  { k=str[i]; str[i]=str[l]; str[l]=k; }                  //
  return this;        // this will point to the object
                      // with changed value of str

}
void main()
{ String my_string;         // declaring object my_string
  puts(my_string.str);
  puts(my_string.rout_string() -> str);
          // instead of the decimal point,
          // the symbol -> is used, since rout_string
          // now returns a pointer to an object

}
```

Objects of the class **String** are initialized by the constructor. The function
**rout_string()** simply reverses the characters in the class member **str** in
both examples. If you inspect the loop in the function you will see that
elements of the string **str** are interchanged starting with the first and last,
and ending in the middle. Elements from each end of the string are
referenced using the indices i and l. The function operates in the first
example to return a **String** class object. This can be seen from the
declaration of the function:

```
String rout_string();
```

The object is returned in the statement:

```
return *this:
```

The second statement in main calling the function **puts** also invokes the
function **rout_string** for the object **my_string** to reverse the order of
**str**. In the second example, the function **rout_string** in the class
**String** returns a pointer to an object.

This is again determined by the declaration in the class:

```
String *rout_string():
```

Note the difference in defining the function in the two examples arising because of the different type of value returned. The results of executing either example is the same and will be as follows:

**MREI-Minsk**
**ksniM-IERM**

## Overloading Operators

As we have seen, operator overloading is a means of defining an alternative function to be attributed to an existing operator, when applied to objects of a specific class. Let us now define operator overloading in greater detail. In the general case, the following syntax applies:

```
type_of_returned_value class_name::operator_symbol(argument_list)
        {operator definition relative to a given class}
```

The word **operator**, in this definition, is a keyword. An operator is always defined in relation to members of a class. As a result, its old meaning always remains valid. The compiler automatically selects the operation to be performed by analyzing the operands in any given instance. When defining an overloaded operator, we are defining an operator function as a member of a class.

The operator function can only be a class member, or have a specifier **friend**. The difference between these two definitions will be explained later. The operator function cannot alter the number of arguments or the precedence and associativity rules from that of the original operator. Instead of just using the operator in the normal way, we can call operator functions directly in the same manner as other class member functions. In the case of overloaded unary operators, operator functions called directly will have no arguments, whereas in the case of binary operators they will have one argument.

The pointer **this** is implicit in references to the object corresponding to the first operand of an operator function. Thus, in the example EX3_4 where the function **operator** is considered, **str[i]** is the same as **this->str[i]**. The second operand in the case of binary operators corresponds to the explicit argument in the operator function definition.

## Example EX3_20

Take a simple example:

```
/*  example  EX3_20  */
#include  <iostream.h>
#include  <graphics.h>
#include  <conio.h>
class  Point
{   int  x,y;
    public:
        Point(int  InitX,int  InitY)  {  x  =  InitX;  y  =  InitY;  }
        Point  operator++(void)  {  return  Point(x++,y++);  }
        Point  operator-(Point  my_p)
            {  return  Point(x-my_p.x,y-my_p.y);}
        void  put_point(void)  {  putpixel(x,y,1);}
};
void  main(void)
{   int  gd  =  DETECT,  gm;
    initgraph(&gd,&gm,"");  //  initializing  the  graphic  system
    Point  my_point(30,30);
    for(int   j=0;j<10;j++)
    {   for(int  i=0;i<100;i++)
    {   my_point++;
        my_point.put_point();
        }
        my_point  =  my_point  -  Point(50,100);
    }
    getch();                //  wait  until  any  key  is  pressed
    closegraph();           //  closing  the  graphic  system
}
```

The first operator function redefines the unary function **++**. It should be noted that it is impossible to redefine **++** and – in such a way that their prefix and postfix versions are interpreted differently. The second operator function redefines the binary operation -. Bearing in mind that the expression **my_point** - **Point(50,100)** returns a value of the type **Point**, it is possible to use the sign - repeatedly with several operands in a single expression. For instance you could write:

**my_point = my_point - Point(50,100) - Point(10,2);**

Executing the sample program results in displaying ten sloping lines on the screen, each consisting of 100 dots. Figure 3.17 illustrates the results of the unary operation **my_point++;**. The **x** and **y** components of the created object, **my_point**, are accessible from the operator function through implicit use of the pointer **this**. As a consequence, it makes it possible to change the values of **x** and **y**.

## Limitations to the Use of the Operator Function

The use of the operator function is subject to the following limitations:

**1.** C++ cannot distinguish between the prefix and postfix versions of ++ and - -.

**2.** The operator priority cannot be changed.

**3.** The number of operands cannot be changed, although the operator function may ignore some of the operands.

**4.** Overloaded operators extend to any derived class, except for the operator =. If necessary, the overloaded operator can be further overloaded in the derived class.

**5.** The following operators cannot be overloaded.

$$., ::, .^*, ?:.$$

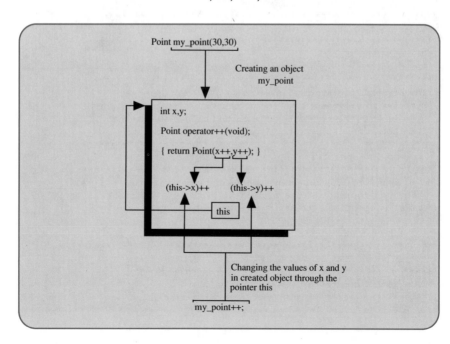

Figure 3.17
**Using the Pointer 'This'**

We will now see how the operator function with the specifier **friend** is defined. The main difference that arises when compared to a class member function, is that all the necessary arguments are now required to be specified, two for binary operations and one for unary. This is due to the fact that a function with the specifier **friend** has no access to the pointer **this**. In addition, the operators =, (), [] and -> cannot be overloaded with functions having the specifier **friend**.

## Example EX3_21

Consider an example:

```
/* example EX3_21 */
#include <stdio.h>
#include <string.h>
class My_str
{ char *str;
  public:
/***********************************************************/
/* The first constructor defines an empty string list.    */
/* (1 Kbyte memory is allocated and a null is written      */
/*                   into it )                             */
/***********************************************************/
  My_str() { str = new char; *str = 0; }
/***********************************************************/
/*The second constructor allocates memory for next string */
/***********************************************************/
  My_str(char *);
  void print() { puts(str); }
/***********************************************************/
/*The keyword, operator, allows you to overload the        */
/*symbol > to provide a function to check the first string is */
/*greater than the second.Keyword friend allows an external */
/*function access to private members of the class My_str   */
/***********************************************************/
  friend int operator > (My_str str1, My_str str2);
/***********************************************************/
/*   The keyword friend need not be used, but in this case */
/* the first operand is always implicit of the type of the */
/* class in question. The statements would be in this case: */
/*   int operator > (My_str str2)                          */
/*    { return strcmp(str, str2.str) > 0; }                */
/***********************************************************/
};          // END OF THE CLASS My_str DESCRIPTION
/***********************************************/
/* The second constructor is defined below     */
/***********************************************/
```

```
My_str::My_str(char *s)
{ str=new char[strlen(s)+1]; // memory for the string str
                  // of length strlen(s)+1 is allocated
  strcpy(str,s);   // string s is copied to string str
}
/******************************************************************/
/*Declaring the function operator (with the specifier friend)*/
/******************************************************************/
int operator > (My_str str1, My_str str2)
{ return strcmp(str1.str, str2.str) > 0;}
/******************************************************************/
/*Function input reads in up to 20 strings and             */
/*returns the count of the number of strings entered.      */
/*Entered strings are stored in a memory region            */
/*   allocated in the class My_str                         */
/******************************************************************/
void input(My_str *s, int &count)
{ static char buf[100];   // next string buffer
  count=0;                        // on termination, count - is number
                          // of strings entered
  puts("Enter strings to be sorted");
  while(count++ < 20)
  if(scanf("%s",buf) == EOF) break; // terminate by Ctrl-Z
    else s[count] = My_str(buf);
}
/******************************************************************/
/*Function output displays the list of string lengths     */
/******************************************************************/
void output(My_str *s,int size)
{ for(int i=0;i<size;i++) s[i].print();}
/****************************************/
/* Function sort sorts strings size       */
/****************************************/
void sort(My_str *s, int size)
{ int pr=1; // pr indicates sorting complete
  while(pr)
  { pr=0;
    for(int i=0;i<size-1;i++)
    if(s[i]>s[i+1])
    { My_str temp=s[i];
      s[i]=s[i+1];
      s[i+1]=temp;
      pr=1;
    }
  }
}
void main(void)
{ int size;
  My_str list_str[20];
  input(list_str,size);        // strings input
  sort(list_str,size);         // strings sorting
  puts("\nThe list of sorted strings is:");
  output(list_str,size);       // Output of sorted strings
}
```

Here, a new keyword, **new**, appears. In **C++**, the keywords **new** and **delete** are employed for dynamic allocation and deallocation of storage just like the library functions **malloc, free**, etc. Their general syntax can be presented as follows:

```
pointer_to_allocated_memory = new component_name
delete pointer_to_allocated_memory
```

The operator **new** attempts to allocate storage for an object with a specified name. If the attempt is successful, a pointer to the beginning of the corresponding storage segment is returned. The operator **delete** releases the allocated storage. Let us now focus our attention on the declaration of the function **input**:

```
void input(My_str *s,int &count)
```

You may recall that in **C**, arguments are passed to a function by value. The function invoked cannot change the original variable values in the calling program. To overcome this limitation, pointers to the corresponding values are passed to the function called. This allows the called program to modify the values directly.

These mechanisms were closely examined in the previous section. **C++** can automatically inform the compiler about a pointer passed to a function. This is achieved by adding the prefix **&** to the name of the object to be passed.

In the example given above, the declaration **int &count** means that the compiler must work with the component **count** through the prefix. Hence, when **input** has completed execution, the value **count** in the calling function will be changed. Those programmers familiar with **Pascal** will note that the use of the operator **&** before an argument is similar to the use of VAR in **Pascal**.

The results of program execution can be presented as:

> **Enter strings for sorting**
> *Minsk <Enter>*
> *Brest<Enter>*
> *Vitebsk<Enter>*
> *Grodno<Enter>*
> *Gomel<Enter>*
> *Mogilev<Enter>*
> *Ctrl-Z<Enter>*
> **The list of sorted strings is:**
> **Brest**
> **Gomel**
> **Grodno**
> **Minsk**
> **Mogilev**
> **Vitebsk**

In the majority of practical applications, it is sufficient to define and use an operator function as a class member rather than as a **friend**. However, there is one disadvantage. Suppose **Ob** is an object and we have overloaded the operator **+** in such a way that it works with the object **Ob**, through the pointer **this**, to add an integer to it. So the statement:

```
Ob = Ob + 10;
```

will be legal. However, the statement:

```
Ob = 10 + Ob;
```

is invalid, since the first operand is an integer and not an object. The next example shows how **Friend** functions can help get around this difficulty.

## Example EX3_22

This obstacle can be overcome by utilizing two functions with the specifier **friend** as illustrated by the following example:

```
/* example EX3_22 */
#include <iostream.h>
struct two_friends
{  int i;
   two_friends operator=(int k) { i=k; return *this; }
   friend two_friends operator*(two_friends F1,int j);
   friend two_friends operator*(int j,two_friends F1);
};
// here the first parameter is a class member,the second is
//                                           integer
two_friends operator*(two_friends F1,int j)
{  two_friends t_f;
   t_f = j * F1.i;
   return t_f;
}
// here the first parameter is integer,the second is a class
//                                           member
two_friends operator*(int j,two_friends F1)
{  two_friends t_f;
   t_f = F1.i * j;
   return t_f;
}
void main(void)
{  two_friends X;
   X = 10;
   X = X * 2;          // an object is multiplied by an integer
   cout << X.i << "\n";  // number 20 will be displayed
   X = 4 * X;          // an integer is multiplied by an object
   cout << X.i << "\n";  // number 80 will be displayed
}
```

The use of an overloaded operator = and the effects of expressions **t_f=j*f1;** and **return t_f** are illustrated in Figure 3.18. Note that types of returned values can be manipulated in a similar way by using several operator functions, not necessarily with the specifier **friend**. For instance, one operator function could define the returned type as an object of a class, whereas the other might define it as a character string.

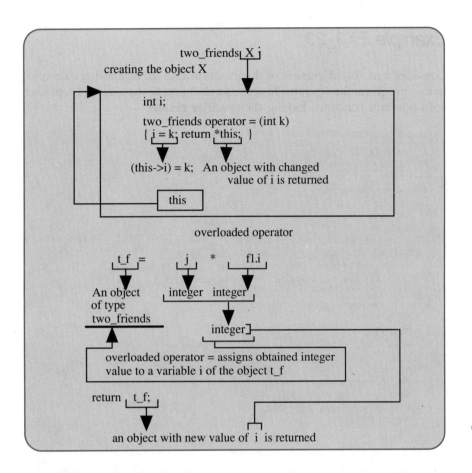

*Figure 3.18*
**Using
Overloaded
Operators**

## Example EX3_23

Consider a modified version of the program EX3_20 as another example. In this program, the operator functions belonging to the class are replaced with operator functions having the specifier **friend**:

```
/* example EX3_23 */
#include <iostream.h>
#include <graphics.h>
#include <conio.h>
class Point
{  int x,y;
   public:
      Point(int InitX,int InitY) { x = InitX; y = InitY; }
      friend Point operator++(Point my_p);
      friend Point operator-(Point my_p1,Point my_p2);
      void put_point(void) { putpixel(x,y,1); }
};
Point operator++(Point my_p)
{  my_p.x++;
   my_p.y++;
   return my_p;
}
Point operator-(Point my_p1,Point my_p2)
{  Point temp(0,0);
   temp.x = my_p1.x-my_p2.x;
   temp.y = my_p1.y-my_p2.y;
   return temp;
}
void main(void)
{  int gd = DETECT, gm;
   initgraph(&gd,&gm,"");      //initializing the graphic system
   Point my_point(30,30);
   for(int  j=0;j<10;j++)
   {  for(int  i=0;i<100;i++)
      {  my_point = my_point++;
         my_point.put_point();
      }
      my_point = my_point  -  Point(50,100);
   }
   getch();                    // wait until any key is pressed
   closegraph();               // closing the graphic system
}
```

Let us examine some features typical of unary operations, using **++** in the example given above. Consider the expression **my_point++;** in the example we are interested in. In this case, the operator function is called and the formal argument **my_p** is replaced by the actual argument **my_point**. Recall that an argument is passed to a function by value.

Thus, the function operator will deal with and change, only a copy of the actual argument. The new value to be returned is identified by prefixing the keyword **return** and needs to be passed to some object. To achieve this, it must occur on the right side of an assignment operator. As a result, the following expression appears in the program:

```
my_point  =  my_point++;
```

Suppose we want to write the more common expression: **my_point++;** . In this case, an object pointer must be passed to the operator function. As mentioned earlier, this can be done as follows:

```
point  operator++(point  &my_p)
```

## Example EX3_24

A new version of the program is given below:

```
/*  example  EX3_24  */
#include  <iostream.h>
#include  <graphics.h>
#include  <conio.h>
class  Point
{   int  x,y;
    public:
        Point(int  InitX,int  InitY)  {  x  =  InitX;  y  =  InitY;  }
        friend  void  operator++(Point  &my_p);          /**********/
        friend  Point  operator-(Point  my_p1,Point  my_p2);
        void  put_point(void)  {  ::putpixel(x,y,1);  }
};
void  operator++(Point  &my_p)                            /**********/
{   my_p.x++;
    my_p.y++;
}
Point  operator-(Point  my_p1,Point  my_p2)
{   Point  temp(0,0);
    temp.x  =  my_p1.x-my_p2.x;
    temp.y  =  my_p1.y-my_p2.y;
    return  temp;
}
```

```
void  main(void)
{   int  gd = DETECT, gm;
    initgraph(&gd,&gm,"");     //initializing the graphic system
    Point my_point(30,30);
    for(int  j=0;j<10;j++)
    {   for(int  i=0;i<100;i++)
        {   my_point++;     /**********/
            my_point.put_point();
        }
        my_point = my_point - Point(50,100);
    }
    getch();                   // suspension until any key is pressed
    closegraph();              // closing the graphics system
}
```

The statements that have been changed are marked with comments thus: **/****../**. It should be noted again that the argument definition, such as **&my_p**, implies that the compiler must deal with the parameter through a pointer. The element **my_p** of the function body need not be preceded with an asterisk.

## *Default Arguments*

In **C++**, function arguments can be assigned values by default. Consider the following definition:

> **void function(int X=0)  { ... }**

With this definition the function can be called with or without an argument, for example, **function(100);** or **function();**. If the argument is omitted, the default value appearing in the function definition will be employed, which in this case is zero.

## Example EX3_25

Consider the following example:

```
/* example EX3_25 */
#include <iostream.h>
void example(char *s,char s1[] = "string2 is missing, ",
     char s2[] = "string3 is missing")
{ cout << s << s1 << s2 << "\n"; }
void main(void)
{ example("Default arguments: ");
  example("Default arguments: ","1st argument, ");
  example("Default arguments: ","1st argument,","2nd argument");
}
```

Here, the function **example** is called three times using one, two and three arguments. The results of program execution will be as follows:

> **Default arguments: string2 is missing,string3 is missing**
> **Default arguments: 1st argument, string3 is missing**
> **Default arguments: 1st argument, 2nd argument**

Note that the following declaration of the function **example** is illegal:

**void example(char *s,char s1[]="string is missing",char*p);**

The default argument **char s1[]= "string is missing"** can only be followed by arguments that also have default values assigned.

Default arguments can also be used in constructors. For instance:

> **Point::Point(int InitX, int InitY, int InitC=1)**

In this case, when

> **Point my_point(10,30);**

is declared, colour number 1 will be specified for the corresponding point.

# *Virtual Functions*

Suppose we have defined a base class, **Base**, and its derivative, **Derived**. We can write the following declarations:

```
Base *p;      // p - is a pointer to a class Base
Base B_ob;    // B_ob - an object of class Base
Derive D_ob;  // D_ob - an object of class Derived
```

One of the rules in **C++** says that any variable declared as a pointer to a base-class object may also be used as a pointer to a derived class object. The following statements will be valid in our example:

```
p=&B_ob;   // p - is a pointer to an object of class
                                            Base
p=&D_ob;   // p - is a pointer to an object of class
                                            Derived
```

Now, using the pointer **p** gives access to all elements of the object, **D_ob**, inherited from the class **base**. However, through this pointer no access is possible to the unique members of the class **Derive** that were not inherited. If a pointer to a derived-class object is declared, it cannot be used for access to base-class members.

If we have declared a pointer **p** to a base-class object, then if it is incremented or decremented by unity the scale factor for the base class is used. If the same pointer is used to refer to the derived class, then incrementing or decrementing the pointer value with respect to the derived class will be performed incorrectly, since the wrong scaling factor will be used.

**Virtual functions** make it possible to resolve the overloading problem (polymorphism) in the course of program execution, rather than at compile time. They represent functions declared with the specifier **virtual** in a base-class and subsequently redefined in one or more derived classes, with their names, types of returned values and the number and types of arguments, being unchanged.

Suppose, we are dealing with the classes **Base** and **Derived** described at the beginning of this chapter. Suppose further that the function **my_virt** is defined with the specifier **virtual** in the class **Base** and without the specifier **virtual** in the class **Derived**. We assume we have also defined the pointer **p**, by means of the statement:

```
p = &B_ob;
```

Then, **p->my_virt** will select the base-class function. Let us now write another statement redefining **p**:

```
p=&D_ob;
```

In this case, **p->my_virt** will select the derived class function. Thus, by redefining the pointer, we can select various versions of the function **my_virt**. An illustration of the mechanisms involved in using virtual functions is given in Figure 3.19.

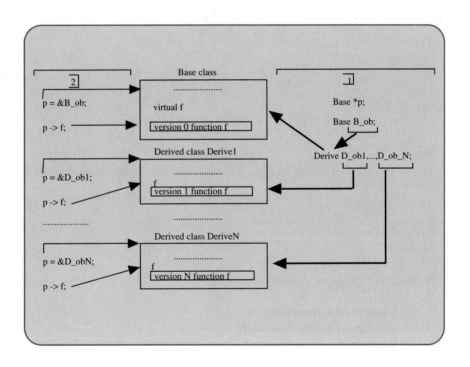

*Figure 3.19*
**Operations
with Virtual
Functions**

## Example EX3_26

Let us consider an example:

```
/* example EX3_26 */
#include <iostream.h>
// defining the base class Base
class Base
{ public:
     virtual void f(void)
     { cout << "version of a class Base\n"; }
};
// defining the derived class Derived1
class Derived1 : public Base
{ public:
     void f(void)    // virtual void f(void) is not an error
     { cout << "version of a class Derived1\n"; }
};
// defining the derived class Derived2
class Derived2 : public Base
{ public:
     void f(void)    // virtual void f(void) is not an error
     { cout << "version of a class Derived2\n"; }
};
void main(void)
{ Base *p, B_ob;
  Derived1 D_ob1;
  Derived2 D_ob2;
  p = &B_ob;
  p->f(); // version of f from the class Base is selected
  p = &D_ob1;
  p->f(); // version of f from the class Derived1 is selected
  p = &D_ob2;
  p->f(); // version of f from the class Derived2 is selected
}
```

The results of program execution will be:

**Version of a class Base**
**Version of a class Derived1**
**Version of a class Derived2**

In the example given above, the required version of the function **f** is selected during program execution by setting the pointer **p** appropriately.

The use of virtual functions is subject to the following limitations:

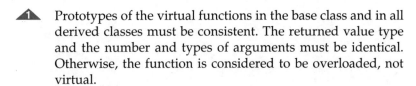 Prototypes of the virtual functions in the base class and in all derived classes must be consistent. The returned value type and the number and types of arguments must be identical. Otherwise, the function is considered to be overloaded, not virtual.

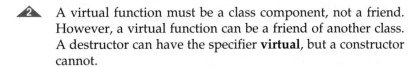 A virtual function must be a class component, not a friend. However, a virtual function can be a friend of another class. A destructor can have the specifier **virtual**, but a constructor cannot.

If a function is declared as virtual, it retains this property for any derived class at any nesting level. If a virtual function definition is omitted in some derived class, then the base-class version is used instead.

## Example EX3_27

This is illustrated by the following example:

```
/* example EX3_27 */
#include <iostream.h>
class Base
{ public:
    virtual void f(void)
    { cout << "version of a class Base\n"; }
};
class Derived1 : public Base
{ public:
    void f(void)
        { cout << "version of a class Derived1\n"; }
};
class Derived2 : public Base
{ public:                        // a virtual function is skipped
    void show(void) { cout << "it's a different function\n"; }
};
// class Derived1_1 is derived from the class Derived1 which in
// its turn is derived from the class Base
class Derived1_1 : public Derived1
{ public:
    void f(void)
        { cout << "version of a class Derived1_1\n"; }
};
```

```
void  main(void)
{ Base  *p,  B_ob;
  Derived1  D_ob1;
  Derived2  D_ob2;
  Derived1_1  D_ob1_1;
  p = &B_ob;
  p->f(); // version f of the class Base is selected
  p = &D_ob1;
  p->f(); // version f of the class Derived1 is selected
  p = &D_ob2;
  p->f(); // version f of the class Base is selected
  p = &D_ob1_1;
  p->f(); // version f of the class Derived1_1 is selected
}
```

The results of program execution will be as follows:

> **Version of a class Base**
> **Version of a class Derived1**
> **Version of a class Base**
> **Version of a class Derived1_1**

A small point worth remembering is that if the function **f** is removed from the class **Derived1_1**, then its version from the class **Derived1** will be used, that is, from the predecessor of the derived class **Derived1_1**.

# *Abstract Classes*

There can be situations where a virtual function that has been omitted in a derived class, cannot be replaced with its version from a base class. Then, **a pure virtual function** is declared, which cannot be called by default. The following syntax is used:

```
virtual  type_of_return_value
function_name(parameter_list)=0;
```

Such declarations require that any derived class should have its own version of the virtual function. If it is omitted, an error message will be displayed. To demonstrate that this is the case, we can execute the program EX3_27 after replacing the statement:

```
virtual  void  f(void)
{       cout << "version of a class Base\n"; }
```

by another statement:

```
virtual  void  f(void)=0;
```

If a class possesses at least one pure virtual function, it is named **an abstract class**. It is impossible to create objects for such a class. It can only be used as a base class from which derived classes can inherit members. Hence, a declaration such as the following statement:

```
Base  *p,B_ob;
```

in the example EX3_27 for creating a pure virtual function, will result in an error message. Therefore, it should be changed to the following:

```
Base  *p;
```

This, in turn, requires removal of some other statements. Declaration of a pointer for the abstract class, such as **p** in the example, is quite legal since it can be used subsequently for addressing derived-class objects.

## Example EX3_28

The final text of the modified program for the example EX3_27 is as follows:

```
/* example EX3_28 */
#include <iostream.h>
// defining an abstract base class Base
class Base
{ public:
    virtual void f(void) = 0;
};
class Derived1 : public Base
{ public:
    void f(void)
       { cout << "version of a class Derived1\n"; }
};
class Derived2 : public Base
{ public:
    void f(void)
        { cout << "version of a class Derived2\n"; }
};
class Derived1_1 : public Derived1
{ public:
    void f(void)
        { cout << " version of a class Derived1_1\n"; }
};
void main(void)
{ Base *p;
  Derived1 D_ob1;
  Derived2 D_ob2;
  Derived1_1 D_ob1_1;
  p = &D_ob1;
  p->f(); // version of f from the class Derived1 is selected
  p = &D_ob2;
  p->f(); // version of f from the class Derived2 is selected
  p = &D_ob1_1;
  p->f(); // version of f from the class Derived1_1 is selected
}
```

The results of program execution will be:

**version of a class Derived1**
**version of a class Derived2**
**version of a class Derived1_1**

Finally, we will have a quick look at another possible application of the keyword **virtual**. Where we have a class derived from multiple base classes, no base class can occur more than once in the definition of the derived class. For instance, the second of the following two declarations is illegal because of the occurrence of the base class twice:

```
class Base
       {...};
class derived  : Base, Base
       { ... };
```

However, there is a perfectly legal way of including a base class indirectly in a derived class more than once. It can be done simply by declaring the derived class in terms of a couple of intermediate classes, each of which inherit the properties of the original base class. There are many practical situations where you will need to do this. The following declarations outline the simplest case:

```
class  Derived1 : public  Base
                          { ... };
class  Derived2 : public  Base
                          { ... };
class  Derived1_2 : public  Derived1,  public  Derived2
                          { ... };
```

Here we have managed to define the class **Derived1_2** such that each of its objects will have two sub–objects inherited from the class **base**. This causes a considerable amount of confusion. A number of things now cannot be satisfactorily decided by the compiler because of the duplication of members of the class **Base** in the class **Derived1_2**. However, we still need to be able to declare **Derived1_2** in this way. The keyword **virtual** comes to the rescue and enables us to prevent this undesirable side effect. We can declare **Derived1_2** with the following statements:

```
class  Derived1 : virtual  public  Base
                                  { ... };
class  Derived2 : virtual  public  Base
                                  { ... };
class  Derived1_2 : public  Derived1,  public  Derived2
                          { ... };
```

Now **Base** is a virtual base class for the classes **Derived1** and **Derived2**. This ensures that the objects of the derived class **Derived1_2** will only contain one sub–object of the class **Base**, regardless of how many inherited copies are implied by the manner of its declaration. To avoid the problems of duplicate sub–objects in a derived class, you simply declare the particular base class as virtual for all intermediate classes involved in the potential inheritance complication.

# OTHER FEATURES OF C++

## The Specifier Inline

The specifier **inline** tells the compiler about the possibility of inline expansions of functions. Similarly to the case with the specifier **register**, the compiler may choose to either accept or ignore this information. Inline expansions considerably reduce the overhead arising from function calls, by replacing the call with the code corresponding to the function body. Inline expansion is usually best applied to small and frequently used functions. There are two possible ways of creating **inline** functions. The first uses the specifier **inline** in the form:

```
inline  function_declaration
```

## Example EX3_29

Consider a simple example:

```
/* example EX3_29 */
#include  <iostream.h>
inline  void  my_func(void)
{   cout << "A way of declaring an inline function \n"; }
void  main(void)
{   my_func();    }
```

The program output will be:

### A way of declaring an inline function

The second way of creating **inline** functions is to include the function body definition in the class pattern. We have already seen this for the function **put_circle** in EX3_12. Any function defined within a class, is automatically assigned the specifier **inline** and the keyword **inline** need not be explicitly written. This approach is justified for very simple functions, where the code requires a relatively insignificant amount of memory. Otherwise, the program will increase in size considerably.

Let's define the circumstances when the compiler will not generate inline code:

1. With functions that return values, have loops or the keywords **switch** or **goto**;

2. With functions that do not return values, but contain the keyword **return**;

3. With functions that are either recursive or contain static variables.

## Operators New and Delete

Let's consider in more detail the **C++** keywords **new** and **delete**, which are operators for dynamic allocation and deallocation of memory. The general form of their use is:

```
pointer_to_name = new name(name_initializer);
delete pointer_to_name;
```

The name can be of any type except function, but pointers to functions are allowed. Initializing values are not necessary. The operator **new** allocates the memory required to accommodate the object and returns a pointer to the beginning of the area allocated. **Null** is returned if any errors occur, or when allocation of memory is not possible. The operator **delete** deallocates previously allocated memory, using the pointer to its beginning which is specified.

The operators **new** and **delete** have the following advantages compared to the **C** library functions **malloc** and **free**:

1. The operator **new** automatically calculates the size of the element for which memory is required, so there's no need to use the operator **sizeof**.

2. You do not have to convert types, since the operator **new** automatically returns a pointer to the desired element.

3. The allocated memory block can be initialized, but with certain restrictions.

4 The operators **new** and **delete** can be overloaded relative to a defined class.

We can take some simple examples. The statements:

```
int *a;
a = new(100);
```

allocate memory for an integer variable and assign it the initial value 100. Memory can be allocated and deallocated for arrays, but they cannot be initialized in the allocation statement. The following syntax is used:

```
pointer_to_element = new element_type[size];
delete[size] pointer_to_element;
```

The **size** parameter determines the number of elements in the array. The returned value points to its first element. The following statements allocate memory for an array of ten integer elements:

```
int *a;
a = new int[10];
```

Deallocation of memory would be carried out in the following manner:

```
delete[10] a;
```

The general form of overloading of the operators **new** and **delete** is as follows:

```
void *operator new(size)
{     memory allocation
return pointer_to_allocated memory;
}

void operator delete(void *p)
{     deallocation of memory
pointed to by p
}
```

The parameter **size** defines the number of bytes in the allocated memory block. It must be of type **size_t**, which is the same as **unsigned int**. The type **size_t** is defined in the **Turbo C++** files **alloc.h, stdio.h, mem.h, stdlib.h, stddef.h** and **string.h**. The returned value can be **NULL**, which is a byte with all zeros, if memory cannot be allocated. Consider an example:

```
void  *my_class::operator  new(size_t  size)
{       return  malloc(size);        }
void  my_class::operator  delete(void  *p)
{       free(p);        }
```

Here the operators **new** and **delete** are overloaded with respect to the class **my_class**. Let's look at one more example of defining overloading:

```
void  *operator  new(size_t,size)
{       return  malloc(size);        }
void  operator  delete(void  *p)
{       free(p);        }
```

Here the operators **new** and **delete** have been overloaded globally.

## Example EX3_30

We can now take a look at some complete program examples of the use of these facilities. The first illustrates overloading of the operators **new** and **delete** with respect to the class **my_class** and dynamic allocation of memory for an array:

```
/* example EX3_30 */
#include <iostream.h>
#include <alloc.h>
#include <string.h>
#include <process.h>
class my_class
{ char *s;
  int count;
  public:
    my_class(int S,char *m);          //constructor
    ~my_class(void) { delete s; }     //destructor
    void *operator new(size_t size);  //overloading operator new
    void operator delete(void *p);    //overloading operator delete
    void show(void);
};
my_class::my_class(int  S,char  *m)
{ if((s = new char[S]) == NULL)
  { cout << "memory allocation error\n"; exit(1); }
  count = S;
  strcpy(s,m);
}
```

```
void *my_class::operator new(size_t size)
  { return malloc(size);}
void my_class::operator delete(void *p)
  { free(p); }
void my_class::show(void)
  { for(int i = 0;i < count;i++)
    cout << s[i] << ((i == count-1)?'\n':' ');
  }
void main(void)
{ char *m;
  if((m = new char[5]) == NULL)   // memory allocation for array
  { cout << "memory allocation error\n"; exit(1);}
  for(char j='0';j<'5';j++)
  m[j-48] = j;                    // ASCII-code of null is 48
  cout << "\nOutput of characters\n";
  my_class m_c(5,m);
  m_c.show();
  delete[5] m;                    // deallocation of memory for array
}
```

Executing the program will produce the following results:

> **Output of characters**
> 0 1 2 3 4

## Example EX3_31

The second example illustrates the use of the operators **new** and **delete**, for allocation and deallocation of memory for objects of a class:

```
/* example EX3_31 */
#include <iostream.h>
#include <string.h>
#include <alloc.h>
#include <process.h>
class String
{ public:
  char *str;
  String(char*);    // constructor
  ~String()         // destructor
    { delete str;
      cout << "~String()" << "\n";
    }
  void print() { cout << str << '\n'; }
};
```

```
String::String(char  *s)
{ if((str  =  new  char[strlen(s)+1])  ==  NULL)
    {    cout  <<  "memory allocation memory\n";  exit(1);  }
    strcpy(str,s);
    cout  <<  "String(char *)"  <<  "\n";
}
void main()
{ String  cp("Minsk"),// initializing  object  cp
    *s[] = { new String("Novosibirsk"),new String("Uljanovsk") };
    // preceding  statement  is  initializing
    // an array  of pointers  s  to objects  of type String
    s[0]->print();  //  output  of  string  "Novosibirsk"
    s[1]->print();  //  output  of  string  "Uljanovsk"
    cp.print();     //  output  of  string  "Minsk"
    delete(s[1]);   //  deallocation  of  memory
    delete(s[0]);   //  deallocation  of  memory
}
```

The program results will be as follows:

> **String(char \*)**
> **String(char \*)**
> **String(char \*)**
> **Novosibirsk**
> **Uljanovsk**
> **Minsk**
> **~String()**
> **~String()**
> **~String()**

# New Features of the Operator &

Take a look at some additional features of the **C++** operator **&**. The easiest way to do that is to take some examples of declarations:

```
int  i;       // declaring  an  integer  variable  i
int  &j = i;  // declaring  a  new  name  j  for  i
              // (j  is  an  alias  for  i)
j = 10;       // here  the  effect  is  the  same  as  i=10
```

Here the element **j** is not the address. The **&** operator is being used as a reference declarator, not as an address operator. The name **j** has been defined as an alternative to the name **i**.

Here are some restrictions for using the operator **&** when declaring references:

1. If the operation **&** is a reference, a reference to a reference cannot be executed.

2. References to bit fields are not allowed.

3. Arrays of references are not allowed.

4. Pointers to references are not allowed.

The reference declarator can be used to declare reference parameters to a function as we have already seen. An example would be:

```
void function(long &my_1);
```

The argument **my_1** will be assigned through the reference. As a result, it can be changed directly in the function, so that when control returns to the calling program, **my_1** will have the new value.

# Using Static Memory

Now turn your attention to some special members of a class, defined with the specifier **static**. With respect to data members **static** has the same significance as in **C** where memory is allocated for the duration of the program.

Regardless of the number of members declared for a class, its static members are stored in a fixed memory region specific to the class, so only one copy of each exists. When creating the first class member, the static memory region is initialized with null values. For the members of that class that are created subsequently, initialization is not performed. If **st** is a static member of the class **my_class** and defined, for example, as:

```
static int st;
```

it can be referenced even if no objects of the class **my_class** have yet been created. Unlike ordinary members, static members can be initialized. For example:

```
my_class::st = 10;
```

The specifier **static** can be used with function members of a class. In this case only one copy of the function is created and will be used then by all objects of the class. Note, that there is one important restriction. A static function can directly access only static data or other static member functions of the class. This is because they have no pointer **this**. Suppose we have two objects, **ob1** and **ob2**, of a class with the static function **f**. Then, if **f** is to access a non-static member **a**, the question arises as to which version of **a** it references. It could be in **ob1** or **ob2**. The compiler cannot determine the answer as it stands.

## Example EX3_32

This can be resolved by explicitly defining the non-static member to be accessed. Consider a simple example:

```
/* example EX3_32 */
#include <iostream.h>
class my_class
{ public:
    int a;
    my_class(int X) { a = X; }
    static void my_func(my_class *p);
};
void my_class::my_func(my_class *p)
{ cout << "a = " << p->a << '\n'; }
void main(void)
{ my_class ob1(100), ob2(200);
    ob1.my_func(&ob1);
    ob1.my_func(&ob2);
}
```

Here we see that the first static function references the member of **ob1** and the second accesses the member of **ob2**. If you run the program, the results will be as follows:

a = 100
a = 200

## Example EX3_33

Consider another example with static class members:

```
/* example EX3_33 */
#include <iostream.h>
class my_static
{ public:
    static int counter;
    static void inc(int n) { counter += n; }
    static void show_counter(void)
    { cout << "counter = " << counter << ".\n"; }
};
void main(void)
{ // reference to static member when an object of
  // class my_static has not been yet created
  cout << "my_static::counter = " << my_static::counter << '\n';
  my_static ob1,ob2;
  ob1.show_counter();// here counter = 0
  ob2.show_counter();// here counter = 0
  ob1.inc(50);       // incrementing by 50 counter in ob1
  ob2.show_counter();// here counter = 50
  ob2.inc(100);      // incrementing by 100 counter in ob2
  ob1.show_counter();// here counter = 150
  // two possible ways of calling static functions
  // are given below
  ob2.show_counter();// here counter = 150 )
  my_static::show_counter();// such a call is allowed for
                      // static functions only (counter = 150)
}
```

The program results will be as follows:

> **my_static::counter = 0**
> **counter = 0.**
> **counter = 0.**
> **counter = 50.**
> **counter = 150.**
> **counter = 150.**
> **counter = 150.**

Static member functions of a class cannot be **virtual**. The static and non-static member functions cannot have the same names.

# Input/Output Organization

We shall now consider some further **C++** features concerning input/output organization. Note that we can still use all of the original **C** input/output functions.

Recall the use of the operators ≪ and ≫. A remarkable feature of **C++** is that it allows the programmer to define their own data types that will be handled by the input/output functions. For example, you can define a class and then input and output all the required members of an object corresponding to the class by using the symbols ≪ and ≫.

## Data Streams

**C++** also operates with **data streams**. Four streams are opened automatically when you start running a program : **cin** corresponding to **stdin**, **cout** corresponding to **stdout**, **cerr** corresponding to **stderr** where errors will be noted and **clog**. We have already used the first two many times in examples. The streams **cerr** and **clog** are connected to the standard output stream. The difference between them is that **clog** is buffered and **cerr** is not. For **clog**, output will occur only when the buffer is full.

As in **C**, standard streams are connected by default with the keyboard and the monitor screen. The types of operands that are sent to an output stream and received from the standard input stream can be: **char** (**signed** and **unsigned**); **short** (**signed** and **unsigned**); **int** (**signed** and **unsigned**); **long** (**signed** and **unsigned**); **char\***; **float**; **double**; **long double**; and **void\***. In the last instance, a pointer is output to the screen in a hexadecimal format.

All definitions of the standard streams are stored in the file **iostream.h**. Now take a look at some of the useful classes included in that file. The first, named **istream**, may be used to create input streams. The second, **ostream**, is used to create output streams. They were all derived from a base class **ios** that includes the functions that support formatted input/output.

We can take a look at some program examples of overloading the operators ≪ and ≫. These show methods for organizing input/output for data types that you have created yourself as classes.

## Example EX3_34

In the first program the operator ≪ is overloaded:

```
/* example EX3_34 */
#include <iostream.h>
class my_class
{   int c;
    char *str;
    public:
        my_class(int  InitA,int  InitB)
        { c = InitA + InitB; str = "c = "; }
        friend ostream &operator<<(ostream &stream,my_class M_C);
};
ostream  &operator<<(ostream  &stream,my_class  M_C)
{
    stream  <<  M_C.str;                                          //**
    stream  <<  M_C.c  <<  ".\n";                                 //**
    return  stream;
}
void  main(void)
{   my_class  X(10,20),  Y(30,40);
    cout << X << Y;
}
```

As you can see from the example, the operator function is defined in the form:

**ostream &operator<<(ostream &stream,my_class M_C)**

The operator function has two parameters. The first is the reference to the object **stream**, of the class **ostream**, that appears to the left of the ≪ symbol. The second parameter is our object that will be written to the right of the ≪ symbol. The operations with the object **stream** in the body of the operator function are carried out through a pointer.

The comments in the example with two asterisks, **//\*\***, mark the program statements that will change if you want to redefine the operator ≪ differently. The specifier **friend** is used to allow access to local members of the class **my_class** with the default attribute **private**. The program output will be:

c = 30.
c = 70.

## Example EX3_35

The next program overloads both the operators << and >>:

```
/* example EX3_35 */
#include <iostream.h>
class my_class
{   int c;
    char str[100];
    public:
        friend istream &operator>>(istream &stream,my_class &M_C);
        friend ostream &operator<<(ostream &stream,my_class M_C);
};
istream &operator>>(istream &stream,my_class &M_C)
{
    cout << "Input a string\n";                             //**
    stream >> M_C.str;                                      //**
    cout << "input an integer\n";                           //**
    stream >> M_C.c;                                        //**
return stream;
}
ostream &operator<<(ostream &stream,my_class M_C)
{
    stream <<"str = " << M_C.str << "; c = "<< M_C.c <<"\n";//**
    return stream;
}
void main(void)
{   my_class X, Y;
    cin >> X;
    cin >> Y;
    cout << X << Y;
}
```

In this instance the class **istream** is also used, and here, the second
parameter of the operator function must be a reference, because the values
of members of the object **M_C** are changed. As in EX3_34, the comments
**//\*\*** mark the program statements that will change when you further
redefine the operators << and >>. The program results will be:

**Input a string**
*Minsk<Enter>*
**Input an integer**
*0<Enter>*
**Input  a string**
*London<Enter>*
**Input  an integer**
*4<Enter>*
**str = Minsk; c = 0**
**str = London; c = 4**

| Manipulator | Syntax | Action |
|---|---|---|
| dec | outs << dec<br>ins >> dec | Output of numbers in decimal format |
| hex | outs << hex<br>ins >> hex | Output of numbers in hexadecimal format |
| oct | outs << oct<br>ins >> oct | Output of numbers in octal format |
| endl | outs << endl | Moves the cursor to the beginning of a new line |
| ends | outs << ends | Puts a terminating null at the end of a line |
| setfill(int) | ins >> setfill(N)<br>outs << setfill(N) | Sets fill-character N |
| setprecision(int) | ins >> setprecision(N)<br>outs << setprecision(N) | Sets output of N digits after the decimal point in float numbers |
| setw(int) | ins >> setw(N)<br>outs << setw(N) | Sets input/output field width equal to N |

*TABLE 3.1*

While using input/output streams in **C++** a number of parameters involved in the process are set by default. They can be changed by using special operators called **manipulators**. Some of these manipulators are given in Table 3.1. The corresponding definitions are held in the file **iomanip.h** that must be included into the program using the **#include** directive.

## Example EX3_36

Consider an example of using a manipulator:

```
/* example EX3_36 */
     #include <iostream.h>
#include <iomanip.h>//file containing the manipulators'
                     // definition
void  main(void)
{    // output of number 20 in decimal, hexadecimal,
     // and octal base number systems
   cout << dec << 20 << endl << hex << 20 << endl;
   cout << oct << 20 << endl;
     // using new characters + and - instead of space,
     //    and setting an output field width
   cout << dec << setw(10) << setfill('+') << 10 << endl;
   cout << setw(20) << setfill('-') << 10 << endl;
     // output of two digits after the decimal point
   cout << setprecision(2) << 123.4567 << endl;
     // output of four digits after the decimal point
   cout << setprecision(4) << 123.4567 << endl;
}
```

The results of the program will be:

> **20**
> **14**
> **24**
> **++++++++10**
> ——————————**10**
> **123.46**
> **123.4567**

# Using Files

Now we can consider some functions specific to **C++** for using files. In order to use them, you must include in your program a standard file, **fstream.h**, that defines several important classes. There are three types of **streams** for using files: **input, output** and **input/output**. The classes **ifstream**, **ofstream** and **fstream** are defined for them, respectively. They all have constructors that open files automatically. To open a file you want to read, you can write the statement:

```
ifstream  in_file("my_file.txt");
```

To open a file you want to write, you can write the statement:

```
ofstream  out_file("my_file.txt");
```

To close a file, you may use the statement:

```
out_file.close();
```

## Examples EX3_37 and EX3_38

We have two pairs of sample programs to illustrate the use of files. The first program of the first pair, EX3_37, writes data to a file as text and the second, EX3_38, reads part of the data back from the file:

```
/* example EX3_37 */
#include  <iostream.h>
#include  <fstream.h>
main(int  argc,  char  *argv[])
{  char *my_text = "text to be written to file";
   if(argc != 2)        // second argument existence check
       {   cout << "File is not defined\n"; return 1; }
   ofstream  out_file(*(argv+1));
   if(!out_file)         // file opening possibility check
       { cout << "can't open file"; return 1; }
   // writing specified string to file
   while(*my_text)  out_file.put(*my_text++);
   out_file.close();    // closing file
   return 0;
}
```

```
/* example EX3_38 */
#include  <iostream.h>
#include  <fstream.h>
main(int  argc,  char  *argv[])
{  char  my_c;         // saving the next argument
   if(argc != 2)       // second argument existence check
       {   cout << "File is not defined\n"; return 1; }
   ifstream  in_file(*(argv+1));
   if(!in_file)        // file opening possibility check
       { cout << "can't open file"; return 1; }
   // reading file from the sixth character
   // from the beginning
   in_file.seekg(5,ios::beg);
   cout << "defined position for reading start = "
           << in_file.tellg() << "\n";
   // reading a line from file
   while(in_file.get(my_c))  cout << my_c;
   in_file.close(); // closing file
   return 0;
}
```

You can execute the first program, for example, by keying at the command line:

*ex3_37 myf.f<Enter>*

Here EX3_37.EXE is the program name and **myf.f** is the name of the file it is assigned. This file must always be defined, otherwise the program will terminate with an error message:

**File is not defined**

The statement **out_file(*(argv+1));** opens the file defined in the command line input, **myf.f** in the example, for output operations. If the file cannot be opened and therefore **out_file = NULL**, the program terminates with an error message **Can't open file**. The text is written byte by byte into the file, as long as there are no errors. For this purpose the function **put** is used. The function has the prototype:

```
ostream  &put(char  c);
```

In the second program, one byte is read using the function **get** with the prototype:

```
istream  &get(char  &c);
```

To provide random access to a file, **C++** uses two functions with the prototypes:

```
istream  &seekg  (shift,reference_position);
ostream  &seekp  (shift,reference_position);
```

The parameter **reference_position** is defined in one of the three forms: **ios::beg,** from the beginning of the file; **ios::cur,** from the current file position; or **ios::end,** from the end of file. The function **seekg** moves the file position pointer relative to the reference position specified, by the specified **shift** number of bytes, for a read operation. The function, **seekp,** positions the pointer in exactly the same way, but for a write operation. The final results of executing the second program EX3_38, after first executing EX3_37, will be:

*ex3_38 myf.f<Enter>*
**defined position for reading start =5**
**to be written to file**

The currently defined position of the file pointer from which reading will start, is returned by the function **tellg()**. The analogous function operating for write, has the name **tellp()**.

For reading and writing blocks of binary data the functions **read** and **write** are used. Their prototypes are as follows:

```
istream &read(unsigned char *buf, int N);
ostream &write(const unsigned char *buf, int N);
```

The first reads **N** bytes from a file and puts them into the buffer pointed to by **buf**. The second writes **N** bytes to a file from the buffer pointed to by **buf**.

## Examples EX3_39 and EX3_40

The following two examples demonstrate binary file input/output.

```
/* example EX3_39 */
#include <iostream.h>
#include <fstream.h>
main(int argc, char *argv[])
{ char *my_text = "new text to be written to file\0";
   if(argc != 2)
      { cout << "File is not defined\n"; return 1; }
   ofstream out_file(*(argv+1));
   if(!out_file)
      { cout << "can't open file"; return 1; }
      // writing specified string to file
   out_file.write(my_text,30);
   out_file.close();
   return 0;
}
```

```
/* example EX3_40 */
#include <iostream.h>
#include <fstream.h>
main(int argc, char *argv[])
{ unsigned char mas[30];
   if(argc != 2)
      { cout << "File is not defined\n"; return 1; }
ifstream in_file(*(argv+1));
if(!in_file)
   { cout << "can't open file"; return 1; }
   // reading file from 26th character
   // to its end
in_file.seekg(-26,ios::end);
cout << "defined position for reading start = "
        << in_file.tellg();
   // reading a line from file
in_file.read((unsigned char *) &mas,26);
cout << "\nread "<<in_file.gcount()<<" characters\n";
for(int i=0;i<26;i++)  cout << mas[i];
cout << "\n";
in_file.close();
return 0;
}
```

The first program can be executed by entering:

> *ex3_39 myf1.f<Enter>*

Then the results of the second program will be:

> *ex3_40 myf1.f<Enter>*
> **defined position for reading start=4**
> **read 26 characters**
> **text to be written to file**

The number of characters read from the file is defined by the function **gcount** with the prototype:

```
int   gcount();
```

One more useful function that is provided has the prototype:

```
int   eof();
```

It returns a non zero value at the end of file and zero otherwise.

## Examples EX3_41 and EX3_42

The last two examples illustrate the rules for writing and reading data to and from text files:

```
/*  example  EX3_41  */
#include  <iostream.h>
#include  <fstream.h>
main(int  argc,  char  *argv[])
{   if(argc  !=  2)
       {   cout  <<  "File  is  not  defined\n";  return  1;  }
    ofstream  out_file(*(argv+1));
    if(!out_file)
       {  cout  <<  "can't  open  file";  return  1;  }
    out_file  <<  345.123456  <<  "  "  <<  123  <<  "  "  <<  123456L
                  <<  "  "  <<  "MREI";
    out_file.close();
    return  0;
}
```

```
/* example EX3_42 */
#include <iostream.h>
#include <fstream.h>
main(int argc, char *argv[])
{  int i;
   double d;
   long l;
   unsigned char s[5];
   if(argc != 2)
      {  cout << "File is not defined\n"; return 1; }
   ifstream in_file(*(argv+1));
   if(!in_file)
      { cout << "can't open file"; return 1; }
   in_file >> d >> i >> l >> s;
   s[5] = 0;  // writing terminating null to string
   cout << d << " " << i << " " << l << " " << s << "\n";
   in_file.close();
   return 0;
}
```

The first program can be executed by entering:

> *ex3_41 myf2.f<Enter>*

After running the first program, the second program will produce the output:

> *ex3_42 myf2.f<Enter>*
> **345.123456 123 123456 MREI**

# *Preprocessor Directives and Macro-names*

Now we will explore the preprocessor directives and macro-names used in the **Turbo C++ IDE**. The operator **defined** is used exclusively with the directives **#if** and **#elif**. It allows you to determine whether a certain identifier is defined or not. The expression:

> **defined (identifier)**

or alternatively:

> **defined identifier**

assumes the value of 1 if an identifier is defined (i.e. does appear in a statement **#define**). Otherwise, the expression will have a **null** value. Thus, we can test whether the identifier **AAA** is defined using either of the directives:

```
#if  defined  AAA
#ifdef  AAA
```

An advantage of the operator **defined** is its ability to be used in expressions, for example:

```
#if  !defined  (AAA)  ||  defined  (BBB)
```

The directive **#pragma** has been considered in a previous section. Its general form is:

```
#pragma  directive_name
```

**Turbo C++** supports the following **directive_names** with **#pragma**: **argsused, exit, inline, option, saveregs, startup, warn**. Let us review them briefly.

The directive **#pragma argsused** can be positioned between two function definitions and affects only the succeeding function. It inhibits a warning that a certain parameter name is never used in the function.

The directives **#pragma startup** and **#pragma exit** define functions to be called prior to the commencement of execution and after the termination of a program respectively. These directives are defined as:

```
#pragma  startup  function_name  priority
#pragma  exit  function_name  priority
```

The function to be called must have the prototype:

```
void  function_name(void);
```

The priority value is an integer from 64 to 255, which by default is set to 100. The smaller number assigns greater priority. The specified **function_name** must have been declared as a function prior to the occurrence of the **#pragma** directive.

The directive **#pragma inline** tells the compiler that the program contains inline assembly language code.

The directive **#pragma option** includes command-line options within your program code. The syntax is:

```
#pragma option options
```

The directive **#pragma saveregs** is needed for interfacing with assembly language code.

The directive **#pragma warn** allows you to control the warning messages given by the compiler. For more detailed information, please consult the original manuals supplied with your compiler.

Now we turn to some global **Turbo C++** identifiers or **macro-names**:

**\_\_CDECL\_\_**   uses **C** calling convention.

**\_\_TINY\_\_, \_\_SMALL\_\_, \_\_COMPACT\_\_, \_\_MEDIUM\_\_, \_\_LARGE\_\_,   \_\_HUGE\_\_**
are defined based on the memory model chosen by a programmer in **Turbo C++**. Only one is defined for any given compilation.

**\_\_cplusplus**   is defined when the **C++** compiler is used.

**\_\_MSDOS\_\_**   provides the integer constant 1 for all compilations.

**\_\_OVERLAY\_\_**   is defined if overlay support is enabled.

**\_\_PASCAL\_\_**   uses **Pascal** calling convention.

**\_\_TURBOC\_\_**   gives the current **Turbo C++** version numbers as a hexadecimal constant.

## Example EX3_43

We can now take a look at an example using preprocessor directives:

```
/* example EX3_43 */
#include <iostream.h>
#pragma option -C     // option -C allows for nested comments
                      // (they are in the next line)
/* 12345 /* 66666 */ 67890 */
void Start1(void)
    {  cout << "Start1\n";   }
void Start2(void)
    {  cout << "Start2\n";   }
#pragma startup Start1  80
#pragma startup Start2  70
void End(void)
    {  cout << "End";   }
#pragma exit End       // default priority is 100
void main(void)
{  void func(int a);
   func(10);
   #if defined __TINY__
        cout << "TINY\n";
     #elif defined __SMALL__
        cout << "SMALL\n";
     #elif defined __COMPACT__
        cout << "COMPACT\n";
     #elif defined __MEDIUM__
        cout << "MEDIUM\n";
     #elif defined __LARGE__
        cout << "LARGE\n";
     #elif defined __HUGE__
        cout << "HUGE\n";
   #endif
}
/****************************************************************/
/* Without the directive pragma a warning will be displayed:    */
/*    Parameter 'a' is never used in function func(int)         */
/****************************************************************/
#pragma argsused
void func(int a)
{  cout << "Called function" << '\n';  }
```

The results of program execution will be:

**Start2**
**Start1**
**Called function**
**SMALL**
**End**

# C and C++ keywords

The **C** language allows for using the following keywords:

```
asm; auto; break; case; cdecl; char; const; continue; _cs;
default; do; double; _ds; else; enum; _es; extern; far;
float;  for; goto; huge; if; int; interrupt; _loadds; long;
near; pascal;  register; return; _saveregs; _seg; short;
signed; sizeof; _ss;  static; struct; switch; typedef; union;
unsigned; void; volatile; while.
```

Keywords **cdecl, _cs, _ds, _es, far, huge, interrupt, loadds, near, pascal, _saveregs, _seg, _ss** do not exist in the **ANSI** standard for **C**.

Now, let us briefly outline the keywords that have not been discussed in the book so far. The keyword **asm** allows you to include assembly language code in your **C** programs. The general form of its use is:

```
asm  opcode  operands  ;  or  newline
```

The modifiers of variables and functions **cdecl** and **pascal** define, for the declared object, the conventions adopted in **C** and **Pascal**, respectively. Consider an example:

```
pascal my_func(int a, int b, int c);
```

The modifier **const** prevents modification of the value of the defined object. A pointer assigned with the modifier **const** cannot be changed. This does not apply to the object to which it points. Typical examples of the use of **const** might be:

```
const float a = 56.218;
const b = 47;
```

The keywords **_cs, _ds, _es, _ss,** modify the value of a pointer of type **near**. They are specifically bound with the corresponding segment registers of the microprocessor (see Figure 2.49). For example, if we declare:

```
char _ss *a;
```

then the variable **a** would contain a 16-bit offset (**SS**) into the stack segment.

The keywords **far, huge** and **near** are used to modify pointers to data. A pointer of type **near** is a 16-bit pointer. It uses the contents of the register **DS** to define the address of an object. A pointer of type **far** is 32-bit and contains both a segment address and an offset (see Figure 2.50). A pointer **huge** is of the same size as **far**. However, it modifies the register **DS**.

The function modifier **_loadds** stores a pointer to the current data segment in the register **DS**. The function modifier **_saveregs** lets you save the values of all registers and then reset them after the function terminates, with the exception of the register containing the return value. The modifier **_seg** can be used to declare the pointers to data, which will be 16-bit segment pointers. The variable modifier **volatile** is the opposite of **const**. It signals that the object can be changed, not only within the program but externally, for example, by an interrupt from an event outside the program.

These are the **C++** keywords:

**catch; class; delete; friend; inline; new; operator; private; protected; public; template; this; virtual.**

The keywords **catch** and **template** have been reserved for the future and are not currently used. All the others have been discussed in the book.

Now to say a few words about priority in **C++**.

| | |
|---|---|
| : : | executes from left to right and is included in group 1 with the highest priority (in Table 2.2 it is at the top). |
| **new, delete** | execute from right to left and are included in group 2 in Table 2.2; |
| .*, ->* | execute from left to right and establish a new group immediately following the second group in Table 2.2. |

# SECTION FOUR

*Examples*

# SECTION FOUR

Chapter Fifteen

**Examples**

# CHAPTER 15

# C++ EXAMPLES

This sections contains examples designed to exercise in a practical way the techniques we have covered for Object Oriented Programming in the previous section. You will find that the examples are constructed in such a fashion that each provides a platform for understanding the successor. You will find that some use almost all of the code of the preceding example. In this way you should be able to absorb the details of the operation of each example with little difficulty, but building to a reasonably complex program.

## Example EX4_1

The first example demonstrates various methods of accessing class members. It models an elapsed time counter. You will see that there are extensive explanations contained in the comments within the program:

```
/* example EX4_1 */
#include <iostream.h>
#include <dos.h>
#include <conio.h>
#include <process.h>
#include <values.h>
struct watch
{
  //alm and als - contain the time for the beep to sound
  //in minutes and seconds; m and s- minutes and seconds counters
  int alm,als,m,s;
  watch(void);            // 1st constructor
  watch(int M,int S);     // 2nd constructor
  void my_time(void);     // time count
    // setting the time for the beep to sound
  void alarm(int m_a,int s_a) { alm = m_a; als = s_a; }
    // resetting time counters m and s to zero
  void set(void)   {  s = 0; m = 0;   }
};
watch::watch(void)
  { alm = als = MAXINT; s = 0; m = 0;        }
watch::watch(int M,int S)
  { alm = als = MAXINT; s = S; m = M;         }
```

```
void watch::my_time(void)
{ for(;;)
  { delay(1000);
    if(s == 60) { s = 0; m++; }
    cout << m << " " << s << '\r';  //output of minutes and seconds
    if(m == alm && s == als)
      cout << '\a';                 // beep sound
    s++;
                          // terminating program by pressing any key
    if(kbhit()) {  getch(); break;  }
  }
  system("cls");   // clearing the screen
}
void main(void)
{ typedef void (watch::*p_func)(int m_a,int s_a);
  p_func pf;
    // pf - a pointer to the class watch function with
    // two integer parameters that does not return values
    // declaring an object w of class watch
    //and a pointer to it, *pw
  watch *pw = new watch,w(10,30);
    // point_int - a pointer to components of
    // type int of the class watch
  int watch::*point_int;
    // x and y - variables used to access integer components
    // of the objects of the class watch
  int x,y;
  pf = &watch::alarm;      // now pf is a pointer to the function
                           // alarm of the class watch objects
  point_int = &watch::m; // now point_int is a pointer to
                     // component m of objects of the class watch
  x = w.*point_int;        // accesses w.m
  y = pw ->* point_int;    // accesses pw->m
    //displaying x = 10, y = 0
  cout << "x = " << x << "; y = " << y << '\n';
    //displaying pw->s = 0, w.s = 30
  cout << "pw->s = " << pw->s << "; w.s = " << w.s << '\n';
    //calling the function alarm in the object w
  w.alarm(10,50);
    //calling the function my_time in the object w
  w.my_time();
    //calling the function alarm in an object pointed to by pw
  pw->alarm(0,10);
    //calling the function my_time in an object pointed to by pw
  pw->my_time();
    //resetting the variables m and s to null in the object w and
    //an object pointed to by pw
  w.set();
  pw -> set();
    //calling the function alarm in the object w via
    //a pointer to the function pf
  (w.*pf)(0,15);
    // calling the function my_time in the object w
```

```
    w.my_time();
    //calling the function alarm in the object pointed to
    //by pw via a pointer to the function pf
    (pw->*pf)(0,20);
    //calling the function my_time in the object pointed to by pw
    pw->my_time();
}
```

**x = 10; y = 0**
**pw->s = 0; w.s = 30**

A digital display of a time counter will appear on the screen, starting at 10 minutes 30 seconds. This will be updated at one second intervals and at 10 minutes 50 seconds a beep signal will sound. The time count will stop when you press any key. The time counter will then reset to start counting from 0 minutes 0 seconds, with a beep signal at 0 minutes 10 seconds.

The time count will stop when you press any key. The counter will again reset and count from 0 minutes 0 seconds, with a beep signal at 0 minutes 15 seconds. The time count will continue until you press any key. Finally the counter will reset and count from 0 minutes 0 seconds with a beep signal at 0 minutes 20 seconds. The time count will stop and the program will terminate when you press any key.

The program includes some new functions. The first one, **system**, has the prototype:

```
int system(const char*command);
```

It is defined in the files **stdlib.h process.h** and lets you execute MS-DOS commands from your **C++** program. At a successful function termination, 0 is returned, otherwise 1 is returned. In our program we have used the MS-DOS command **cls** that clears the screen.

The second function, **delay**, is defined in the file **dos.h** and has the following prototype:

```
void delay(unsigned milliseconds);
```

It ensures program execution is delayed for the number of milliseconds specified as a parameter.

The constant **MAXINT** used in the program has the value 32767 and is defined in the file **values.h**.

# Example EX4_2

The second program lets you display a stopwatch at any position on the screen, with timing and position parameters specified by your input. The time count is indicated by the seconds pointer movement similar to that of a mechanical watch. You can specify the time at which a beep signal is to sound in minutes and seconds. You can also define a maximum count period for the stopwatch in minutes. The program code is given below:

```cpp
/* example EX4_2 */
#include <graphics.h>
#include <dos.h>
#include <process.h>
#include <stdio.h>
#include <conio.h>
#include <values.h>
#define ESC 27
class watch
{ int x_c,y_c,size,min,alm,als;
  public:
    watch(void);      // constructor
    void arrow(void);
    void move_arrow(int x,int y);
    void size_watch(int z) { size = z; };
    void time_m(int m) { min = m; }
    void alarm(int m_a,int s_a) {  alm = m_a; als = s_a; }
};
watch::watch(void)
  { x_c = getmaxx()/2;
    y_c = getmaxy()/2;
    min = 1;
    size = 100;
    alm = als = MAXINT;
  }
    // displaying the stopwatch on the screen
    // and the seconds pointer movement
void watch::arrow(void)
{ struct arccoordstype a;
  int c;
  setcolor(7);
  setlinestyle(0,0,3);    // thick line
    // displaying the external circle of the watch
  circle(x_c,y_c,size);
  setlinestyle(0,0,0);    // normal line
    // displaying the numbers 0,5,10,...,55 around the dial
  for(int i=0;  i<=360;i+=6)
  { arc(x_c,y_c,90,90-i,size-25);
    getarccoords(&a);
    setcolor(5);
```

```
        // displaying a small circle to mark the point
        // on the dial a beep is to sound
    if(als*6 == i) circle(a.xend,a.yend,2);
    switch (i)
    { case 30:   outtextxy(a.xend+5,a.yend-10,"5");  break;
      case 60:   outtextxy(a.xend+3,a.yend-8,"10");  break;
      case 90:   outtextxy(a.xend+4,a.yend-4,"15");  break;
      case 120:  outtextxy(a.xend+3,a.yend,"20");  break;
      case 150:  outtextxy(a.xend+1,a.yend+4,"25");  break;
      case 180:  outtextxy(a.xend-7,a.yend+6,"30");  break;
      case 210:  outtextxy(a.xend-17,a.yend+4,"35");  break;
      case 240:  outtextxy(a.xend-22,a.yend,"40");  break;
      case 270:  outtextxy(a.xend-20,a.yend-4,"45");  break;
      case 300:  outtextxy(a.xend-17,a.yend-8,"50");  break;
      case 330:  outtextxy(a.xend-17,a.yend-10,"55");  break;
      case 360:  outtextxy(a.xend-2,a.yend-12,"0");
    };
    setcolor(0);
  }
  for(int  j=0;j<min;j++)
  {      // this loop controls the movement
         // of the seconds pointer
    for(i=0;  i<=360;i+=6)
    { arc(x_c,y_c,90,90-i,size-25);
      getarccoords(&a);
         // generating a beep sound
      if(j == alm && i == als*6) puts("\a");
      setcolor(3);
         // terminating the program by pressing the ESC key
      if(kbhit()) if((c = getch()) == ESC) break;
         // displaying the seconds pointer
      line(x_c,y_c,a.xend,a.yend);
         // delay for 1 second
      if(i !=360)delay(1000);
         // setting the background colour
      setcolor(0);
         // deleting the seconds pointer
      line(x_c,y_c,a.xend,a.yend);
    }
         //terminating the program after Esc key is pressed
    if(c == ESC) break;
  }
}
    //positioning the watch at the desired place on the screen
void watch::move_arrow(int x,int y)
{ x_c = x; y_c = y;  }
void main(void)
{ watch w1;
  int gd=DETECT,gm,er,x,y,m,s,ss,t;
  puts("Time of beep sound signal (minutes and seconds)?");
  scanf("%d%d",&m,&s);
  puts("The size of the watch in screen pixels?");
  scanf("%d",&ss);
```

```
puts("Number of minutes?");
scanf("%d",&t);
puts("Coordinates for displaying the watch(x,y)?");
scanf("%d%d",&x,&y);
puts("Press ESC to exit to DOS");
delay(300);
initgraph(&gd,&gm,"");
er = graphresult();
if (er != grOk)    // errors check
{ printf("Graphics error: %s\n",grapherrormsg(er));
  printf("Press any key");
  getch();
  exit(1);
}
w1.size_watch(ss);
w1.time_m(t);
w1.alarm(m,s);
w1.move_arrow(x,y);
w1.arrow();
closegraph();
}
```

The program results will be as follows:

**Time of beep sound signal (minutes and seconds)?**
*0 42<Enter>*
**The size of the watch in screen pixels?**
*150<Enter>*
**Number of minutes?**
*3<Enter>*
**Coordinates for displaying the watch(x,y)?**
*320 175<Enter>*
**Press ESC to exit to DOS**

If you enter input as above, you'll see the stopwatch displayed on the screen as shown in Figure 4.1. The time at which the beep signal will sound is marked on the perimeter of the watch by a large dot, which in Figure 4.1 is adjacent to the value 42.

Let us briefly review the new library functions that were used in the program. They are defined in the file **graphics.h** and you will find comprehensive details of their operation in your **Turbo C++** library reference manual.

The functions **getmaxx** and **getmaxy** have the prototypes:

```
int  far  getmaxx(void);
int  far  getmaxy(void);
```

They return the value of the horizontal and vertical screen size, respectively.

The function **setlinestyle** has the following prototype:

```
void  far  setlinestyle(int  l_s,unsigned  pat,int  thickness);
```

It defines the line style to be used when creating subsequent graphic entities. The parameter **l_s** determines the type of line to be drawn, with values 0, 1, 2 ,3 and 4 corresponding to solid, dotted, centre line, dashed line and user- defined line respectively. With **l_s** set to 4, **pat**  is a bit pattern defining line segments where a 1 bit corresponds to a pixel  on and a 0 bit to a pixel off. The parameter **thickness** defines the line width, 0 being normal width and 3 being thick lines.

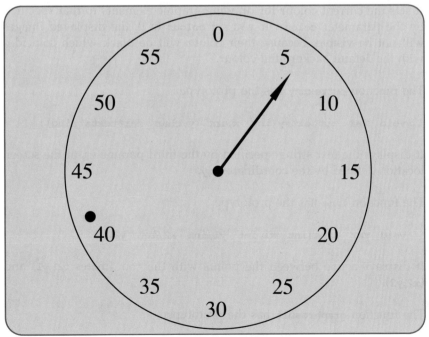

*Figure 4.1*
**The Stopwatch Display**

The function **getarccoords** has the prototype:

```
void far getarccoords(struct arccoordstype far *arccoords);
```

It returns a structure of type **arccoordstype**, with the coordinates of the last arc displayed using the function **arc**. The structure of type **arccoordstype** is presented in the form:

```
struct  arccoordstype
{ int  x,y;
   int  xstart,ystart,xend,yend;
};
```

In the example, **x** and **y** are the coordinates of the arc centre,  **xstart** and **ystart** are the coordinates of the arc start point  and   **xend** and **yend** are the coordinates of the arc end point.

The function **setcolor** has the prototype:

```
void far  setcolor(int  colour);
```

It sets the current colour for drawing graphic elements to that specified by the parameter **colour**. If you set **colour** to 0, the displayed images will not be visible, because their colour will be black which coincides with the default background colour.

The function **outtextxy** has the prototype:

```
void far  outtextxy(int  x,int  y,char  far*textstring);
```

It displays the text string specified by the third parameter, at the screen location defined by the coordinates **x,y**.

The function **line** has the prototype:

```
void far  line(int  x1,int  y1,int  x2,int  y2);
```

It displays a line between the points with the coordinates (**x1,y1**) and (**x2,y2**).

The function **graphresult** has the prototype:

```
int  far  graphresult(void);
```

It returns the error code for the last unsuccessful graphic operation. Otherwise, zero or the constant **grOk** is returned.

The function **grapherrormsg** has the prototype:

```
char *far grapherrormsg(int errorcode);
```

Depending on the specified error code, it returns a pointer to a text line consisting of an appropriate error message.

The function **circle** has the prototype:

```
void far circle(int x,int y,int r);
```

It draws a circle on the screen with radius **r**, and the centre at the point (**x,y**).

The function **arc** has the prototype:

```
void far arc(int x,int y,int stangle,int endangle,int r);
```

It draws an arc on the screen with radius **r** and the centre at the point (**x,y**). The parameter **stangle** is the arc start angle in degrees and **endangle** is the arc end angle. Positive angles are defined counterclockwise, with the horizontal at zero degrees. The arc is drawn anti-clockwise from the end point of the radius at **stangle**, to the end point of the radius at **endangle**.

Further explanation of the operation of the example is given in the comments within the source code.

# Menu Creating Program

## Example EX4_3

For all the examples given below, the file **conio.h** will be a basic standard include file. The first program draws a rectangle on the screen and lets you move and copy it:

```
/* example EX4_3 */                                              ***//
// *** THIS PART IS TO BE SAVED IN THE FILE RECT.H              ***//
#define Visible 1                                                   //
#define Nonvisible 0                                                //
#include <conio.h>                                                  //
#include <dos.h>                                                    //
//***********************************************/                  //
/* Keys on the numeric key pad for controlling       */            //
/*     movement of the rectangle:                     */           //
/*                                                    */            //
/*     left_up        up        right_up             */            //
/*                                                    */            //
/*                                                    */            //
/*     left                     right                */            //
/*                                                    */            //
/*                                                    */            //
/*     left_down     down       right_down           */            //
/*                                                    */            //
/***********************************************/                   //
enum  arrow_key                                                     //
   // setting symbolic names for specific keys                      //
{ CR=13, ESC=27, left_up=71, up=72, right_up=73, left=75,           //
   right=77, left_down=79, down=80, right_down=81 };                //
class Point                                                         //
{ int x,y;                                                          //
   public:                                                          //
   Point(int a, int b) { x=a; y=b; } // a constructor               //
   Point() { x=0; y=0; }          // another constructor that will  //
                                  // be used later in the program   //
   Point operator += (Point t)                                      //
   { return Point(x+=t.x,y+=t.y); }                                 //
   Point operator + (Point t)                                       //
   { return Point(x+t.x,y+t.y); }                                   //
   Point operator -= (Point t)                                      //
   { return Point(x-=t.x,y-=t.y); }                                 //
   Point operator - (Point t)                                       //
   { return Point(x-t.x,y-t.y); }                                   //
   int operator <= (Point t),                                       //
   { return x<=t.x && y<=t.y; }                                     //
   int operator < (Point t)                                         //
```

```
  { return x<t.x && y<t.y; }                             //
  int operator >= (Point t)                              //
  { return x>=t.x && y>=t.y; }                           //
  int operator > (Point t)                               //
  { return x>t.x && y>t.y; }                             //
  void putch(char ch) { gotoxy(x,y); ::putch(ch); }      //
/********************************************************/   //
/* These two functions are introduced for later use.   */   //
/* They return the coordinates x and y, respectively    */   //
/********************************************************/   //
  int get_x() { return x; }                              //
  int get_y() { return y; }                              //
};                                                       //
class Rect                                               //
{ protected:                                             //
  Point left_top, right_bot;                             //
  public:                                                //
  Rect(Point l_t, Point r_b)                             //
  { left_top = l_t;                                      //
    right_bot = r_b;                                     //
  }                                                      //
  void draw_hide(int d_h);                               //
  void Copy(Point NewL_T);                               //
  void MoveTo(Point NewL_T);                             //
  void Move();                                           //
};                                                       //
/************************************/                   //
/* The function draw_hide is defined */                 //
/************************************/                   //
void Rect::draw_hide(int d_h)                            //
// a rectangle is built from graphic characters          //
{ Point t=left_top;                                      //
  d_h ? t.putch(218) : t.putch(32);      // 32 - space code //
  for(t+=Point(1,0);t<right_bot;t+=Point(1,0))           //
  d_h ? t.putch(196) : t.putch(32);                      //
  d_h ? t.putch(191) : t.putch(32);                      //
  for(t+=Point(0,1);t<(right_bot+Point(1,0));t+=Point(0,1)) //
  d_h ? t.putch(179) : t.putch(32);                      //
  d_h ? t.putch(217) : t.putch(32);                      //
  for(t-=Point(1,0);t>left_top;t-=Point(1,0))            //
  d_h ? t.putch(196) : t.putch(32);                      //
  d_h ? t.putch(192) : t.putch(32);                      //
  for(t-=Point(0,1);t>(left_top-Point(1,0));t-=Point(0,1)) //
  d_h ? t.putch(179) : t.putch(32);                      //
}                                                        //
/*****************************/                          //
/* The function Copy is defined */                       //
/*****************************/                           //
void Rect::Copy(Point NewL_T)                            //
{ right_bot += (NewL_T - left_top);                      //
  left_top = NewL_T;                                     //
  draw_hide(Visible);                                    //
}                                                        //
```

```
/**********************************/                           //
/* The function MoveTo is defined */                          //
/**********************************/                           //
void Rect::MoveTo(Point NewL_T)                               //
{ draw_hide(Nonvisible);                                      //
  right_bot += (NewL_T - left_top);                           //
  left_top = NewL_T;                                          //
  draw_hide(Visible);                                         //
}                                                             //
inline int get_key()                                          //
{ unsigned char ch = 0;                                       //
  if (!(ch=getch())) ch = getch();                            //
  return(ch);                                                 //
}                                                             //
/**********************************/                           //
/* The function Move is defined */                            //
/**********************************/                           //
void Rect::Move()                                             //
{ unsigned char my_key;                                       //
  //The loop will execute until ESC is pressed                //
  while((my_key=get_key())!=ESC)                              //
  { Point Init = left_top;                                    //
  /********************************************************/   //
  /* The next four lines position the watch in the    */      //
  /* centre of the screen if it strikes any screen    */      //
  /*   border whilst being moved                      */      //
  /********************************************************/   //
    if (!(left_top>Point(1,1)))                               //
    { MoveTo(Point(35,10)); continue; }                       //
    if (!(right_bot<Point(80,25)))                            //
    { MoveTo(Point(35,10)); continue; }                       //
  /********************************************************/   //
  /*    The rectangle can move in vertical, horizontal, */    //
  /*    and diagonal directions                      */       //
  /********************************************************/   //
    if (my_key == up) MoveTo(Init+=Point(0,-1));              //
    else                                                      //
    if (my_key == left) MoveTo(Init+=Point(-1,0));            //
    else                                                      //
    if (my_key == down) MoveTo(Init+=Point(0,1));             //
    else                                                      //
    if (my_key == right) MoveTo(Init+=Point(1,0));            //
    else                                                      //
    if (my_key == left_up) MoveTo(Init+=Point(-1,-1));        //
    else                                                      //
    if (my_key == left_down) MoveTo(Init+=Point(-1,1));       //
    else                                                      //
    if (my_key == right_down) MoveTo(Init+=Point(1,1));       //
    else                                                      //
    if (my_key == right_up) MoveTo(Init+=Point(1,-1));        //
    delay(15);                                                //
    } // the end of the while loop                            //
}                                                             //
// ***************************************************** *****//
```

```
void main()
{ clrscr();
Rect my_rect(Point(10,10),Point(15,15));
my_rect.draw_hide(Visible);     // building a rectangle
getch();                        // wait until any key is pressed
my_rect.Copy(Point(50,10));     // copying a rectangle
my_rect.Move();                 // moving a rectangle until
                                // the ESC key is pressed
clrscr();                       // clearing the screen
}
```

Let's review the classes we are using in this example.

The class **Point** includes a function for displaying characters at a specified coordinate position and of course the constructors which define coordinate positions. It also includes the operators +=, +, -=,-, <=, <, >=, > overloaded for use with objects of the class **Point**.

The class **Rect** includes the functions for displaying or hiding a rectangle (**draw_hide**), copying it to a different position on the screen (**Copy**), moving it to a different position on the screen (**MoveTo**, or moving it using the arrow keys (**Move**).

You need to take note of the part of the program highlighted with terminating pairs of slashes. Since we are going to use it in subsequent examples, it should be saved in a file named **RECT.H**. Before saving it you should insert the following preprocessor directives preceding the lines of code marked with **//** :

**#if  !define  (_RECT_)**
**#define  _RECT_**

and immediately after the marked code, the directive:

**#endif**

This will ensure that only one copy is compiled in any program including this block of code, even if it occurs more than once.

When you start running the program you'll see a rectangle on the screen. Press any key to copy it to any other place on the screen. Now you can move it on the screen using the keys on the numeric keypad shown at the beginning of the program. If you move a rectangle such that it touches the screen border, it will jump back to the centre of the screen. The program terminates as soon as you press the *ESC* key.

Let's discuss the new library functions used in the program. They are defined in the file **conio.h**. The function **gotoxy** has the prototype:

```
void gotoxy(int  x,int  y);
```

It positions the cursor at the screen coordinate position (**x,y**) in the current text window.

The function **putch** has the prototype:

```
int  putch(int  c);
```

It outputs the character **c** to the cursor position in the current text window. The character **c** is returned at a successful termination, otherwise the constant **EOF** is returned. In the program, the function **putch** is used extensively to output graphic characters to the screen:

**putch(218)** - output of the character     ⌐
**putch(196)** - output of the character     –
**putch(191)** - output of the character     ¬
**putch(179)** - output of the character     |
**putch(217)** - output of the character     ⌟
**putch(192)** - output of the character     L

The function **clrscr** has the following prototype:

```
void  clrscr(void);
```

It clears the current text window.

We now need to consider an additional aspect of the operation of the function **getch** that we have not discussed previously. If the first call to **getch** returns a null, the second call to **getch** returns what is called the extended **ASCII-code** of the key pressed. Use of this facility is necessary for analysing the status of the arrow keys on the numeric keypad: 71 - left_up, 72 - up, 73 - right_up, 75 - left, 77 - right, 79 - left_down, 80 - down, 81 - right_down. The key nomenclature here is as we have used in the program.

## Example EX4_4

The next program example, EX4_4, introduces a new class **Window** that is
derived from the class **Rect**:

```
/* example EX4_4 */
#include "rect.h"
#include <process.h>
#include <iostream.h>
//*** THIS PART IS TO BE SAVED IN THE FILE WINDOW.H ********/      //
/*********************************************************/      //
/* Derived class Window is derived from a base class     */  //
/* Rect with an attribute public. As a result, the base  */  //
/* class members with the attributes public and protected */  //
/* become the members with the same attributes in the    */  //
/* derived class. Private members of the base class       */  //
/* are not accessible in the derived class.               */  //
/*********************************************************/      //
class Window : public Rect                                      //
{ char *mem;          // a pointer to the memory region         //
                      // for saving the text                    //
  Point cur_place;  // a pointer to the cursor position         //
  public:                                                       //
  Window(Point lt, Point rb);         // creating a window      //
  void w_save();        // saving the cursor coordinates and    //
                        // position of the text in a window     //
  void w_restore();   // restoring the saved cursor             //
                        // and text in a window                 //
  void w_open();        // window opening function              //
  void set_window();  // window setting function                //
  void my_text(char *text) { cputs(text); }                     //
                // a function for text output in a window       //
  void w_Copy(Point NewL_T);     // similar to function Copy    //
  void w_MoveTo(Point NewL_T); // similar to function MoveTo     //
  void w_Move(Window scr);       // Similar to function Move     //
};                                                              //
/*********************************************************/      //
/* Window setting. The library function window from the  */  //
/*              conio.h is used                          */  //
/*********************************************************/      //
void Window::set_window()                                       //
{ window(left_top.get_x()+1,left_top.get_y()+1,                 //
    right_bot.get_x()-1,right_bot.get_y()-1);                   //
}                                                               //
/*********************************************************/      //
/* Function that sets a window to the whole screen       */  //
/* (a mode of 25 lines with 80 characters each is set) */  //
/*********************************************************/      //
inline void hole_scr() {   window(1,1,80,25); }                 //
/*********************************************************/      //
```

```
/* The function w_save saves the cursor coordinates and */    //
/*     the window text in RAM                           */    //
/***********************************************************/   //
void Window::w_save()                                          //
{ cur_place = Point(wherex(),wherey());                        //
          // saving the cursor coordinates                     //
  gettext(left_top.get_x(),left_top.get_y(),                   //
  right_bot.get_x(),right_bot.get_y(),mem);                    //
      // saving the window text by using                       //
      // the library function gettext                          //
}                                                              //
/***********************************************************/   //
/* The function restore, restores the saved cursor and  */    //
/*                  the text in the window              */    //
/***********************************************************/   //
void Window::w_restore()                                       //
{ puttext(left_top.get_x(),left_top.get_y(),                   //
  right_bot.get_x(),right_bot.get_y(), mem);                   //
      // restoring the text in the window                      //
      // by using the library function puttext                 //
  gotoxy(cur_place.get_x(),cur_place.get_y());                 //
      // restoring the cursor position                         //
}                                                              //
/**************************************/                        //
/* The function w_open opens a window */                       //
/**************************************/                        //
void Window::w_open()                                          //
{ set_window(); clrscr();                                      //
  hole_scr();      draw_hide(Visible);                         //
  set_window(); w_save();                                      //
}                                                              //
/***********************************************************/   //
/* The function Window creates a window.It first builds */     //
/* a rectangle, the cursor moves to its left corner and */     //
/* memory is allocated for storing text in the window    */    //
/***********************************************************/   //
Window::Window(Point lt,Point rb)  : Rect(lt,rb)               //
{ cur_place = lt + Point(1,1); // placing the cursor at        //
      // the top left corner of a rectangle                    //
  Point for_mem = rb - lt;                                     //
      // defining the size of a rectangle                      //
  int l_r = for_mem.get_x() + 1;  // l_r - width                //
  int t_b = for_mem.get_y() + 1;  // t_b - height               //
/*********************************************/                 //
/* The operator new allocates the memory       */               //
/*********************************************/                 //
  mem = new char [l_r * t_b * 2]; // mem - a pointer to         //
  if(mem == NULL) {   cout << '\a'; exit(1);   }               //
  // memory region for saving the text inside the rectangle    //
}                                                              //
/********************************************************/      //
/* Similar to the function Copy in the file rect.h */          //
/********************************************************/      //
```

```
void Window::w_Copy(Point NewL_T)                          //
{ w_save();            // saving the image                 //
  Copy(NewL_T);        // copying a rectangle              //
  cur_place = NewL_T + Point(1,1); // moving the cursor    //
  w_restore();         // copying the saved image          //
}                                                          //
/*********************************************************/ //
/* Similar to the function MoveTo in the file rect.h */    //
/*********************************************************/ //
void Window::w_MoveTo(Point NewL_T)                        //
{ w_save();            // saving the image                 //
  set_window();                                            //
  clrscr();            // clearing the old image from the screen //
  hole_scr();                                              //
  MoveTo(NewL_T);  // moving the rectangle                 //
  cur_place = NewL_T + Point(1,1);   // moving the cursor  //
  w_restore();     // restoring the saved image            //
}                                                          //
/***********************************************************/ //
/* Similar to the function Move in the file rect.h. This */ //
/* function is additionally assigned the object scr of   */ //
/* type Window that contains screen image that will      */ //
/*       serve as a background for the window movements  */ //
/***********************************************************/ //
void Window::w_Move(Window scr)                            //
{ unsigned char my_key;                                    //
  w_save();                                                //
  while((my_key=get_key())!=ESC)                           //
  { Point Init = left_top;                                 //
    w_save();                         // saving the image  //
    if (!(left_top>Point(1,1)))                            //
    { w_MoveTo(Point(35,10)); goto cont; }                //
    if (!(right_bot<Point(80,24)))                         //
    { w_MoveTo(Point(35,10)); goto cont; }                //
    if (my_key == up) MoveTo(Init+=Point(0,-1));           //
    else                                                   //
    if (my_key == left) MoveTo(Init+=Point(-1,0));         //
    else                                                   //
    if (my_key == down) MoveTo(Init+=Point(0,1));          //
    else                                                   //
    if (my_key == right) MoveTo(Init+=Point(1,0));         //
    else                                                   //
    if (my_key == left_up) MoveTo(Init+=Point(-1,-1));     //
    else                                                   //
    if (my_key == left_down) MoveTo(Init+=Point(-1,1));    //
    else                                                   //
    if (my_key == right_down) MoveTo(Init+=Point(1,1));    //
    else                                                   //
    if (my_key == right_up) MoveTo(Init+=Point(1,-1));     //
    delay(15);                                             //
    cur_place = left_top + Point(1,1);                     //
                    // restoring the cursor position       //
    cont:    scr.w_restore();                              //
```

```
        w_restore();// restoring the image              //
   }         // end of the while loop                   //
   w_restore();                                         //
}                                                       //
// ********************************************************//
void main()
{ clrscr();
  Window my_w(Point(10,10),Point(27,16));
  my_w.w_open();                    // opening the window
  my_w.my_text("   Demonstration "); gotoxy(1,2);
  my_w.my_text("        MoveTo         "); gotoxy(1,3);
  my_w.my_text("   Press      any "); gotoxy(1,4);
  my_w.my_text("          key        ");
  getch();
  clrscr();
  my_w.w_MoveTo(Point(1,1));// moving the window
  my_w.set_window();
  my_w.my_text("   Demonstration "); gotoxy(1,2);
  my_w.my_text("          Copy        "); gotoxy(1,3);
  my_w.my_text(" Press        any     "); gotoxy(1,4);
  my_w.my_text("          key        ");
  getch();
  hole_scr();
  my_w.w_Copy(Point(50,5));         // copying the window
  getch();
  Window scr(Point(1,1),Point(80,25));    // saving the image
  scr.w_save();                     // that will serve as a background
                                    // when moving the window
  my_w.set_window();
  my_w.my_text("   Demonstration "); gotoxy(1,2);
  my_w.my_text("          Move        "); gotoxy(1,3);
  my_w.my_text("   Press        ESC "); gotoxy(1,4);
  my_w.my_text("    to exit        ");
  hole_scr();
  my_w.w_Move(scr);                 // moving the window by using
                                    // the arrow keys

  clrscr();
}
```

Because we will be using it in a subsequent example, the part of the
program marked with **//** needs to be saved in a new file   **WINDOW.H**. As
with the previous example, in order to prevent the possibility of duplicate
copies of the code being included in the compilation, you should add the
following lines before the code marked with **//** :

```
#if !define (_WINDOW_)
#define _WINDOW_
```

and at the end of the marked code, you should add the line:

**#endif**.

A description of the new class **Window**, and the functions it contains, is given in the program comments. When you start running the program you'll see on the screen a window with the text:

**Demonstration MoveTo Press any key**

Pressing any key will move the window to another part of the screen and new text will be displayed:

**Demonstration Copy Press any key**

A further depression of any key copies the window with the text to another part of the screen. If you then press any key, the window will display the text:

**Demonstration Move Press ESC to exit**

Now you can move the new window using the arrow keys as described in the program EX4_3. To terminate the program, press **ESC**.

Let's have a quick look at the new library functions used in this program. They are defined in the file **conio.h**.

The function **window** has the prototype:

```
void window(int left,int top,int right,int bottom);
```

It sets a text window defined by the (x,y) coordinates of its upper left and bottom right corners.

The functions **wherex** and **wherey** have the following prototypes:

```
int wherex(void);
int wherey(void);
```

They return the horizontal and vertical positions of the cursor, respectively.

The function **gettext** has the prototype:

```
int gettext(int left,int top,
int right,int bottom,void *mem);
```

It copies the text from the defined window to the memory region pointed to
by the variable **mem**.

The function **puttext** has the prototype:

```
    int  puttext (int  left, int  top, int  right, int  bottom, void
*mem) ;
```

It copies the text from the memory region pointed to by the variable **mem** to
the defined window.

## Example EX4_5

The program EX4_5 demonstrates some useful mechanisms for handling
lists.

```
  /* example EX4_5 */
#include <conio.h>
#include <process.h>
#include <iostream.h>
inline int get_key()
{ unsigned char ch = 0;
  if (!(ch=getch())) ch = getch();
  return(ch);
}
enum arrow_key
{ CR=13, ESC=27, left_up=71, up=72, right_up=73, left=75,
  right=77, left_down=79, down=80, right_down=81 };
// *** THIS PART IS TO BE SAVED IN THE FILE LIST.H ****        //
#include <string.h>                                           //
/**********************************************************/    //
/* The function on_light causes the inverse text image */      //
/**********************************************************/    //
inline void on_light() { textattr(0x70); }                     //
/**********************************************************/    //
/* The function off_light cancels the inverse image    */      //
/* of the text (sets it to normal mode)                */      //
/**********************************************************/    //
inline void off_light() { textattr(0x07); }                    //
/**********************************************************/    //
/* The class New_Element allows you to add new elements, */    //
/*    and delete existing elements from the list        */     //
/**********************************************************/    //
class New_Element                                              //
{ public:                                                      //
  char *str; //a list element - a pointer to string            //
  New_Element *next__;// a list element -                      //
```

```
                            // a pointer to the next list element    //
   New_Element *__prev; // a list element -                          //
                            // a pointer to a previous list element   //
   New_Element(char *s) // a constructor that                        //
      // allocates memory for storing a new element                  //
   { str=new char[strlen(s)+1];                                      //
      if(str == NULL) {   cout << '\a';   exit(1);}                  //
      strcpy(str,s);                                                 //
   }                                                                 //
   ~New_Element() { delete str; } //  a destructor                  //
      // deallocates memory for an element                           //
   void my_text() { cputs(str); } // text output function           //
};                                                                  //
/*************************************************************/       //
/* The class List allows you to carry out a variety      */          //
/*         of operations on the list                     */          //
/*************************************************************/       //
class List                                                          //
{ int counter;         // number of elements in the list            //
   int current_str;     // current line number                      //
   New_Element *head;  // a pointer to the line start               //
   public:                                                          //
   //constructor assigns initial values to the list elements        //
   List() { head=0; counter=current_str=0; }                        //
   void add(char *s);           // adding elements to the list      //
   void pr_list(int shift);  // displaying the                      //
                                // list elements on the screen       //
   New_Element* first() { return head; }                           //
      // the function first, returns a pointer to the first         //
      // element in the list                                        //
   int l_choice(int shift);                                        //
      // the function l_choice returns the position number          //
      // of the list element selected in the function              //
      // (shift - the position number of the line on the           //
      // screen from which the list will be displayed              //
};                                                                 //
/*************************************************************/       //
/* The function add, adds an object to the class List.   */          //
/* One of this object's fields will point to the string s*/          //
/* The list is held as a ring structure. Thus each object*/          //
/* contains pointers to the next and preceding list       */         //
/* members. If the list has only one member, the next    */          //
/* member, and the previous member, is itself.           */          //
/*************************************************************/       //
void List::add(char *s)                                            //
{ New_Element *temp = new New_Element(s);                          //
   if(temp == NULL) {   cout << '\a'; exit(1);   }                 //
      // The previous statements allocates memory for a new         //
      // element of the list.                                       //
// temp - is a pointer to the new element                          //
if(head)                                                           //
// If head is not 0, THE LIST CONTAINS ELEMENTS.                   //
   { temp->next__=head;                                            //
```

```
// For the last element in the list, the next element        //
// is the first list element, which is pointed to by head    //
   temp->__prev=head->__prev;                                 //
// the last element is the previous element for the          //
// first element of the ring structure.                      //
// That is why head->__prev pointed to the last element      //
// before a new element is added. When a new element is      //
// added, the previous to it will be the element pointed     //
// to by head->__prev                                        //
   head->__prev->next__=temp;                                 //
// the pointer next__ for the element that was previously    //
// the last, must now point to the new element, so we        //
// set it to the value of temp                               //
   head->__prev=temp;                                         //
// the pointer __prev of the first element, must now         //
// point to our new last element, so we set it to temp       //
  }                                                           //
// IF head - 0, THE LIST IS EMPTY                             //
// Our new element will become the first, and the last       //
// element. Both next__ and prev__ pointers will be          //
// set to temp, as will the pointer head                     //
  else                                                        //
  { temp->__prev=temp;                                        //
    temp->next__=temp;                                        //
    head=temp;                                                //
  };   counter++;                                             //
     // the count of list elements will increase by 1        //
}                                                             //
/***********************************************************/ //
/* The function pr_list displays on the screen all the    */ //
/* list elements (the parameter shift indicates the       */ //
/* horizontal screen position from which it is            */ //
/* to be displayed                                        */ //
/***********************************************************/ //
void List::pr_list(int shift)                                 //
{ New_Element *pf = first();                                  //
// pf - a pointer to the first element in the list            //
  for(int i=0;i<counter;i++,pf=pf->next__)                    //
// In the for loop, pf will point successively                //
// to each of the elements in the list.                       //
// The cursor will be positioned horizontally                 //
// determined by shift, and stepped down one line for         //
// each successive element to be displayed                    //
  { gotoxy(shift,i+1);                                        //
// a selected line is highlighted                             //
    if(i==current_str)                                        //
    on_light(); else off_light();                             //
    pf->my_text();                                            //
// the function my_text outputs to the screen,                //
// a line for the next element in the list                    //
  }                                                           //
}                                                             //
/***********************************************************/ //
```

```
/* The function l_choice causes different actions when    */    //
/* you press the keys ESC, CR - Enter, down - down arrow,*/     //
/*              and up - up arrow                        */     //
/***********************************************************/    //
int List::l_choice(int shift)                                   //
{ pr_list(shift);                                               //
// display the list elements at position shift                  //
  for(;;) // an endless loop                                    //
  { switch(get_key())                                           //
// get_key returns the code of the key pressed button           //
    { case ESC : return -1;                                     //
//    if ESC is pressed, the value of -1 is returned            //
      case CR  : return current_str;                            //
// if CR is pressed, the current string number is returned      //
      case down:                                                //
// if the down key is pressed, increment the current string     //
// number, current_str, to the next string                      //
        if(++current_str>=counter)                              //
// The next string after the last, is the first string...       //
        current_str=0;                                          //
        pr_list(shift);                                         //
// for moving the highlighted string, all are redisplayed       //
        break;                                                  //
      case up:                                                  //
// for up, analogous actions to down are carried out            //
        if(-current_str<0)                                      //
        current_str=counter-1;                                  //
        pr_list(shift);                                         //
        break;                                                  //
    }                                                           //
  }                                                             //
}                                                               //
// ********************************************************     //
void main()
{ clrscr();
  List my_list;              // the object my_list is of type list
  gotoxy(30,10); cputs("Press ESC to exit");
  my_list.add("Minsk");  // a four-element list is
  my_list.add("Moscow"); // being created
  my_list.add("Kiev");
  my_list.add("Riga");
  while(my_list.l_choice(10)!=-1); // press ESC to exit
}
```

Figure 4.2 illustrates how a list is structured in this example. Given the list is as we have constructed in our example, let us suppose the second element, **Moscow**, is active in the displayed list. If you press the up arrow key, the value in the field **__prev** will tell you that you must go to the first element which is the word **Minsk**.

In the same manner, pressing the down arrow key will result in transition from the word **Moscow** to the word **Kiev**. If you press the down arrow key once again, a transition to the word **Minsk** will occur. Such a mechanism can be useful for choosing and making active items of a menu on the screen. The part of the program marked with **//** should be saved in a file called **LIST.H** for use in the next example. As before you need to insert the following, preceding the marked lines of code:

```
#if  !define  (_LIST_)
define  _LIST_
```

and at the end of the marked code, the line:

```
#endif.
```

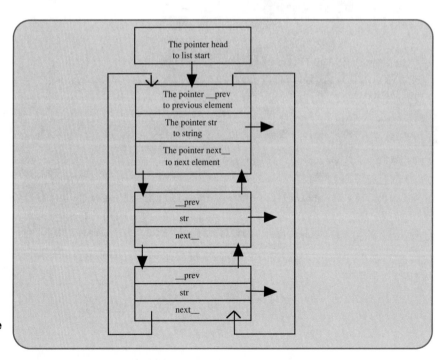

*Figure 4.2*
**The Structure
of the List**

## Example EX4_6

The program EX4_6 uses all the previous examples in this section (**rect.h**, **window.h**, and **list.h**). It also introduces a new class **Menu**:

```
/* example EX4_6 */
#include <string.h>
#include "rect.h"
#include "window.h"
#include "list.h"
class Menu                    // Class Menu
{ List ll;                    // ll - a list for a menu
  Point left_top;             // left_top - the coordinates of the
                              // upper left corner of a menu
  public:
    Menu() { }                    // constructor
    Menu(Point p) { left_top=p; }          // constructor
    void add(char *s) { ll.add(s); }    // adding an element
    int m_choice();                      // for choosing a menu
    Window make_window(Window w);        // making a menu window
    void show_window(Window w) { w.w_restore(); }
          // the show_window function shows a created window
};
/******************************************************/
/* The function m_choice returns an integer, connected     */
/* with a menu number, chosen by the function ll.l_choice */
/*     (here the possible integers can be from  -1 to 4)  */
/******************************************************/
int Menu::m_choice()
{ return ll.l_choice(2);      // an integer value from -1 to 4
}                             // is returned
/******************************************************/
/* The  function  make_window  saves  the  whole  screen, */
/* creates a prompt line, opens a window received as a     */
/* parameter, lets you to type in some text and move it    */
/*       to any desired position on the screen             */
/******************************************************/
Window Menu::make_window(Window w)
{ char c;
  Window scr(Point(1,1),Point(80,24));
  scr.w_save(); // saving the screen before displaying a window
  gotoxy(1,25); cputs("ESC - the end of input");
  w.w_open();    // opening a window
  cputs("     Enter some text"); gotoxy(1,2);
  cputs("   (ESC  - the end of input)");
  gotoxy(1,3);
  while((c = getch())!=ESC)
  putch(c);      // input and display of text
  hole_scr();
  gotoxy(1,25); cputs("ESC - stop moving a window");
```

```
   w.w_Move(scr);     // moving a window
   return(w);         // a created window is returned
}
void main()
{ clrscr();
  Point left_top;    // a point for the upper left corner
                     // of a main menu
     int l,t;        // the coordinates of the upper left
                     // corner of a main menu
   Menu m1, m2, m3, m4;
   Window w1(Point(48,13),Point(78,23)),
   w2(Point(48,13),Point(78,23)),
   w3(Point(48,13),Point(78,23)),
   w4(Point(48,13),Point(78,23));
   w1=m1.make_window(w1);   //     creating
   w2=m2.make_window(w2);   //     four windows
   w3=m3.make_window(w3);   //     in a
   w4=m4.make_window(w4);   //     menu
   hole_scr();
   gotoxy(1,25); cputs("Assign the menu coordinates (x and y)? ");
   cscanf("%d%d",&l,&t);  // input the menu coordinates
   left_top = Point(l,t);
   delline();              //deleting the bottom line of the screen
   gotoxy(1,25); cputs("ESC - program termination");
   Menu mm(left_top);     // creating a main menu mm
   mm.add("Window 1");    // these lines
   mm.add("Window 2");    // select
   mm.add("Window 3");    // one of
   mm.add("Window 4");    // the menus
   mm.add("Exit");
   Window w(left_top,left_top+Point(10,6));
   w.w_open();
   int no_exit = 1;
   while(no_exit)          // choosing an active menu
   { switch(mm.m_choice())
               // m_choice returns integer value from -1 to 4
     { case 0 : m1.show_window(w1); break; // window 1
       case 1 : m2.show_window(w2); break; // window 2
       case 2 : m3.show_window(w3); break; // window 3
       case 3 : m4.show_window(w4); break; // window 4
       case -1:      // ESC key is pressed
       case 4 : no_exit = 0; break;
         // the fifth string, "Exit", is chosen
     }
   }
   off_light();    // restoring
   hole_scr();     // and clearing
   clrscr();       // the whole screen
}
```

When you start running the program, you'll see a window on the screen. You can type in any text you like. After pressing *Esc* you can move the window around on the screen using the arrow keys. They are shown in the comments in the program code we included from the file **RECT.H**. Pressing *Esc* once again will display a new window on the screen. Similar actions may be carried out until a prompt appears on the screen:

**Assign the menu coordinates (x and y)?**

Enter any coordinates, for example:

*60 15<Enter>*

The menu rectangle will appear on the screen. Only one line of the menu will be highlighted. Using the arrows keys, you can choose a new line from the menu. Pressing *<Enter>* will activate on the screen a rectangular window, containing the text corresponding to the highlighted line. Press *Esc*, or choose the line Exit, to quit the program. Figure 4.3 illustrates one possible set of window positions on the screen.

We have used another new library function, **delline**, in the program. It is defined in the file **conio.h** and has the prototype:

```
void  delline(void);
```

This function deletes the line of text in the text window in which the cursor is positioned.

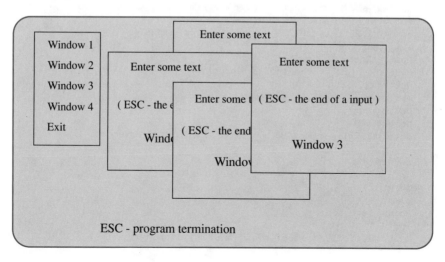

*Figure 4.3*
**Displaying Windows**

## Example EX4_7

Let's modify the program EX4_6 in order to display a reference book on the screen organised alphabetically. In this case, the menu will contain the letters from A to Z. As a result, you can choose any letter and activate the corresponding page of the reference book. You can write any desired information in the page. You could enter names and telephone numbers for example.

```
/* example EX4_7 */
#include <iostream.h>
#include <string.h>
#include "rect.h"
#include "window.h"
#include "list.h"
class Menu
{ List ll;
  Point left_top;
  public:
    Menu() {  }
    Menu(Point p) {  left_top=p;  }
    void add(char *s) {  ll.add(s);  }
    int m_choice();
    Window make_window(Window w);
    void show_window(Window w) {  w.w_restore();  }
};
int Menu::m_choice()
{ return ll.l_choice(2);    }
Window Menu::make_window(Window w)
{ char c;
  Window scr(Point(1,1),Point(80,24));
  scr.w_save();
  gotoxy(1,25); cputs("ESC - the end of input");
  w.w_open();
  cputs("Enter a text"); gotoxy(1,2);
  cputs("   (ESC - the end of input)");
  gotoxy(1,3);
  while((c = getch())!=ESC)
  putch(c);
  hole_scr();
  gotoxy(1,25); cputs("ESC - stop the window movements");
  w.w_Move(scr);
  return(w);
}
void main()
{ clrscr();
  Point left_top;
  int l,t;
  Menu m1,m2,m3,m4,m5,m6,m7,m8,m9,m10,m11,m12,m13;
```

```
Window w1(Point(1,1),Point(31,11)),
  w2(Point(2,2),Point(32,12)),
  w3(Point(3,3),Point(33,13)),
  w4(Point(4,4),Point(34,14)),
  w5(Point(5,5),Point(35,15)),
  w6(Point(6,6),Point(36,16)),
  w7(Point(7,7),Point(37,17)),
  w8(Point(8,8),Point(38,18)),
  w9(Point(9,9),Point(39,19)),
  w10(Point(10,10),Point(40,20)),
  w11(Point(11,11),Point(41,21)),
  w12(Point(12,12),Point(42,22)),
  w13(Point(13,13),Point(43,23));
w1=m1.make_window(w1);
w2=m2.make_window(w2);
w3=m3.make_window(w3);
w4=m4.make_window(w4);
w5=m5.make_window(w5);
w6=m6.make_window(w6);
w7=m7.make_window(w7);
w8=m8.make_window(w8);
w9=m9.make_window(w9);
w10=m10.make_window(w10);
w11=m11.make_window(w11);
w12=m12.make_window(w12);
w13=m13.make_window(w13);
hole_scr();
left_top = Point(70,1);
gotoxy(1,25); cputs("ESC - the program termination");
Menu mm(left_top);      // creating a main menu
mm.add("A - B");
mm.add("C - D");
mm.add("E - F");
mm.add("G - H");
mm.add("I - J");
mm.add("K - L");
mm.add("M - N");
mm.add("O - P");
mm.add("Q - R");
mm.add("S - T");
mm.add("U - V");
mm.add("W - X");
mm.add("Y - Z");
mm.add("Exit");
Window w(left_top,left_top+Point(10,15));
w.w_open();
int no_exit = 1;
while(no_exit)
{ switch(mm.m_choice())
  { case 0   :  m1.show_window(w1); break;
    case 1   :  m2.show_window(w2); break;
    case 2   :  m3.show_window(w3); break;
    case 3   :  m4.show_window(w4); break;
```

```
        case  4   :  m1.show_window(w5);  break;
        case  5   :  m2.show_window(w6);  break;
        case  6   :  m3.show_window(w7);  break;
        case  7   :  m4.show_window(w8);  break;
        case  8   :  m1.show_window(w9);  break;
        case  9   :  m2.show_window(w10);  break;
        case 10  :  m3.show_window(w11);  break;
        case 11  :  m4.show_window(w12);  break;
        case 12  :  m4.show_window(w13);  break;
        case -1:
        case 13  :  no_exit = 0;  break;
    }
  }
  off_light();
  hole_scr();
  clrscr();
}
```

When you start running the program, the reference book pages will appear on the screen in succession. All in all there should be 13 pages. You can write any information you wish in the page, and move it to any position on the screen. Press the *Esc* key to list the pages. The pages overlap in the left part of the screen. After the last page, a menu appears in the right part of the screen. As far as other details of the program operation are concerned, they are similar to those of the program EX4_6.

## *Displaying and Using a Calculator*

Lastly, we would like to present you with an example which should provide a real test of how well you understand **C++**. It should also provide some fun in looking at how it works.

The program simulates a pocket calculator. The listing appears at the end of this chapter. It comprises three modules, two **include** files **BUTTON.H** and **CALC.H** and the file **EX4_9.CPP**. To run the program simply open the file **EX4_9.CPP** in the **IDE** and run it. The calculator is operated using the numeric keys and . to enter numbers and +, -, *, and / for add, subtract multiply and divide. The = key or *<Enter>* evaluates a result. The *Tab* key will change the sign of the displayed value. To terminate operation of the program press the *Esc* key. You will see that it operates in quite a realistic fashion. As each key is pressed there are visual and audible cues to the key operation. There is no operator precedence but you can enter repeated operations such as 3+4*5. The result in this case will be 35 since the addition is performed as soon as the second operator is keyed.

The program was written by a group of graduate students as an entertaining exercise in **C++**. It makes extensive use of classes as well as the graphics library routines available with **Turbo C++**. Whilst the program consists of quite a lot of code, its organisation is relatively simple. The primary program file, `EX4_9.CPP`, brings in the `include` file `CALC.H`, which in turn brings in the `include` file `BUTTON.H`. As well as the function `main()` and a function `calcdemo`, `EX4_9.CPP` also contains the definitions of the member functions of the class `Calc`.

`BUTTON.H` is very straightforward. It contains the class `Button` and its member functions. Objects of the class `Button` are the physical keys of the calculator displayed on the screen. The member functions of the class `Button` display a `Button` object and provide for displaying a `Button` object in pressed and released states.

The include file `CALC.H` defines three classes, `Operand`, `Indicator` and `Calc`. The class `Operand` defines the operands of the calculator. The numeric input is processed by a member function of this class corresponding to the overloaded operator <<. The arithmetic operators +, -, *, / and the = operator are also overloaded for use with `Operand` objects. The class `Indicator` corresponds to the display on the calculator and is a base class for the class `Calc`. The function `Display` in the class `Indicator` will display `Operand` objects.

If you have any difficulty in following the operation of any of these examples, try running them with some tracing of the program operation using Debug in the **IDE**. You can also refer back to the tutorial program for any concepts you feel unsure about. If, on the other hand, you find them quite easy, you could try extending them in various ways. The last example simulating a calculator could be extended by adding memory functions. You could also add functionality to handle operator precedence and parentheses. If you can do that, you can be sure you are really quite proficient in Object Oriented Programming with **C++**. We wish you the best of luck!

```
/*          File BUTTON.H      */
/***********************************************/
/* This include file contains the class Button */
/* and its member functions. The objects of    */
/* the class Button are the keys on a          */
/* calculator.                                 */
/***********************************************/


#ifndef __BUTTON_H__
#define __BUTTON_H__

#define Color      15
#define TextColor  0
#define ShColor    7
#define BordColor  0
#define DeskColor  15

class Button {
    int    x;        // coordinated for
    int    y;        // position of key
    int    xx;       // Key width
    int    yy;       // Key height
    int    xt;       // Coordinates for annotation
    int    yt;       // on a key
    char * text;     // Annotation for a key

    int flag;        // Key state indicator
    int    color;
    int    shcolor;
    int    textcolor;
  public:
    Button( int width , int high , char * name="" //constructor
       int color=Color , int shcolor=ShColor ,
       int tcolor=TextColor );
    void Show( int x , int y );                  // Display key
    void Press (void);                           // Depress key
    void Unpress (void);                         // Release key
    void put_text(int x,int y);
    void text_press(void)  {put_text(xt+1,yt+1);}
    void text_unpress(void)  {put_text(xt,yt);}
};

Button::Button( int width , int high ,
    char * name , int bcolor , int scolor , int tcolor )
{                        // Constructor for Button object (a key)
    xx=width;            // Key width
    yy=high;             // Key height
    text=name;           // Annotation on key
    color=bcolor;        // Set background color
    shcolor=scolor;      // Set key show color
    textcolor=tcolor;    // Set text color
    flag=0;
}
```

```cpp
void Button::Show( int px , int py )            // Display a key
{
    int xx_,yy_;
    x=px;
    y=py;
    xt=(xx-textwidth(text))/2+x;   //Calculate the coordinates for
    yt=(yy-textheight(text))/2+y; //displaying the text on the key
    xx_=xx+x;
    yy_=yy+y;
    flag=0;                                  // Key not pressed indicator
    setfillstyle ( 1,color );
    bar( x+2,y+1,xx_-2,yy_-1 );      // Drawing a fancy key...
    setcolor(color);
    line( x+1,y+2,x+1,yy_-2 );
    line( xx_-1,y+2,xx_-1,yy_-2 );
    setcolor(BordColor);
    line( x+2,y,xx_-2,y );
    line( x+2,yy_,xx_-2,yy_ );
    line( x,y+2,x,yy_-2 );
    putpixel(x+1,y+1,BordColor);
    putpixel(x+2,y,BordColor);
    putpixel(x+1,yy_-1,BordColor);
    putpixel(x+2,yy_,BordColor);
    line( xx_,y+2,xx_,yy_-2 );
    putpixel(xx_-1,y+1,BordColor);
    putpixel(xx_-2,y,BordColor);
    putpixel(xx_-1,yy_-1,BordColor);
    putpixel(xx_-2,yy_,BordColor);
    setcolor( shcolor );
    line( xx_-1,y+2,xx_-1,yy_-2 );
    line( xx_-2,y+3,xx_-2,yy_-2 );
    line( x+3,yy_-2,xx_-1,yy_-2 );
    line( x+2,yy_-1,xx_-2,yy_-1 );   //...down to here
    text_unpress();                      //Display the text on the key
}
void Button::Press(void)              // Displays a key depressed
{
    int xx_,yy_;
    xx_=xx+x;
    yy_=yy+y;
    if( flag!=1 )
    { setcolor(color);
    line( x+1,y+2,x+1,yy_-2 );         // Redisplaying the key
    line( xx_-1,y+2,xx_-1,yy_-2 );  // outline in different
    line( xx_-2,y+3,xx_-2,yy_-2 );  // colors...
    line( x+3,yy_-2,xx_-1,yy_-2 );
    line( x+2,yy_-1,xx_-2,yy_-1 );
    setcolor( shcolor );
    line( x+2,y+1,xx_-2,y+1 );
    line( x+1,y+2,x+1,yy_-2 );
    line( x+2,y+1,x+2,yy_-1 );
    text_press();              // ...and move the annotation
    flag=1;                    //Set state indicator to pressed
    }
}
```

```
void Button::Unpress(void)    // Resets a key to normal state on
                              // screen
{
    int xx_,yy_;
    xx_=xx+x;
    yy_=yy+y;
    if( flag==1 )
    { setcolor(color);          // Redraw outline and annotation
  line( x+2,y+1,xx_-2,y+1 );// as normal...
  line( x+1,y+2,x+1,yy_-2 );
  line( x+2,y+1,x+2,yy_-1 );
  line( xx_-1,y+2,xx_-1,yy_-2 );
  setcolor( shcolor );
  line( xx_-1,y+2,xx_-1,yy_-2 );
  line( xx_-2,y+3,xx_-2,yy_-2 );
  line( x+3,yy_-2,xx_-1,yy_-2 );
  line( x+2,yy_-1,xx_-2,yy_-1 );
  text_unpress();
  flag=0;                     // set indicator to unpressed
    }
}


void Button::put_text(int x_,int y_)  // display annotation on key
{
    setfillstyle(1,color);
    bar(x+2,y+2,xx+x-3,yy+y-3 );
    setcolor(textcolor);
    settextstyle(0,HORIZ_DIR,1);
    outtextxy(x_,y_,text);
}

#endif

/*      End of BUTTON.H     */

/*   File CALC.H     */

/*************************************************/
/* This include file contains the class Calc    */
/* for the calculator, the class Indicator for  */
/* the display on the calculator, and the       */
/* Operand for the operands of the calculator.  */
/*************************************************/

#ifndef __CALC_H__
#define __CALC_H__

#include "button.h"
#define TAB 9

class Operand {    // Objects are calculator operands
protected:
```

```
      float n;   // Value of an operand
   private:
     int isPoint;              // Decimal point indicator
     int isNew;                // Object value reset indicator
     float fraction;// Factor for digits to right of
   public:   // decimal point
     Operand(float num=0){ n=num;isPoint=0;isNew=1;fraction=1; };
     float Value(void){ return n; };      // Returns the value of
                                          //object
     void New(void){ isNew=1;isPoint=0; };// Resets object
     Operand& operator << (int keyval);   // Processes digits &
                                          //point
              // for operand value
   /********************************************************/
   /* The following functions overload operators for      */
   /* use with Operand objects. The overloaded =          */
   /* operator returns and processes as a right argument  */
   /* a reference to an Operand object.                   */
   /********************************************************/
     Operand& operator = (Operand& op)
     { n=op.n;               // Assign left Operand value of right
     op.New();     // Reset right Operand
     isNew=1;      // Set left Operand
     isPoint=0;    // indicators...
     fraction=1;
     return *this;        // Return left Operand
     };
     Operand operator + (Operand o) { return Operand(n+o.n); };
     Operand operator - (Operand o) { return Operand(n-o.n); };
     Operand operator * (Operand o) { return Operand(n*o.n); };
     Operand operator / (Operand o) { return Operand(n/o.n); };
};

Operand& Operand::operator << (int keyval)
   // This function overloads the operator << to process
   // digits, decimal point, or Tab (change sign key), to
   // form Operand value.
{
   switch( keyval )
   { case '.':
     if( isNew )
     {   isNew=0; // Input starts with a decimal
         n=0;                     // so reset new operand indicator
         fraction=1;              // and set object value and
     }   // factor for decimals.
     isPoint=1; // Set indicator for decimal digits
     break;
   case TAB:   // Change sign key
     n = -n;
     break;
   case '0':   // All digits treated
   case '1':   // the same
   case '2':
```

```
    case '3':
    case '4':
    case '5':
    case '6':
    case '7':
    case '8':
    case '9':
      if( isNew )
      {   isNew=0;    // First digit of new value
          n=0;        // so set initial values
          fraction=1;
      }

          int neg=0;
          if( n<0 )
      {   neg=1;      // Switch negative number
          n=-n;       // to positive temporarily
      }
          if( !isPoint )
      {   if( n<20000001 )  n= n*10 + (keyval-'0');
      }
          else
      {   fraction=fraction/10;    // decimal digit factor
          n=n+fraction*(keyval-'0');
      }
      if( neg ) n=-n;                 // Switch negative number back
          break;
      }
      return *this;
}

class Indicator {     // Object is the display for a calculator
protected:            // which displays input and results
          int top;
    int left;
    int w;
    int h;
    public:
     Indicator(int width=50,int height=10)  // Constructor
     { top=0;
       left=0;
       w=width;
       h=height;
     };
     void Display(Operand o);   // Displays value of Operand
};


void Indicator::Display(Operand o)   // Display Operand
{
    char buf[30];
    setfillstyle(1,15);
    bar(left,top,left+w-1,top+h-1);   // Display indicator
    sprintf(buf,"%- g",o.Value());      // Form formatted o/p
```

```
        setcolor(0);
        outtextxy(left+w-2-textwidth(buf),top+2,buf);  // Write
                                                //formatted o/p
}                                               // to indicator


class Calc:public Indicator {           // Object is calculator
    private:
      int old_operation;
      Operand X,Y;
      Button * key_0,* key_1,* key_2,* key_3,* key_4,// Pointers
        * key_5,* key_6,* key_7,* key_8,* key_9,      // to keys...
        * key_point,* key_sign,
        * key_add,* key_sub,* key_mul,* key_div,
        * key_calc,* key_clear;
      void InitCalc(void);              //Function to Initialise a
                                        //calculator
      void ServeKey(int keyval);        //Function to service an operator
                                        //key
    public:
      Calc();                           // Constructor
      ~Calc();                          // Destructor
      void Show(int x=0,int y=0);       // Function to display a
                                        //calculator
      void PressKey(int keyval);        // Function to simulate key
                                        //operation
};

#endif
/*        End of File CALC.H        */



/* example EX4_9 */
#include <graphics.h>
#include <dos.h>
#include <stdio.h>
#include <conio.h>

#include "calc.h"

#define STEPX 37
#define STEPY 17
#define TONE  4000
#define PAUSE 50
#define ESC 27


void Calc::InitCalc(void)              // Initialise calculator
{
```

```
    old_operation=0;              // no previous operation
    key_0=new Button(30,14,"0",15,7,0);      // Create keys for
    key_1=new Button(30,14,"1",15,7,0);      // calculator
    key_2=new Button(30,14,"2",15,7,0);
     key_3=new  Button(30,14,"3",15,7,0);
     key_4=new  Button(30,14,"4",15,7,0);
     key_5=new  Button(30,14,"5",15,7,0);
     key_6=new  Button(30,14,"6",15,7,0);
     key_7=new  Button(30,14,"7",15,7,0);
     key_8=new  Button(30,14,"8",15,7,0);
     key_9=new  Button(30,14,"9",15,7,0);
     key_point=new Button(30,14,".",15,7,0);
     key_sign=new Button(30,14,"+/-",15,7,0);
     key_add=new Button(30,14,"+",15,7,0);
     key_sub=new Button(30,14,"-",15,7,0);
     key_mul=new Button(30,14,"*",15,7,0);
     key_div=new Button(30,14,"_",15,7,0);
     key_calc=new Button(30,14,"=",7,8,15);
     key_clear=new Button(30,14,"C",12,4,15);
}


Calc::Calc():Indicator(177,14)    // Constructor for calculator
{                                 // calls indicator constructor
    InitCalc();
}



Calc::~Calc()                     // Calculator destructor
{
    delete key_0;                 // Removes keys from memory
    delete key_1;
    delete key_2;
    delete key_3;
    delete key_4;
    delete key_5;
    delete key_6;
    delete key_7;
    delete key_8;
    delete key_9;
    delete key_point;
    delete key_sign;

    delete key_add;
    delete key_sub;
    delete key_mul;
    delete key_div;

    delete key_calc;
    delete key_clear;
}


void Calc::Show(int x, int y) // Display Calculator at x,y
{
```

```
    top=y+12;
    left=x+14;

    setfillstyle(SOLID_FILL,7);
    bar(x,y,x+208,y+106);                // Draw filled rectangle
    setcolor(0);
    rectangle(x,y,x+208,y+106);          // Draw rectangle
    rectangle(left-1,top-1,left+178,top+15);
    Display( X );                        // Display indicator with
                                         //value of X

  key_7->Show( x+9+STEPX*0 , y+32+STEPY*0 );        // Display
                                                    //calculator keys
  key_8->Show( x+9+STEPX*1 , y+32+STEPY*0 );        // using function
                                                    //Show of
  key_9->Show( x+9+STEPX*2 , y+32+STEPY*0 );        // Button
                                                    //objects...
  key_4->Show( x+9+STEPX*0 , y+32+STEPY*1 );        // Values of STEPX
                                                    //and
  key_5->Show( x+9+STEPX*1 , y+32+STEPY*1 );        // STEPY control
                                                    //horizontal
  key_6->Show( x+9+STEPX*2 , y+32+STEPY*1 );        // and vertical
                                                    //key spacing

    key_1->Show( x+9+STEPX*0 , y+32+STEPY*2 );
    key_2->Show( x+9+STEPX*1 , y+32+STEPY*2 );
    key_3->Show( x+9+STEPX*2 , y+32+STEPY*2 );

    key_0->Show    ( x+9+STEPX*0 , y+32+STEPY*3 );
    key_point->Show( x+9+STEPX*1 , y+32+STEPY*3 );
    key_sign->Show ( x+9+STEPX*2 , y+32+STEPY*3 );

    key_calc-> Show( x+125+STEPX*0 , y+32+STEPY*1 );
    key_clear->Show( x+125+STEPX*1 , y+32+STEPY*1 );

    key_add->Show( x+125+STEPX*0 , y+32+STEPY*2 );
    key_sub->Show( x+125+STEPX*1 , y+32+STEPY*2 );

    key_mul->Show( x+125+STEPX*0 , y+32+STEPY*3 );
    key_div->Show( x+125+STEPX*1 , y+32+STEPY*3 );
}

void Calc::PressKey(int keyval)  // Simulates pressing a key
{        // with visual and audible cues
    switch( keyval )
    { case '0':          // For the appropriate key, show
        key_0->Press();  // the key depressed, sound a brief
        sound(TONE);     // tone, then display the key
        delay(PAUSE);    // released.
        nosound();
        key_0->Unpress();    // Call Display for keys defining
        Display( Y << keyval );  // the value of an Operand.
        break;
```

```
case '1':
      key_1->Press();
      sound(TONE);
      delay(PAUSE);
      nosound();
      key_1->Unpress();
      Display( Y << keyval );
      break;
case '2':
      key_2->Press();
      sound(TONE);
      delay(PAUSE);
      nosound();
      key_2->Unpress();
      Display( Y << keyval );
      break;
case '3':
      key_3->Press();
      sound(TONE);
      delay(PAUSE);
      nosound();
      key_3->Unpress();
      Display( Y << keyval );
      break;
case '4':
      key_4->Press();
      sound(TONE);
      delay(PAUSE);
      nosound();
      key_4->Unpress();
      Display( Y << keyval );
      break;
case '5':
      key_5->Press();
      sound(TONE);
      delay(PAUSE);
      nosound();
      key_5->Unpress();
      Display( Y << keyval );
      break;
case '6':
      key_6->Press();
      sound(TONE);
      delay(PAUSE);
      nosound();
      key_6->Unpress();
      Display( Y << keyval );
      break;
case '7':
      key_7->Press();
      sound(TONE);
      delay(PAUSE);
      nosound();
```

```
            key_7->Unpress();
            Display( Y << keyval );
            break;
    case '8':
            key_8->Press();
            sound(TONE);
            delay(PAUSE);
            nosound();
            key_8->Unpress();
            Display( Y << keyval );
            break;
    case '9':
            key_9->Press();
            sound(TONE);
            delay(PAUSE);
            nosound();
            key_9->Unpress();
            Display( Y << keyval );
            break;
    case '.':
            key_point->Press();
            sound(TONE);
            delay(PAUSE);
            nosound();
            key_point->Unpress();
            Display( Y << keyval );
            break;
    case TAB:
            key_sign->Press();
            sound(TONE);
            delay(PAUSE);
            nosound();
            key_sign->Unpress();
            Display( Y << keyval );
            break;
    case '+':
            key_add->Press();
            sound(TONE);
            delay(PAUSE);
            nosound();
            key_add->Unpress();
            ServeKey(keyval); // Call Servekey for
            break;            // operators
    case '-':
            key_sub->Press();
            sound(TONE);
            delay(PAUSE);
            nosound();
            key_sub->Unpress();
            ServeKey(keyval);
            break;
    case '*':
            key_mul->Press();
```

```
           sound(TONE);
           delay(PAUSE);
           nosound();
            key_mul->Unpress();
            ServeKey(keyval);
           break;
     case  '/':
            key_div->Press();
            sound(TONE);
            delay(PAUSE);
            nosound();
            key_div->Unpress();
            ServeKey(keyval);
           break;
     case  '=':
     case  13:              // ENTER key equivalent to =
            key_calc->Press();
            sound(TONE);
            delay(PAUSE);
            nosound();
            key_calc->Unpress();
            ServeKey(keyval);
           break;
     case  'c':              // Upper or lower case is
     case  'C':              // Clear operation for calculator
            key_clear->Press();
            sound(TONE);
            delay(PAUSE);
            nosound();
            key_clear->Unpress();
            Display( Y=0 );
           break;
   }
}

void Calc::ServeKey(int keyval)   // Process operator keys
{
   switch( keyval ) {
     case '+':
     case '-':
     case '*':
     case '/':
        if( old_operation==0 )
        {                      // If there is no previous operation
   X=Y;                        // in effect, store current Operand Y
        }                      // in Operand X
        else
        {
   switch( old_operation )
   {  w            // If there is a previous operation
      case '+':    // in effect, execute with old
         Display( X=X+Y ); // operand X and current operand Y
        break;     // and store result in X.
      case '-':
```

```
            Display( X=X-Y );
            break;
        case `*':
            Display( X=X*Y );
            break;
        case `/':
            Display( X=X/Y );
            break;
    }
        }
        old_operation=keyval; // Set old operation to key entry
        Y.New();              // Reset operand Y
        break;
    case `=':
    case 13:                  // Enter key equivalent to =
        if( old_operation!=0 ) {
    switch( old_operation ) {
        case `+':
            Display( Y=X+Y );  // Execute old operation in effect
            break;             // with result in operand Y...
        case `-':
            Display( Y=X-Y );
            break;
        case `*':
            Display( Y=X*Y );
            break;
        case `/':
            Display( Y=X/Y );
            break;
    }
    old_operation=0;          // Reset to no old operation
    Y.New();                  // Reset operand Y
        }
        break;
    }
}

void CalcDemo(void)
{
    int ch;
    int endcalc=0;
    Calc a;                   // Create a calculator
    a.Show(100,100);          // Display it at 100,100
    while( ! endcalc )
        if( (ch=getch())==0 ) getch();
        else switch( ch )
        {   case ESC:         // Exit if Esc key pressed
            endcalc=1;
            break;
    default :
            a.PressKey(ch);   // Call member function of
            break;            // calculator object a
        }
}
```

```
void main()
{
    int gdriver = EGA, gmode = EGAHI;
    initgraph(&gdriver, &gmode, ""); //.BGI file needs to be in
    setfillstyle(1,15);                 // current directory
    bar(0,0,639,349);
    CalcDemo();                         //Start demo for calculator
    closegraph();
}
```

# Index

## Symbols

## A